AUTOMOTIVE ELECTRICAL EQUIPMENT

The Institution of Mechanical Engineers

AUTOMOTIVE ELECTRICAL EQUIPMENT

A conference arranged by the
Automobile Division
of the Institution of Mechanical Engineers
13–14th September 1972

1 BIRDCAGE WALK · WESTMINSTER · LONDON

© The Institution of Mechanical Engineers 1973

ISBN 0 85298 060 4

Library of Congress Catalog Card Number 73–184589

CONTENTS

Automotive Electrical Equipment

A conference on Automotive Electrical Equipment, arranged by the Automobile Division of the Institution of Mechanical Engineers, was held at the University of Sussex, Brighton, on 13th and 14th September 1972. 125 delegates registered to attend.

The conference was formally opened by Mr J. H. H. Barrow, C Eng, F I Mech E, Chairman of the Organizing Committee, and closed by Mr C. D. Brewer, C Eng, F I Mech E.

The presentation of papers and the discussions were arranged in four sessions as follows.

Session 1   Chairman: Mr R. W. Mellor, B Sc (Eng), C Eng, M I Mech E. Opening of conference. Presentation of papers C89/72, C106/72, C61/72 and C65/72. Discussion.

Session 2   Chairman: Mr Mellor. Presentation of papers C63/72, C72/72, C115/72 and C111/72. Discussion.

Session 3   Chairman: Mr C. D. Brewer, C Eng, F I Mech E. Presentation of papers C90/72, C75/72, C113/72 and C79/72. Discussion.

Session 4   Chairman: Mr Brewer. Presentation of papers C108/72, C114/72, C88/72 and C107/72. Discussion. Summing-up and closure.

The members of the organizing committee were Mr J. H. H. Barrow, C Eng, F I Mech E (Chairman), Mr E. G. Bareham, Mr K. J. Leech, B Sc, C Eng, M I Mech E, Mr E. J. McArdell and Mr J. V. B. Robson, C Eng, M I Mech E.

C61/72 ELECTRONIC FUEL INJECTION

H. SCHOLL*

The introduction of electronic control has resulted in a considerable increase in popularity of fuel injection systems. The application of fuel injection helps to boost engine performance and reduce fuel consumption and also has an increasingly important contribution to make to the solution of air pollution problems. The particular advantage offered by the electronic control system is in its ability to process at low cost those additional signals necessary to ensure compliance with future exhaust emission requirements. This paper will cover the latest state of development of a new generation fuel injection system incorporating integrated circuit techniques.

1 INTRODUCTION

FUEL INJECTION for spark ignition engines offers a number of advantages, in particular more power output per cubic inch displacement, smaller brake specific fuel consumption and a smaller amount of unburnt components in the exhaust gas (1)–(6)†. Only to a minor degree are these advantages related directly to the injection of fuel. More important is the fact that the fuel injection systems offer additional possibilities and degrees of freedom to the designer of engines. It facilitates an optimum design of the induction system for the engine. It also allows for the numerous control inputs required to ideally adapt the amount of fuel to the various operating conditions of the engines. Electronically controlled fuel injection (6)–(13) offers special advantages concerning controllability. By electronic means it is possible to sense as many variables in as many locations of the vehicle as is desired and to combine these variables following a specified programme.

Jetronic—the electronic fuel injection system developed by Bosch—went into production in 1967 and has since seen an ever-widening application. Today it is used for 15 different types of passenger cars with four- six- and eight-cylinder engines.

The Jetronic system has been improved continually during recent years and has met the more and more stringent requirements laid down by the engine manufacturers. Parallel to this effort the development of a new injection system, called the 'L-Jetronic', was started approximately two years ago. It combines improved performance at considerably reduced cost. These advantages are obtained by the use of the principle of air flow measurement and by the application of integrated circuits in the electronic control unit.

Following is a short description of the present Jetronic system with manifold pressure control which will then serve as a basis for the discussion of the characteristics of the new L-Jetronic.

The MS. of this paper was received at the Institution on 12th January 1972 and accepted for publication on 14th March 1972.
34
* Robert Bosch GmbH, Automotive Products Div. 1, 7141 Schwieberdingen bei Stuttgart, Robert-Bosch-Strasse, Germany.
† References are given in Appendix 61.1.

2 BASICS OF THE JETRONIC SYSTEM

The Jetronic system was covered to a great extent in ealier publications (12)–(14). The basic system is shown in Fig. 61.1.

2.1 Fuel circulation system

The electrically driven fuel pump delivers the fuel and generates the fuel pressure. From the tank the fuel is drawn to a filter and is forced into the pressure line. The filter may also be located in the pressure line provided the suction side of the pump is protected from dirt particles by a small strainer. At the end of the pressure line a pressure regulator of the overflow type controls the fuel pressure with a very high accuracy at 2·0 atu regardless of the delivered and injected amount of fuel. The pump delivers 20–40 litres/h fuel in excess of the maximum engine requirement. The excess fuel flows back to the tank from the pressure regulator through a second line. Branch lines lead from the pressure line to the individual injectors.

2.2 Air induction system

The inducted air flows from the air filter past a throttle valve to the intake manifold. From there separate manifolds lead to the individual cylinders.

Each cylinder is equipped with an electromagnetically actuated injection valve. Dependent on engine design, the injector is located either in the intake tube or in the cylinder head.

To achieve good driveability and low exhaust gas emissions the injectors have to be mounted near the inlet valves. However, this means that the distance to the cylinder is short and at extremely low temperatures the fuel will not vaporize and be mixed with air adequately during a cold start. To achieve a perfect cold start down to approximately −30°C with the Jetronic system, a special magnetic injection valve was developed. This valve has an exceptionally good fuel atomizing characteristic and is used during a cold start to inject additional fuel into the intake manifold directly behind the throttle valve. By this, the fuel added during the start is completely atomized and mixed with air and the light ends vaporize while travelling through the intake tubes to the cylinders.

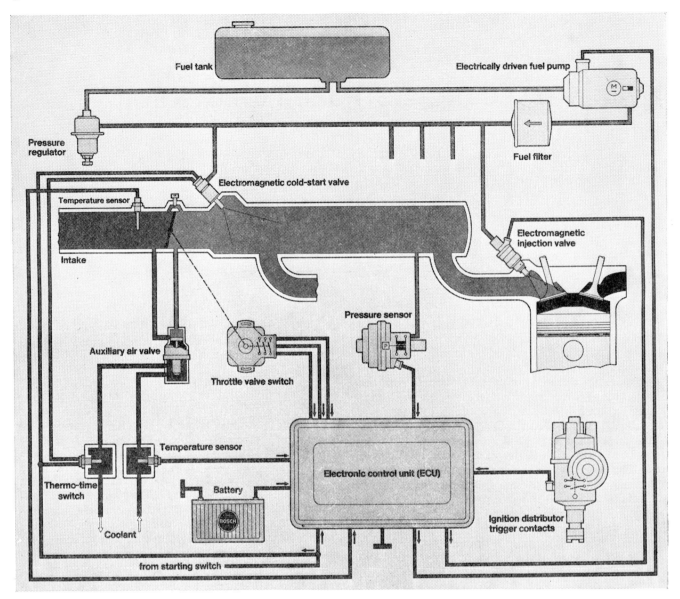

Fig. 61.1. Jetronic with manifold pressure control

2.3 Control of the injected amount of fuel by means of manifold pressure, engine speed and air intake temperature

In the individual air intake tubes near the cylinders fuel is injected once for every engine cycle. The injectors are arranged in groups to keep the number of electronic components at a minimum. For a four-cylinder engine always two, and for a six-cylinder engine always three, injectors are connected electrically in parallel and thus inject simultaneously. The injectors within one group belong to cylinders following each other in the firing sequence. For an eight-cylinder engine either 4 × 2 or 2 × 4 injectors are operated simultaneously.

The injection timing for the different groups is determined by trigger contacts located in the distributor. This trigger unit marks the start of the current pulses. The amount of fuel injected during each engine cycle is determined by the duration of the current pulses which the electronic control unit computes from the operating data of the engine. The operating data are measured at different

locations of the engine by sensors and then transmitted electrically to the electronic control unit.

The amount of fuel determined for each cycle of the engine must be related directly to the air taken in for every stroke. As a first approximation, the amount of air is proportional to the absolute pressure in the intake manifold. It also depends on the engine speed. It is therefore possible to control the amount of injected fuel using the absolute pressure in the manifold with a correction factor for engine speed (13)–(16). In this way the first Jetronic generation was implemented.

The variable inductance of a pressure sensor connected to the intake manifold controls the duration of the pulses. The inductance is changed by evacuated aneroids which move a plunger in the magnetic circuit of the pressure sensor.

A separate engine speed input to the electronic control unit is unnecessary since the control unit senses the time between trigger pulses coming from the distributor.

The computation of the amount of injected fuel as a

function of manifold pressure and engine speed is only correct at a constant temperature since the air density, and thus the amount of air drawn in per stroke, changes with temperature. This is taken into account by a temperature sensor located in the intake manifold which shortens the injector open time with increasing temperature corresponding to the decrease of air density.

2.4 Cold start and warm-up control

The engine requires a richer mixture during a cold start and the following warm-up period. During starting this enrichment is mainly supplied by a cold start valve which injects fuel as long as the starter switch is operated. The amount of injected fuel ranges between 70 and 200 cm³/min, dependent on engine size. A thermo switch with a switching point between 0 and 15°C—dependent on engine type—ensures that the cold start valve is only operated at cooling water temperatures below the switching point.

With a rich mixture during start, some engines tend to spark plug wetting. In this case it is advantageous to replace the thermo switch with a thermo time switch. This limits the on-time of the cold start valve. The switch is sized to hold the on-time between 5 and 20 s, dependent on engine type, at a cooling water temperature of −20°C. The on-time decreases with higher cooling water temperature and finally reaches 0 at 20–40°C.

The time following cold start until the engine reaches the normal operating temperature is called the warm-up phase. During this operating mode the engine requires a warm-up enrichment. Immediately following a start at −20°C two to three times the quantity of fuel required at normal operating temperatures must be injected. The enrichment during the warm-up period is decreased continuously with increasing engine temperature and is eliminated as soon as the operating temperature is reached. The warm-up enrichment is also provided during the start. At low temperatures it is added to the quantity injected by the cold start valve. Above the switching temperature of the thermo switch it serves as start-up enrichment.

The enrichment is controlled by a temperature sensor. The temperature must be sensed at engine locations which assume the temperature representative for fuel mixture preparation and the combustion process. For the fuel injection system of a water-cooled engine shown in Fig. 61.1, the warm-up enrichment is controlled by a temperature sensor installed in the coolant. For air-cooled engines the temperature sensor is located at the cylinder head.

With a cold start, and during the following warm-up period, a larger volume of air is required for idling in addition to a richer air–fuel mixture. The additional air is necessary to increase the engine speed and to ensure acceptable idling. Furthermore, the cold engine has to generate considerably more torque to overcome the increased friction. The auxiliary air is controlled by a so-called auxiliary air valve which bypasses the throttle valve. It consists of a valve in which the open cross-section is varied as a function of the engine temperature or the temperature of an electric heating coil by means of a bi-metal coil or a thermal expansion element.

2.5 Additional controls

The so-called throttle valve switch, which is connected mechanically to the throttle valve, serves to generate a signal that is used for acceleration enrichment during a movement of the throttle valve. For this purpose the throttle valve switch is equipped with a set of contacts which generate a sequence of voltage pulses during opening of the throttle valve. These voltage pulses result in the injection of additional fuel during the opening movement. The added quantities are small and hardly affect fuel consumption.

For part load operation of the engine, the fuel quantity is calculated to minimize the specific fuel consumption and the content of unburnt exhaust gas. At full load, however, the fuel quantity is determined to reach maximum output power from the engine. The necessary large increase of injected fuel during full load operation is called full load enrichment. It is determined by the manifold vacuum and not by the absolute pressure in the manifold to make the enrichment independent of elevation. On an optional basis, the throttle valve switch can also be used for full load enrichment. For this, a contact in the throttle valve switch is closed when a certain opening angle is reached, and causes the widening of the injection pulses.

In addition, another contact in the throttle valve switch can be used to adjust the air–fuel mixture during idling. Furthermore, a potentiometer mounted in the electronic control unit allows an individual idling setting for each engine.

The opening and closing times of the electromagnetic injectors depend on the operating voltage. The opening time increases and the closing time decreases with higher operating voltage. For the same duration of the current pulses, this results in a longer opening of the injectors and thus more injected fuel. To stabilize the supply voltage is very expensive and therefore the effect of voltage changes is compensated in the electronic control unit by an inverse relation between pulse duration and supply voltage.

The fuel pump is switched on by an electrical circuit in the electronic control unit and not by the ignition switch. The pump logic prevents the operation of the pump with turned on ignition as long as the engine is not running. This prevents the flooding of a cylinder in case an injector should fail to close properly because of dirt particles.

3 THE L-JETRONIC SYSTEM

Following is the description of the new Jetronic system with air flow metering shown in Fig. 61.2. The emphasis will be on the differences between the present method and the new system.

3.1 Fuel circulation and air induction system

There is only a small difference to the present system which pertains to the pressure regulator. The spring chamber (see Section 4.9) is now connected to the intake manifold through a hose and is no longer in contact with the atmospheric pressure. This means that the pressure differential between fuel pressure and manifold pressure is constant, and thus the injected fuel quantity is now only dependent on the injector open time.

3.2 Control of the fuel quantity by air flow and engine speed

The essential task of a fuel injection system is to add to the amount of air drawn in by the engine an exact quantity

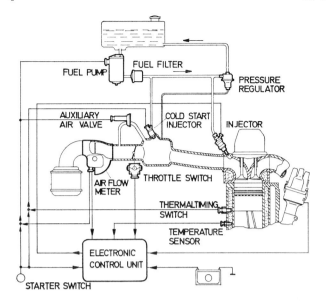

Fig. 61.2. L-Jetronic with air flow metering

of fuel to obtain the desired air/fuel ratio. From a technical standpoint, the direct measurement of air quantity is somewhat difficult. It is possible to use substitute variables that have a determined relationship to the quantities of interest. The present Jetronic system employs as substitute inputs the manifold pressure and the engine speed. This solution appeared attractive since the measurement of the manifold pressure is relatively simple. However, manifold pressure is a function of many parameters and it can only be used as a control input under the assumption that all these parameters are constant.

The more and more stringent emission control regulations, especially in the U.S.A., make it desirable to measure directly the amount of air drawn in by the engine. Measuring the air quantity offers the following advantages for a fuel injection system:

(1) Compensation of differences in volumetric efficiency caused by manufacturing tolerances, wear, deposits in the combustion chamber or variations of valve settings between engines.

(2) Compensation of variations in volumetric efficiency which are the result of speed-dependent manifold dynamics.

(3) Since the signal from the air flow metering device precedes the entry of the air into the cylinder, an acceleration enrichment is no longer required and the stability in the idling mode is improved.

(4) Compensation of changes of the exhaust pressure which are caused by thermal and catalytic reactors and by the wear and deterioration of these devices.

(5) Insensitivity of the system to exhaust gas recirculation, since the air flow meter is measuring only the inlet air.

The last two items are of particular importance considering the more severe standards of the emission control regulations proposed in the U.S.A. for 1976.

The air drawn in by the engine moves a measuring plate positioned in the air stream inside the air flow metering device. The measuring plate is turned to a defined angular position due to the force from the air flow and the effective

return force of a spring. A voltage signal for the electronic control unit is taken from a potentiometer which is connected mechanically to the measuring plate.

The fuel quantity is computed for each engine cycle and is adapted to the amount of intake air on a 'per stroke' basis. The signal from the air flow meter is a measure for the air quantity per unit time. From this, a signal proportional to air quantity per stroke is obtained, dividing the input signal by engine speed in the electronic control unit.

No separate control input is required for engine speed. This information is obtained inside the electronic control unit from the time interval between trigger pulses coming from the distributor.

3.3 Injection timing

In the new system all injectors are connected electrically in parallel to reduce the number of electronic components in the control unit. Therefore, the injectors are operated simultaneously although, with reference to the individual cylinders, at different phases of the operating cycle. To achieve, in spite of this, an adequate conformity of the combustion process, fuel is injected twice for every revolution of the camshaft; each injection contributes half of the fuel quantity required for the engine cycle.

The procedure has the additional advantage that no co-ordination is required between the angular position of the camshaft and the start of the fuel injection. This considerably simplifies the triggering of the fuel injection system; the trigger pulses are derived directly from the breaker points of the distributor and no additional trigger contacts are required. Since, for a four-cylinder engine, the breaker points open four times for every engine cycle, the electronic control unit has to divide this frequency by 2. For six- or eight-cylinder engines a frequency division by a factor of 3 or 4, respectively, is required.

3.4 Cold start and warm-up control

The cold start and warm-up control is basically the same as in the present Jetronic systems. Further improvements have been made, however, to reduce the exhaust gas emission during the warm-up period and to adapt in an optimum manner to the requirements of different types of engines.

3.5 Additional controls and correction factors

The principle of direct air flow metering already takes into account a large number of parameters which affect the required amount of fuel in the engine. Therefore, fewer corrections are necessary than in the present system. The very expensive building blocks in the electronic control unit used for a speed-dependent adjustment of the injected fuel quantity and for the acceleration enrichment are no longer required.

The adjustments for full load and idling are initiated again by contacts in the throttle valve switch. To adjust the air/fuel ratio at idling, a variable air bypass in parallel to the air flow meter is provided.

As in the present system, the time duration of the injection is corrected, dependent on battery voltage.

As is practised today, electrical interlocking prevents the operation of the fuel pump with turned-on ignition but stalled engine. This is achieved by a contact which is closed with the air measuring plate in its rest position. An override eliminates this interlocking during starting.

3.6 Centralized electronic control unit for exhaust emission control

The development of systems designed to control exhaust gas emission within the limits proposed for the U.S.A. after 1976 is still in a state of flux. However, it is already obvious that fuel injection will be applied increasingly to European and American cars for exhaust gas emission control.

The future emission limits cannot be achieved by such measures in the fuel system only. Additional equipment, particularly as part of the exhaust system, will be required. However, as far as can be predicted at present, the number of additional sub-systems will be considerably less by the application of fuel injection.

The added equipment has to be controlled partially in dependence of engine parameters (speed, load, temperature, etc.). In many cases it has to be monitored to prevent it from being destroyed. The following are a few examples:

(1) Additional variation of the ignition timing dependent on engine temperature and throttle valve opening.

(2) Control of the amount of fresh air supplied to the motor during overrun, dependent on engine speed and load.

(3) Control of exhaust gas recirculation as a function of engine speed, engine torque and engine temperature.

(4) Control of a bypass valve to protect the thermal reactor or catalyst dependent on exhaust gas temperature.

(5) Control of the air/fuel ratio dependent on exhaust gas temperature.

It is advisable to implement the control and monitoring functions required for the added emission control equipment electrically or electronically. This is especially economical in connection with an electronically controlled fuel injection system since most of the required engine parameters are already available in the electronic control unit. A combination of the additional control and monitoring circuits with the electronics of the Jetronic system in the Jetronic control unit represents an optimum solution and is already the start for a centralized engine electronic module.

4 DESIGN AND FUNCTION OF THE DIFFERENT JETRONIC SUBSYSTEMS

A description of the presently used Jetronic subsystems was given above (12) (13). In the following, components used unchanged in the new Jetronic system will only be mentioned briefly. Changes on existing subsystems and newly developed components will be covered in more detail.

4.1 Electronic control unit

The electronic control unit (Fig. 61.3) is designed using printed circuit boards. For reasons of higher reliability and lower cost, a solution was chosen where integrated circuits are employed extensively. Besides three integrated

Fig. 61.3. L-Jetronic, electronic control unit

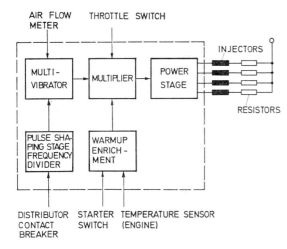

Fig. 61.4. **Block diagram of the L-Jetronic control unit**

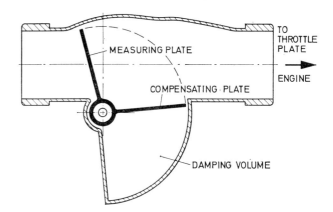

Fig. 61.5. **Cross-section of the air flow meter**

circuits which represent the major portion of the design, the unit contains very few discrete electronic components and a number of capacitors and resistors selected on test. Including everything, approximately 80 electronic components are being used, compared with about 300 in the present Jetronic control unit. The control unit is connected through a multi-pin connector with the wiring harness which then leads to the other subsystems.

Fig. 61.4 shows the block diagram of the control unit. The trigger pulses from the breaker points of the distributor are fed to the pulse-shaping network and the frequency divider. There the trigger frequency is divided and rectangular-shaped output pulses with a mark space ratio of 1:1 are generated. These pulses trigger the division multivibrator. The on-time or pulse width of the multivibrator is inversely proportional to speed and directly proportional to air quantity (see Section 4.2). This way the on-time of the multivibrator is proportional to the amount of air drawn in on a per stroke basis.

In the multiplication stage, the output pulses from the division multivibrator are extended by a factor of at least 2. The compensation for variations of the battery voltage prolongs the output pulses of the multiplication stage by a voltage-dependent increment. The generated pulse is fed to the output stage which applies battery voltage to the injectors during the duration of the pulse.

Temperature sensor, starter switch and throttle valve switch provide the input signals to the multiplication stage for the necessary adjustments regarding warm-up enrichment, cold start enrichment, idling and full load.

The power resistors connected in series with the injectors are mounted in a special housing and located between the coils of the injectors and the plus terminal of the battery.

4.2 Air flow meter

Fig. 61.5 shows a schematic view of the air flow meter. The meter is designed to generate a voltage signal which is dependent on air flow. For this, a number of measuring principles are suitable, and one of the most frequently used is based on the principle of measuring the force exerted on a body located in a stream of air. In this case, a rectangular measuring plate is used which can turn in a rectangular-shaped channel to a defined angular position

dependent on the pressure from the flowing air and the return torque of a coil spring. This return torque is chosen to be a multiple of the bearing friction torque and also to minimize the pressure loss on the measuring plate. To dampen the movement of the plate, a compensation plate is provided which is connected to the damping volume through a small gap. The damping volume and gap are designed to optimize the dynamic response. Employment of the compensation plate ensures that the manifold pressure pulsations caused by the piston strokes have only a negligible influence on the angular position of the plate.

The functional relationship between the angle of the measuring plate and the air flow can be varied by a change of the open cross-section. In our case, the cross-section is designed to yield approximately a logarithmic function for angular position versus air flow per unit time. This means that the relative measuring error is almost constant over the full range, which offers advantages for an accurate setting in the idling and partial load mode. The angular position of the measuring plate is transformed into a voltage by a potentiometer.

A small part of the drawn-in air can circumvent the measuring plate through an adjustable bypass. This gives the opportunity to influence the air/fuel ratio at low air flow (idling) by changing the cross-section of the bypass.

4.3 Throttle plate switch

The elimination of the acceleration enrichment in the new Jetronic system simplifies this component considerably (Fig. 61.6). Now the throttle valve switch contains only one set of contacts each for idling and full load respectively.

4.4 Temperature sensor

The temperature sensors consist of resistors with a high-temperature coefficient (NTC-resistor). The resistor is mounted in a hollow threaded stud and then coated with plastic. Fig. 61.7 shows two different designs of temperature sensor.

4.5 Injector

Fig. 61.8 shows a cross-section of the injector. It consists mainly of the valve housing and the injector spindle connected to the magnetic plunger. On the right, the housing contains the magnetic coil and on the left the guiding arrangement for the injector spindle. If the coil is not excited, the injector spindle is forced by a coil spring

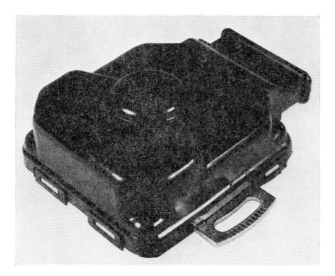

Fig. 61.6. Throttle valve switch

Fig. 61.7. Temperature sensors

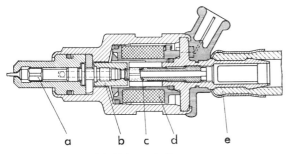

(a) Valve spindle.
(b) Solenoid plunger.
(c) Helical spring.
(d) Solenoid coil.
(e) Fuel line.

Fig. 61.8. Injector

against a leakage proof seat located on the left end of the injector.

Excitation of the magnet causes the spindle to lift approximately 0·15 mm and the fuel can discharge through a calibrated annulus. The front end of the injector spindle is shaped as an atomizing pintle with a ground tip. The opening and closing time of the injector is approximately 1 ms.

4.6 Cold start valve

Short opening and closing times are not essential for the cold start valve. The important factor is an extremely fine atomization of the fuel. Therefore, a valve specially suited

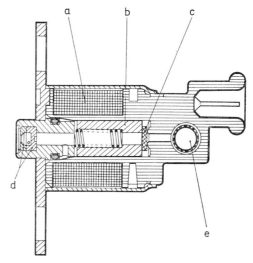

(a) Magnetic coil.
(b) Solenoid plunger.
(c) Seal.
(d) Turbulence nozzle.
(e) Fuel inlet.

Fig. 61.9. Cold start valve

for this purpose was developed and its cross-section is shown in Fig. 61.9.

In the unexcited state the solenoid plunger of the magnetic circuit is forced, with its seal, against the valve seat by the helical spring and seals it. The valve seat is freed if the plunger is attracted. The fuel flows laterally past flats on the plunger and reaches the turbulence nozzle through a transverse and longitudinal bore of the part of the magnetic circuit forming the nozzle holder. In the turbulence nozzle the fuel is brought into rotation by two tangential intake ducts, and it is discharged from the nozzle in a finely atomized condition on the envelope of a cone of about ±45° angle.

4.7 Auxiliary air valve

The auxiliary air valve (Fig. 61.10) contains an electrically heated bimetal spring as an actuator. The device is mounted on the engine in a location where the temperature is characteristic for the operating state. The electrical heating offers the advantage that the time constant determining the cut-off of auxiliary air can be chosen freely.

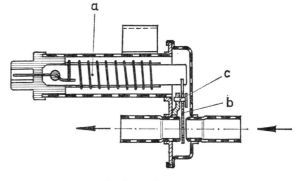

(a) Bimetal spring.
(b) Movable plate.
(c) Pivot point.

Fig. 61.10. Auxiliary air valve

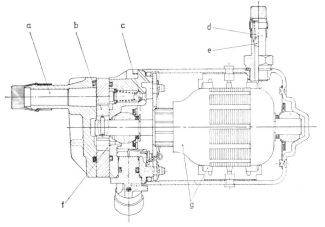

(a) Fuel inlet.
(b) Pump rotor.
(c) Relief valve.
(d) Fuel outlet.
(e) Check valve.
(f) Roller.
(g) Permanent magnet electric motor.

Fig. 61.11. Fuel pump

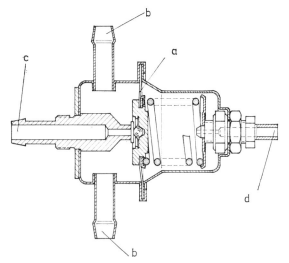

(a) Diaphragm.
(b) Pressure line.
(c) Return flow.
(d) Line to intake manifold.

Fig. 61.12. Pressure regulator

4.8 Fuel pump

The pump is a roller type pump (Fig. 61.11) driven by a permanent-magnet electric motor.

The pump consists of a cylindrical chamber in which the turning rotor is mounted eccentrically. The rotor has pocket-shaped openings along the circumference in which metal rollers are located. When the rotor is turning, the rollers are pushed to the outside by centrifugal force and act as circulating seals. Pumping is accomplished by the fact that the rotating rollers provide a periodically increasing volume at the fuel inlet and a decreasing volume at the outlet.

4.9 Pressure regulator

The pressure regulator (Fig. 61.12) consists of a two-part metal housing with a diaphragm crimped in between. The

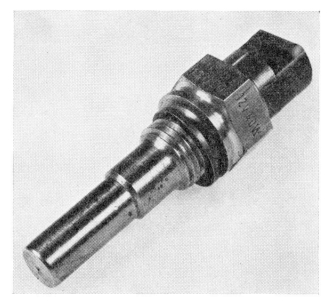

Fig. 61.13. Thermo time switch

fuel enters through one or several radial inlets and presses against the spring loaded diaphragm. The spring chamber is connected through a hose to the induction manifold. This means that the pressure in the fuel system is dependent on the manifold pressure, thus keeping the pressure differential across the injectors constant for all load conditions. The diaphragm opens an overflow outlet to maintain constant fuel pressure where this differs from the set value. The fuel pressure can be adjusted by changing the preloading of the spring.

4.10 Fuel filter

The filter contains a paper insert with an average pore size of 20 μm. The useful life is approximately 20 000 km. It is replaced as a unit. Different sizes are available according to the applied pump capacity. When installed on the suction side of the pump, a filter in a plastic housing is used. For a pressure side installation, the housing is of aluminium.

4.11 Thermo time switch

The thermo time switch used to control the cold start injector is an electrically heated bimetal switch (Fig. 61.13). It is mounted on a location of the engine where the temperature is representative for the operating state. The turn-on time decreases with higher engine temperature.

5 SUMMARY

The fuel injection system 'L-Jetronic' described above shows simultaneously a considerable increase in performance combined with a reduction of cost. The progress is due to the application of air flow metering and the introduction of integrated circuits. The electronic control unit can be employed with few additions to perform controlling and monitoring functions for additional equipment used in the future for exhaust emission control. Thus the L-Jetronic is an effective and economic contribution towards meeting the more stringent standards of exhaust emission control in the future. The system still offers the traditional advantages of fuel injection, increased engine power and reduced fuel consumption.

APPENDIX 61.1

REFERENCES

(1) EBERLE, O. 'Bosch-Einspritzausrüstung für Viertakt-Otto-motoren mit Mengenteiler-Saugrohreinspritzung', *MTZ* 1959 **29**, 331.

(2) SCHERENBERG, H. 'Erfolg der Benzineinspritzung bei Daimler-Benz', *MTZ* 1961 **22**, 241.

(3) ANDERS, U. 'Entwicklungsprobleme der Benzineinspritzung von Personenwagenmotoren', *ATZ* 1961 **63**, 315.

(4) GRÖZINGER, H. 'Die Benzineinspritzung des 230-SL-Motors von Daimler-Benz', *ATZ* 1963 **65**, 166.

(5) SCHENK, R. 'Kraftstoffeinspritzung beim Peugeot 404', *ATZ* 1963 **65**, 169.

(6) KNAPP, H., JOACHIM, E.-U. and BAUMANN, G. 'Beeinfluss-ung der Kraftfahrzeugabgase durch Benzineinspritzung', *Bosch Techn. Ber.* 1965 **1**, 206; *MTZ* 1965 **26**, 353.

(7) WINKLER, A. H. and SUTTON, R. W. 'Electrojector—Bendix electronic fuel injection system', *S.A.E. Trans.* 1957 **65**, 758.

(8) BRÜNING, R. 'Elektronisch gesteuerte Benzineinspritzung für Verbrennungsmotoren', *Funktech.* 1963 **18**, 862.

(9) 'Electronically controlled petrol injection', *Auto. Engr* 1966 **56**, 461.

(10) ZEYNS, J. and MÜLLER, K. 'Elektronisch gesteuerte Benzin-einspritzung. I. Aufbau der elektronisch gesteuerten Ben-zineinspritzung', *MTZ* 1967 **28**, 10.

(11) ZEYNS, J. and MÜLLER, K. 'Elektronisch gesteuerte Ben-zineinspritzung. II. Versuchsergebnisse an einem Sechs-zylinder-Einspritzmotor', *MTZ* 1967 **28**, 13.

(12) BAUMANN, G. 'Eine elektronisch gesteuerte Benzineinsprit-zung für Ottomotoren', *Bosch Techn. Ber.* 1967 **2** (No. 3), 107; *MTZ* 1967 **28**, 475.

(13) SCHOLL, H. 'Elektronische Benzineinspritzung', *ATZ* 1968 **70**, 115.

(14) GLÖCKLER, O., RITTMANNSBERGER, N. and SCHOLL, H. 'Weiterentwicklung der elektronisch gesteuerten Ben-zineinspritzung "Jetronic"', *ATZ* 1971 **4**.

C63/72 STARTING GAS TURBINE ENGINES

E. WHARTON*   E. CARR†

The basic requirements for starting gas turbine engines are described. Engine resistance with accessory drag is considered in relation to fuel, ignition, starter motor and electrical power supply characteristics. Each aspect is examined individually and in relation to the overall system. Combustion-chamber operating conditions, air/fuel ratio, ignition energy and atomizing techniques are given consideration. The performance of the system in cold-weather conditions is given particular attention to show the interdependence of one subsystem with another. The effect of trends in design will be discussed and the effects likely to result compared with operational requirements and optimization objectives.

1 OBJECTIVE

THE STARTING of a gas turbine engine presents special problems. This paper deals only with starting by an electric motor. It is necessary to accelerate the engine up to a condition known as self-sustaining speed (defined later). This differs from the piston engine in that relatively high speeds are necessary before self-sustaining speed is reached.

Turbine compressor speeds may be as high as 80 000 rev/min; since the mechanical aspects of the starter motor become limiting at high speeds, and to obtain optimum performance from the motor, it is necessary in most cases to employ a suitable gear ratio and mechanical disconnect between the engine and the starter motor. A requirement for automotive gas turbines is to achieve a start under normal temperature conditions within a few seconds; a normal well-designed system will achieve this consistently. If through deterioration the engine should fail to start the first time, it may be necessary to make repeated attempts. Under such circumstances heating of the starter motor could become a problem, unless this is allowed for in the design.

The function of the starter motor is to accelerate the engine by the provision of an excess amount of torque over the drag imposed by the engine during the run-up period to self-sustaining speed. The amount of torque required is then determined by the engine inertia and the specified starting time.

A typical small engine resistance curve is shown in Fig. 63.1 on which is superimposed a starter motor output curve. The difference between the two curves is the amount of torque available for acceleration. It should be noted that it is customary to depict the motor characteristic in this inverted form for convenience in comparison with the engine performance.

During the starting cycle it is necessary to provide fuel and electrical power for the ignition, solenoids, relays and starter motor. The capability of the starter motor is deter-

mined not only by the excellence of the motor design but by the supply characteristics. The battery, cables, connections and any switches between battery and starter motor will all affect the starting system. Each aspect of the starting system will therefore be discussed, since the system should be optimized as a whole.

2 ENGINE CHARACTERISTICS

By reference to Fig. 63.1 it will be seen that under normal temperature conditions there is an initial friction torque to be overcome, following which there is an increasing engine resistance torque loading due to compressor windage drag loss and the loads of directly driven accessories.

At a certain point along this curve the fuel–air mixture attains proportions suitable for ignition. This is provided by the igniter plug, which has been repetitively energized from commencement of the start cycle by the ignition unit.

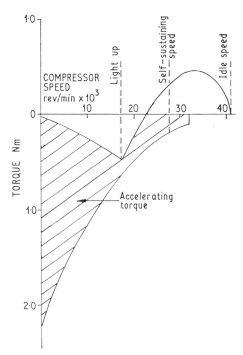

Fig. 63.1. Typical engine–starter motor characteristics

The MS. of this paper was received at the Institution on 18th January 1972 and accepted for publication on 23rd March 1972. 23
* Chief Electrical Equipment Engineer, Lucas Aerospace Ltd, Electrical Group, Hemel Hempstead.
† Assistant Chief Development Engineer, Lucas Aerospace Ltd, Fabrication Group, Hemel Hempstead.

From this point onwards the engine provides an assisting torque of increasing magnitude. The power obtained from the engine is, however, insufficient in itself to accelerate the engine and results merely in a reduction in the net required torque. Consequently, to continue the process of engine acceleration, the starter motor must continue to provide this net torque. The speed of the engine therefore continues to increase until a point is reached when no additional assistance is required from the starter motor. This is called the self-sustaining speed, and at this point the starter motor can be de-energized. Although self-sustaining speed would logically occur at zero torque where the curve crosses the axis, it is necessary to continue starter assistance to avoid engine overheating and to ensure smooth acceleration to idling.

A most important aspect of the engine characteristic is the increase in viscous drag in cold weather conditions. At very low temperatures this will be considerable; but when compared with the internal-combustion engine having large, wetted, surface areas, the cold temperature effect is less pronounced and starting is correspondingly easier.

The period between engine light-up and self-sustaining speed is critical in terms of engine life. On light-up of the engine, combustion takes place, resulting in a rapid temperature increase. The turbine blades are capable of withstanding a maximum temperature beyond which strength is lost and creep will take place. In order to avoid this condition it is necessary to increase the gas flow, which will inhibit the temperature rise by increasing the speed of the compressor at a satisfactory rate.

Under normal ambient temperature conditions, usually $+15°C$, the time taken from the initiation of the starting cycle to light-up will be in the order of 1 s. After a further 4 s, or thereabouts, the starter cut-out speed will have been reached; approximately 2 s later the turbine will have reached idling speed. The complete starting cycle, therefore, for a typical 100-hp gas turbine engine will be in the order of 7–10 s, of which the starter motor is in use for 50–70 per cent of the run-up time.

Adverse climatic conditions and deterioration of components with time are factors that will undermine the starting capability of the system in a similar way to the circumstances applicable to the internal-combustion engine. The depressed voltage that inevitably results detracts not only from the performance of the starter motor but also the ignition system and electrical fuel pumps.

3 ELECTRICAL POWER SUPPLY CONSIDERATIONS

The battery is the prime source of energy, and the objective must be to utilize this power as effectively as possible. The resistance of cables between the battery and starter motor must be kept as low as is practicably possible. Similarly, connections and contact breakers will add to the losses in the power feeder system to the starter motor.

The maximum output obtainable from a starter motor can be derived from the following expression:

$$W_o = \frac{(V_b - V_d)^2}{4(R_b + R_f + R_m)} - W_m$$

where W_o is the starter motor maximum output, watts; V_b the battery open circuit voltage; V_d the starter motor brush voltage drop; R_b the battery internal resistance, ohms; R_f the feeder resistance, ohms; R_m the starter motor resistance, ohms; and W_m the copper, iron and mechanical watts loss of motor. From the above it will be clearly seen that the maximum output of the starter motor is dependent on the combined resistances of the motor, feeder resistance and internal battery resistance.

It is an advantage to have a high voltage for starting wherever this is possible. It will be observed that the net voltage available for the motor is that figure which results after deducting the brush voltage drop and the feeder and battery voltage drops. It is of interest, therefore, to compare the merits of an identical starter motor system operating both on a 24-V system and a 12-V system.

A typical 24-V battery at normal temperatures would have an internal resistance of 20 mΩ. In this example a feeder cable resistance of 4 mΩ and a motor resistance of 40 mΩ is assumed, making a total circuit resistance of 64 mΩ. Substituting these figures in the above expression and allowing 1-V drop for brushes, the maximum motor output is calculated to be 2065 W, minus the motor copper and iron losses.

It could be assumed that a 12-V starter system designed to have the direct equivalent system resistance of the 24-V example would give the same motor output. This would certainly be true if it were possible to achieve this in practice. The brush voltage drop is, however, more likely to be similar to the 24-V machine, i.e. 1 V. This would then yield a calculated maximum output, ignoring motor losses, of 1890 W. The 12-V starter motor would therefore give some $8\frac{1}{2}$ per cent lower output than the 24-V machine, primarily due to the effect of brush drop.

4 STARTER MOTORS

Starter motors are almost always series- or compound-wound commutator-type direct current machines. Because the duty cycle is short it is possible to obtain a relatively high specific output through the use of high magnetic and electrical loadings, together with relatively high speeds.

The importance of the selection of a suitable gear ratio can best be illustrated by reference to the curves on Fig. 63.2. A study of the three examples shows that, for a given supply characteristic, the torque–speed relationship obtained by using a gear ratio of 1:1·75 between the armature and output shaft should provide a satisfactory engine start.

The speed–torque characteristic of the motor with a direct drive will produce a greater accelerating torque over the speed range 0 to 10 000 rev/min but fail to assist the engine up to the minimum self-sustaining speed. An increase in gear ratio 1:2·75 is unsuitable for this application as insufficient torque is available to accelerate the engine under extreme cold weather conditions due to the high resistance torques that are encountered on those occasions.

Experience indicates that the starter torque available at light-up speed should provide a margin of at least 20 per cent above the engine resistance torque for that condition. A typical starter motor (Fig. 63.3) for starting a 100-hp gas turbine that might be fitted to a small automobile is described. Electrically, the motor would consist of a conventional four-pole, compound-wound, field system using a wave-wound armature assembly.

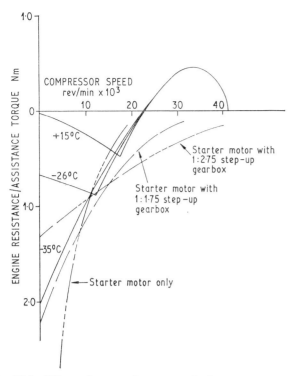

Fig. 63.2. Effect of gear ratio on a particular starter motor

Fig. 63.3. Starter motor

During the starting phase the motor would exhibit a predominantly series characteristic with the shunt winding designed to provide an upper speed limitation on no-load. A no-load speed of some 22 000 rev/min is not uncommon, although this varies with the size of the machine. The commutator and windings tend to be a limiting factor in the choice of maximum speed, and it is for this reason that the shunt winding is provided.

High-permeability iron is used for the yoke, pole shoes and armature laminations. Mechanically, the unit comprises three main assemblies consisting of an integral yoke and housing assembly, a pole shoe assembly and an armature. The pole shoes are usually bolted to the yoke but in some instances they can form an integral part of the yoke in the form of a one-piece lamination.

With the newer insulation materials now available it is possible to operate windings as high as 300°C for the short duty of the starter motor. This facilitates a number of repetitive starts being made before the limiting tem-

perature is reached. Cost will be a factor in choice of materials.

Quite high brush-current densities are employed. For this reason brushes having a high copper content are selected to achieve a low-contact voltage drop. A starter engagement mechanism with associated gearbox may be incorporated into the starter unit. The simplest arrangement is the ratchet type of drive brought into engagement by means of a coarse screw-thread. This is limited to slow-speed applications due to the friction necessary to prevent initial rotation of the engaging jaw.

An alternative method is to actuate the jaw with a solenoid connected in the series field circuit. Disengagement is not then engine dependent, since the solenoid becomes ineffective as the motor approaches no-load speed.

Shock loadings, and even failure to engage, will result if much rotation takes place before axial engagement occurs. Careful design is required to avoid such difficulties and a clutch may be necessary. Another mechanism is a sprag clutch with drive shaft in continuous engagement. Suitable lubrication is necessary, together with appropriate shaft seals. The latter may influence service reliability.

Certain applications can lend themselves to the adoption of a starter generator. This is a machine serving a dual role whereby on completion of the starting cycle the engine drives the machine as a generator throughout the complete engine speed range. The requirement for maximum acceleration during starting normally results in the fitting of accessories such as the alternator, air conditioning and air compressors to the power turbine side.

Starter generators offer the advantage of lower system cost through the use of a single machine. The complication of the engaging and disengaging mechanism is eliminated, and there is no added burden during the starting phase.

The speed range of the internal-combustion engine is typically 10:1; and whereas the commutator machine would give useful output over a speed range of 5:1, the alternator extended this range to 10:1. On the other hand, the gas turbine engine has a comparatively narrow speed range of operation. Usually, the idling speed will be approximately 50 per cent of maximum speed, resulting in a reduced generator speed range of 2:1.

A fundamental problem with starter generators is the incompatibility between maximum magnetic utilization and a speed range extending from zero to full-rated speed covering both motor and generator modes of operation. It is therefore possible to improve upon the normal performance of a machine by adopting a series–parallel battery arrangement; for example, 24 V starting and 12 V generating.

Alternatively, variable ratio gear drives can be arranged whereby, on starting, the motor drives the engine through the particular gear ratio most suitable for the starting operation. When the transmission power is reversed and the unit is driven as a generator, an alternative gear ratio gives the most desirable generator speed.

The arrangements described must be assessed against cost, reliability, size and life and operating requirements.

5 STARTER CONTROL SYSTEMS

The operation of the starting cycle should be simple and automatic. Turning the ignition key momentarily to the start position will initiate through an interlocking circuit the complete starting cycle, during which time the engine will run up to idle speed.

The starter motor and ignition system are energized by the operation of a power relay. It is then necessary for the control system to actuate the nozzle guide vanes into the starting position and to operate the fuel valve.

It is possible to arrange for what might be described as a soft start by means of in-line resistors arranged to limit the starting current and torques. One or more resistance stages can be brought into effect in sequence to avoid peak torques, which may be damaging to the gear mechanism.

The simplest of controllers for such applications are based on a clockwork mechanism that controls the starting cycle sequence as the spring unwinds. On completion of the cycle, the spring can be rewound by means of an electromagnet.

In the Lucas automotive gas turbine engine unit (Fig. 63.4), thick-film circuitry is employed and solid-state components are used throughout. Thermocouple sensors are used to determine intake air temperature and compressor turbine blade temperature. Magnetic pick-up probes register an impulse frequency appropriate to the gasifier speed and the power turbine speed. A transducer determines the power demand after starting, according to the position of the accelerator pedal.

The engine is monitored during start-up by means of these sensors feeding information into a small analogue computer, which forms the starter portion of the control system. A satisfactory rate of temperature change indicating successful light-up will permit the starting cycle to continue. If, however, the rate of temperature change fails to be positive after approximately 4 s, the starting cycle will be terminated. In a similar manner the fuel flow will be modified during the run-up phase according to the limiting temperature governor.

In this unit the starter motor and ignition circuits are switched off to allow disengagement at approximately 40 per cent of maximum engine revolutions. In the case of an abortive start, the driver should allow the engine to come to rest before the starting sequence is re-initiated. Under certain circumstances where compound-wound starter motors are employed, abnormally high transient

Fig. 63.4. Lucas automotive gas turbine engine control unit of which 10 per cent volume is connected with the starting circuit

torques can result if the shunt field and armature circuits are not switched simultaneously.

If the shunt field, having a high inductance relative to the armature, is energized prior to the armature circuit, it is possible for the field strength to build up to the maximum value for that voltage before the effects of armature reaction have time to reduce the net overall field strength. It is not unusual in such circumstances for the instantaneous transient torque to reach a value of twice the normal maximum starting torque, which could lead to serious damage.

6 IGNITION

The basic ignition system comprises a voltage generator unit, lead and igniter plug. Its function is to draw power from the electrical supply and to release energy repetitively in the form of short-duration pulses, which produce high-intensity sparks at the active surface or gap of an igniter plug situated at the edge of a combustion chamber.

Two basic approaches can be employed. The first is a simple high-tension system producing a voltage of about 12–15 kV discharging through an air-gap igniter plug at the rate of 300 sparks/min, or thereabouts, with a discharge energy in the order of 50 mJ.

The second approach, more commonly found in industrial gas turbine applications, is the use of a high-energy ignition system. The working voltage is usually 2 kV, controlled by means of a sealed barrier gap and differing from the high-tension unit in that the energy is not immediately released to the spark gap but allowed to build up to a certain level before being discharged. Units of this kind for small gas turbine engine applications have ratings of approximately 2 J with a typical spark rate of 250 sparks/min, discharging through an igniter plug consisting of two concentric electrodes with ceramic insulation.

The basic voltage generator common to both units contains an electromechanical vibrator, in its simplest form, so that when connected to a direct-current supply the vibrator interrupts the input current at a high rate, creating a flux change within the magnetic circuit. This change of flux induces the high voltage in the secondary output winding. The primary capacitor is present to control the rate of current decrease at the opening of the contacts, as well as to reduce arcing.

A logical improvement is the replacement of the vibrating contact voltage generator (Fig. 63.5) by a transistorized charging unit (Fig. 63.6), thereby improving life, which would otherwise be limited by contact wear. A typical circuit used mainly for stored energy systems is shown in Fig. 63.7. Similar circuits can be used for the high-tension system (Fig. 63.8).

When the supply is switched on, the starting and base resistors form a potential divider across the supply, putting a small positive potential on the base of the transistor making it conductive; the current in the primary winding rises almost linearly, producing a further positive drive to the base. The base current is determined by the primary-to-base winding turns ratio, and the value of the base resistor. While the base drive exceeds the value necessary to maintain full conduction, the primary current continues to rise at a rate determined by the effective resistance and inductance of the primary circuit.

Fig. 63.5. Lucas H.T. ignition unit vibrator type 2TC

Fig. 63.6. Lucas transistorized H.T. ignition unit

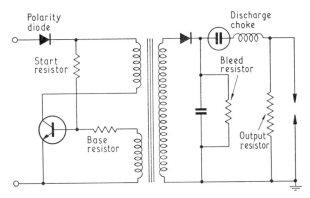

Fig. 63.7. Transistorized high-energy ignition

When the base current is no longer sufficient to keep the transistor fully conductive, the rate of current rise decreases, the base drive decreases and, in a cumulative manner, the transistor rapidly switches off. The secondary discharge current maintains a negative voltage at the base of the transistor. When this current ceases, the direct current potential switches the transistor on and the cycle repeats.

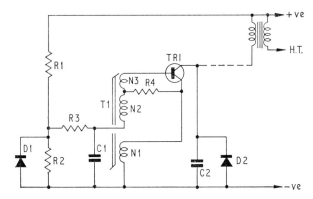

Fig. 63.8. Circuit diagram of electronic igniter

The secondary circuit of the high-tension system is simply a high-tension lead and igniter with an electrode gap length in the order of 0·1 in. The high-energy ignition unit, on the other hand, comprises a rectifier, large storage capacitor and a barrier gap to control the voltage break-down level. This latter type of unit is consequently more sophisticated and expensive.

The igniter for the high-tension system is also much simpler and cheaper than the concentric electrode type required for the high-energy ignition unit. The usual practice with this type of igniter is to implant a semi-conductor coating across the ceramic insulator to promote break-down at a potential less than 2 kV.

7 COMBUSTION SYSTEM

The combustion problems experienced during light-up and acceleration of an engine to a self-sustaining condition depend largely upon the type of combustion chamber adopted. Two basic types of combustion chamber are available, namely, annular or pipe chambers (see Figs 63.9 and 63.10), and the choice of system for a particular application is usually made in the light of the overall engine requirements. For example, if the over-riding need is for a compact lightweight engine, an annular combustion chamber will be used; but if simplicity, cheapness and ease of inspection are more important, a pipe chamber will probably be adopted.

The main combustion system requirements during starting and acceleration of the engine are outlined below, together with the influence of the choice of either pipe or annular combustion chambers on their achievement.

Light-up should be obtained as early in the engine-cranking cycle as possible and the maximum tolerable heat release obtained in order to minimize the starter power demanded, and also to achieve rapid engine acceleration. The level of ignition energy and the maximum fuel pressure should be kept as low as possible to minimize the cost, weight and power consumption of the ancillary equipment. It is therefore necessary to ensure stable combustion at very low engine speeds and to achieve a standard of fuel atomization and placement that gives reliable light-up with the type of ignition system to be used. Observations of the ignition process in transparent models show two distinct phases, namely, ignition of some proportion of the mixture adjacent to the igniter and the subsequent propagation of this flame kernel back to the source of flame stabilization to initiate the main combustion reaction.

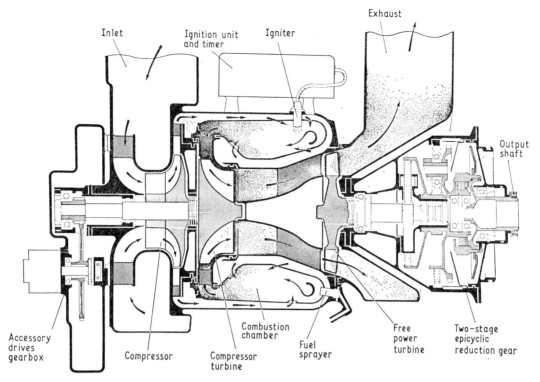

Fig. 63.9

Operation at low ambient temperature, or operation with the reduced temperatures and pressures experienced at high altitudes, increases the severity of the light-up problems and, in general, demands that engines be cranked to higher speeds to ensure reliable light-up. Reduction of both air temperature and pressure reduce the chemical reaction rate of the combustion process and thus tend to inhibit the light-up performance. However, if a combustion chamber has adequate stability limits at normal ambient temperatures and pressures, the reduction of the combustion reaction rate occurring at the most severe conditions specified for an automotive engine (approximately 3000 m altitude and −40°C) does not produce a significant narrowing of the combustion stability or ignition limits. Any deterioration of performance observed is, in the main, usually caused by an increase of fuel viscosity reducing the quality of fuel atomization.

Having achieved reliable light-up early in the cranking cycle, it is necessary to ensure the maximum tolerable temperature rise from the combustion system to ensure rapid acceleration of the engine. This resolves into a compromise between limitations imposed by the engine fuel control system, the maximum temperature the turbine can withstand for a short period, the combustion stability range (particularly at the lower cranking speeds) and the air/fuel ratio conditions giving the maximum temperature rise.

In order that a simple control system can be used, it may be preferable to schedule an essentially constant air/fuel ratio to the engine during light-up and acceleration. The air/fuel ratio at the lower cranking speeds will then probably be weaker than that required to give the highest acceptable turbine entry temperatures, since the combustion efficiency tends to be reduced at the lower cranking speeds. It is necessary, therefore, either to tolerate a combustion temperature rise below the maximum per-

missible or, alternatively, to 'cut back' the scheduled fuel flows at the higher cranking speeds as the combustion efficiency increases.

The permissible short-term maximum temperature is dependent upon the design and material of the turbine-nozzle assembly and can probably only be established by tests. The stability limits and the conditions giving the maximum temperature rise also have to be established by test for each particular type of combustion chamber. At cold crank conditions it is possible that the highest temperature rise is achieved at very rich air/fuel ratios and that a significant proportion of the fuel passes through the combustion chamber without burning. With the new legislation limiting the permissible level of exhaust pollutants, it becomes increasingly necessary to achieve rapid, efficient and smoke-free starts. This, in turn, will make it impractical to have very rich starts and will demand more powerful starters.

The cranking conditions of non-heat exchanger, heat exchanger and single- or twin-shaft engines are usually essentially of a similar order. However, the non-heat exchanger engines have to cater for a larger range of fuel flows than the heat exchanger engines, and hence present more problems when ensuring adequate atomization at low fuel flows. Conversely, by comparison with the full-load conditions, the degree of richening of the primary zone experienced during light-up is greater on the heat exchanger engines than on the non-heat exchanger designs; and if the primary zones are designed to operate in the normal manner with a full-load primary zone air/fuel ratio of approximately 18/1, excessively rich primary conditions may be experienced during light-up and acceleration. The combustion systems of heat exchanger engines are therefore usually designed to have a weaker full-load primary zone air/fuel ratio. Weaker conditions can be tolerated on heat exchanger engines because of the

Fig. 63.10. Regenerative automotive gas turbine with pipe combustion chamber

high combustion air-inlet temperature and, in fact, prove beneficial in other respects.

Although an annular combustion chamber configuration is normally preferred when a compact lightweight arrangement is essential, it is more difficult to achieve satisfactory light-up and acceleration with this type of chamber. Annular combustion systems for engines of less than 400 hp output normally have very narrow combustion annuli, possibly only of the order of 1-in depth, and this tends to give narrow stability limits even though by normal parameters the combustion chambers are lightly loaded. On some small engines this aspect has been further exaggerated by the omission of flow-straightener vanes from compressor delivery, in order to cheapen and lighten the engine. Deletion of these straightener vanes gives a swirling flow condition throughout the combustion chamber and, by significantly increasing the absolute gas velocity levels, further narrows the stability range. The combustion volume chosen for a particular design and the degree of flow straightening adopted are therefore dependent upon the operating requirements of the engine.

In the case of the small annular combustion chamber it is necessary to use several fuel injectors. In addition, particular attention must be paid to the positioning of the fuel within the combustion chamber to achieve adequate fuel distribution and to avoid fuel impingement on to the flame tube walls. Fuel injection is usually either by means of sprayers injecting directly into the flame tube or through vaporizer tubes.

Of these two alternatives, the latter are the more difficult to light; it is invariably necessary to fit a torch igniter comprising a small pressure-jet atomizer and some form of igniter plug to ensure reliable light-up. This is an unacceptable complication on the smaller gas turbine engines.

With the pressure-jet atomizers, the quality of atomization achieved is dependent upon the pressure drop across the atomizer; as the number of fuel injectors is increased, it is necessary to reduce the size of the individual atomizer orifices to maintain the required standard of atomization. In fact, on the smaller engines it is possible that the available fuel-pump pressure cannot be utilized without using atomizer orifice sizes below the minimum recommended from blockage considerations.

Whilst it may be possible to achieve light-up on either one or a reduced number of sprayers, this invariably leads to a more complex arrangement and an inferior exhaust temperature distribution during engine acceleration. It is possible to improve the quality of atomization at the low fuel flows by assisting the atomization by means of a

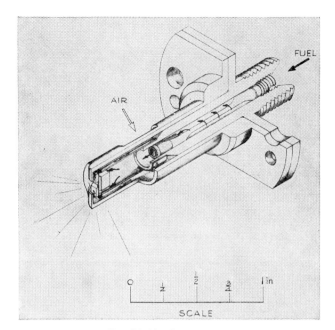

Fig. 63.11. Fan sprayer

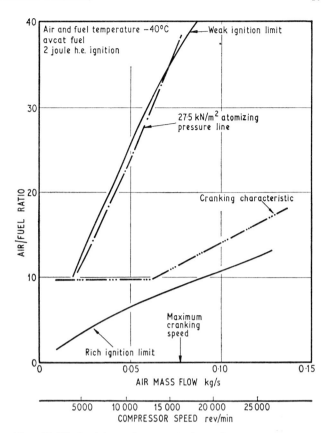

Fig. 63.12. Ignition characteristics of a small annular combustion system

separate air feed to each sprayer. If 'air assistance' is used on these small engines, it is necessary to fit a small air pump to supply the air flows required.

With engines of the type under consideration it has not proved feasible to utilize the flame tube wall pressure loss to provide the air flow required for air assistance, because the pressure loss across the flame tube wall at starting is too low, normally only 0.125 kN/m^2. There is thus a considerable incentive to avoid using air assistance and to achieve the required standard of atomization with pressure-jet atomizers, particularly on engines using several sprayers.

A novel type of atomizer, shown in Fig. 63.11, has been developed to satisfy this requirement. This atomizer gives a flat spray of fuel, which provides a good fuel distribution within the narrow flame tube annulus without causing fuel impingement on to the flame tube walls, thus allowing a reduction in the number of atomizers required. In addition, as the atomization is achieved by the impingement of opposing jets of fuel, the parasitic losses within the atomizers are low, resulting in excellent low flow atomizing characteristics being obtained.

Nevertheless, the standard of atomization achieved at the lowest flow conditions is still below the ideal level, and it is necessary to use a high-energy ignition system to obtain light-up. These high-energy systems are potentially dangerous if misused; therefore they are not favoured for domestic automotive applications. Further, if light-up is required within 1 or 2 s of the initiation of the starting cycle, it is obviously desirable to use a high-spark frequency. The 12-J high-energy ignition systems normally used on large aero or industrial engines have a frequency of 80 sparks/min and are obviously unsuitable for an engine demanding rapid light-up; however, the 2-J system fitted to some small engines has a frequency of 250 sparks/min. This latter is more suitable for an engine demanding rapid light-up, although improved atomization is required to compensate for the reduced ignition energy.

The ignition limits for a small annular combustion chamber operating with AVCAT fuel at air and fuel temperatures of $-40°C$ are shown in Fig. 63.12, together with the cranking characteristics for the engine. It will be seen that ignition would occur at approximately 3000 rev/min and that the weak ignition limit is virtually coincident with a line denoting an atomizing pressure of 27.5 kN/m^2.

With a single-pipe combustion chamber, several potential problem areas are eased. The basic stability limits of this type of chamber are wider than those of the small annular chamber; although asymmetrical flow conditions may be obtained, a satisfactory solution can be obtained by the use of plenum chambers or deflectors, because small size and light weight are not usually demanded on these applications. Similarly, only one fuel atomizer is required; it is therefore possible to size the orifice in relation to the pump capability and hence achieve higher atomizing pressures without resorting to very small passage sizes.

In addition, as there is only one sprayer, a slightly more complex design can be fitted, and it is normally acceptable to use air assistance to improve the low flow atomization. The procedure usually followed is to provide air assistance from a small electrically driven air pump during the starting cycle only, and to utilize a tapping at compressor delivery to give an air feed through the sprayer air passages once the engine is self-sustaining. The quality of atomization obtained during cranking with this arrangement is good enough to allow ignition to be obtained down to low ambient temperatures using only a car-type high-tension ignition system.

The weak ignition limits for a typical automotive

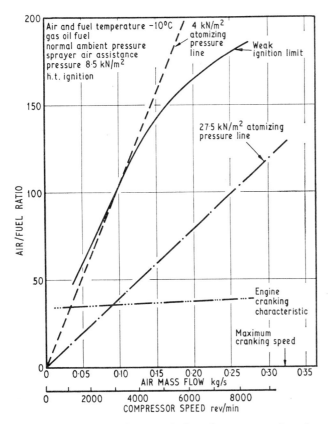

Fig. 63.13. Ignition characteristics of an automotive pipe
combustion chamber

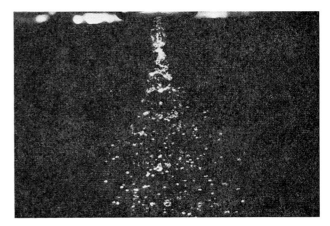

a Without air assistance.

b With 8·5 kN/m² air assistance.

Fig. 63.14. Performance of a F.N. 1·2/90° sprayer, fuel
flow 6·8 litre/h of gas oil

combustion chamber are shown in Fig. 63.13. This shows ignition to be achieved at an engine speed of only 1000 rev/min and the weak ignition limit to occur at fuel pressures of approximately 4 kN/m²; a 27·5 kN/m² atomizing pressure line is shown for comparison with Fig. 63.12. In this case it proved to be impracticable to establish the rich ignition limits without risking damage to the test equipment. The improvement of atomization achieved by the use of air assistance is shown by Figs 63.14*a* and 63.14*b*; these show the fuel spray at a 6·8 litre/h light-up condition both with and without air assistance.

8 TRENDS

It was shown earlier that the effect of brush-drop could show a marked difference in starter motor output when considering system voltage. In that example, the resistances of the system were converted in relation to the system voltage.

In the practical situation, discrete battery sizes only may be available, and therefore the merits of individual systems must be assessed with specific battery values obtained in each instance. A higher system voltage is nearly always to be preferred wherever possible. Not only will there be a benefit in maximum power utilization through reduced brush-drop but the effects of contactor voltage drop and termination voltage drops will be minimized.

Future trends are difficult to predict with any accuracy, but it is unlikely that any significant improvement can be seen in the specific output of starter motors other than by using better quality magnetic materials at increased cost.

Permanent magnet field poles reduce the machine resistance and heating. Ceramic-type magnets have good properties under demagnetizing forces such as those that occur during starting, but low overall flux levels when compared to an electromagnetic field. The cost of magnetic materials such as Permendur, a cobalt alloy, is more than a hundred times that of silicon iron magnetic materials, and the net gain in reduced machine resistance may be no more than 10 per cent.

Brush voltage drop is an obvious area in which to seek future improvements. Although commutators have been in use for decades there is still much to be learnt on commutation. Improved brush-grades and current collection techniques that tend to give a more uniform current density at the surface of the brush could result in lower contact drops.

9 CONCLUSIONS

The basic requirement for the starting of gas turbine engines has been outlined. These requirements differ from the internal-combustion engine in that the starting cycle consists of several phases in which the turbine blade and jet pipe temperature are critical considerations. Automatic means must therefore be provided for run-up to idle.

Anti-pollution trends may result in larger starter motors,

but little significant improvement is foreseen in the development of greater specific output from conventional starter motors, as the actual output is dependent to a great extent on the prime energy source, the battery. Permanent magnet starter motor designs could perhaps offer better system optimization advantages in certain applications due to the lower machine resistance.

Starter generators could serve a useful role in certain applications due to the narrow power–speed range, and their use may be more suitably optimized through the introduction of twin-ratio gearboxes or series–parallel battery arrangements. Brush life, probably in the order of 50 000 miles, will, however, influence such a choice, as will the need for ventilation in exposed installations.

10 ACKNOWLEDGEMENTS

The authors wish to thank friends and colleagues who have contributed opinions and information in the preparation of this paper, Mr A. C. Mason of our Computer Department for Appendix 63.1, and also the Directors of Joseph Lucas Ltd and Lucas Aerospace Ltd for permission to publish.

APPENDIX 63.1

ESTIMATION OF ENGINE STARTING TIME

The time taken for any driven load to attain a particular speed is determined by the combined torque, T, and the combined inertia, I, of the system. These parameters have the following relationship:

$$T = I \frac{d\omega}{dt}$$

where $d\omega/dt$ is the instantaneous angular acceleration.

Rearranging and integrating this expression gives the time to change the angular speed from ω_1 to ω_2, which is:

$$\text{Time} = \int_{\omega_1}^{\omega_2} \frac{I}{T} \, d\omega$$

Since the torque is usually a function ω but not of a known mathematical form, it is necessary to use approximate methods to evaluate this integral. The integral is equivalent to finding the area under the curve of I/T $V.\omega$ between ω_1 and ω_2; one method is to divide the speed into a number of intervals and to compute the time for each interval, assuming a simple trapezoidal area for each.

This method results in the following equation for the time taken to run-up a load from rest to a speed of ω_n:

$$\text{Time} = \frac{I}{2} \left\{ \left(\frac{1}{T\omega_0} + \frac{1}{T\omega_1} \right) (\omega_1 - \omega_0) \right.$$
$$+ \left(\frac{1}{T\omega_1} + \frac{1}{T\omega_2} \right) (\omega_2 - \omega_1) + \cdots$$
$$\left. + \left(\frac{1}{T\omega_{(n-1)}} + \frac{1}{T\omega_n} \right) (\omega_n - \omega_{(n-1)}) \right\}$$

where I is the motor+load inertia and $T\omega$ the algebraic sum of the motor and load torques at speed ω.

This series of calculations may be performed quite easily using a computer, and the accuracy of the method is improved by increasing the number of speed intervals.

C65/72 COLD CHAMBER DEVELOPMENT WORK AND TESTING

A. J. BARBER*

Cold chamber testing has for many years been a normal part of vehicle equipment specification programmes carried out throughout the automobile industry. Procedures and techniques have been developed at the author's company that are aimed at ensuring the best possible utilization of the cold room facility and minimization of possible error. The primary objective of this paper is to detail the techniques currently in use in order that standardization of the procedures used in the industry for this type of testing can be discussed. The variations in performance of the starter motor, battery and ignition system with reduction in temperature are discussed together with the effect of changes in oil viscosity. In addition, the problems associated with cold starting of petrol and diesel engines are outlined. Reference is made to the instrumentation employed during cold chamber testing.

1 INTRODUCTION

WITH THE INCREASING EMPHASIS on export in the motor industry, it is important that vehicles are correctly specified for the environment in which they will be required to operate. Since these markets include North America and Scandinavia, where temperatures down to −40°C are not uncommon, testing of vehicle starting systems in depressed temperatures is essential. The engineer responsible for specifying this system has two alternatives: either to equip a vehicle and carry out tests in a country with a suitable environment, or to test in a cold chamber. The former has many disadvantages including cost, variation in temperature, difficulty with instrumentation and, since testing can only be carried out during the winter months, the time available for testing is limited. It is advisable, therefore, to use the cold chamber, where greater experimental control is available, for the original specification of the system and to confine field testing to confirmation and validation of complete vehicle systems. In addition, testing of prototypes, either in complete vehicle form or engines and transmissions, can be carried out without prematurely exposing new body designs.

Many variables that exist in cold chamber testing are discussed in this paper, but the temperature control of the facility itself is of the utmost importance. To ensure accuracy, the equipment must be capable of controlling to within ±1°C and of testing down to −40°C. The Lucas facility consists of two rooms both capable of reducing complete vehicles to −40°C in 15 h; the larger of the two rooms (Fig. 65.1) is suitable for testing medium-size trucks or tractor units. Vehicular access is by large, sliding doors with an hydraulic closing mechanism at the front of each room; personnel access is via an airlock at the side of each room. The majority of the tests carried out in this facility are designed to establish suitable starter–battery combinations for both temperate and cold climate areas. This involves testing at −12°C (+10°F) and −29°C (−20°F) respectively, these being the agreed minimum test temperatures in the British motor industry. The latter temperature is selected for cold climate specifications because it is the minimum long-term temperature normally experienced in North America and Scandinavia.

This paper discusses cold chamber testing under six main headings, viz. (a) starter motor, (b) battery, (c) engine resistance, (d) cold cranking, (e) cold starting, and (f) instrumentation.

2 STARTER MOTOR

Low-temperature starter motor rig tests, to establish performance, are virtually confined to proving tests, where it is necessary to establish the characteristics of the motor at various temperatures down to −29°C. Starters used for cold cranking are normally tested at room temperature to ensure that they conform to the expected performance and to establish a torque–current line, which is necessary for obtaining the engine resistive torque.

For a given battery volt–ampere characteristic, the starter motor performance will appreciate with reducing temperature due to reductions in the overall electrical resistance of the machine. This change in performance occurs to the speed–current characteristic with the torque–current characteristic remaining virtually constant, except for a negligible change due to bearing losses. It follows, therefore, that the speed–torque characteristic varies with temperature. Fig. 65.2 shows the change in this characteristic at −29°C from that measured at 20°C. From this it will be seen that, if all other variables remained constant and assuming a 10:1 starter-to-engine gear ratio, for an engine resistance of 100 N m, there would be an approximate increase in cranking speed of 18 per cent.

It is not always possible to obtain the particular starter

The MS. of this paper was received at the Institution on 19th January 1972 and accepted for publication on 13th April 1972. 33
* Project Engineer, Joseph Lucas (Elect.) Ltd, Great King Street, Birmingham 19.

motor for a prototype engine for which a cold climate specification is required. However, with a knowledge of the torque–speed characteristic of the starter at the relevant temperature, and using the specified battery volt-ampere, the engine/starter gear ratio and the resistive torque–speed characteristic of the engine, it is possible to predict accurately the crank-performance by plotting the two torque characteristics (Fig. 65.3) to a base of engine speed. Where the two curves intersect is the cranking point.

Fig. 65.1. The Lucas No. 1 cold room

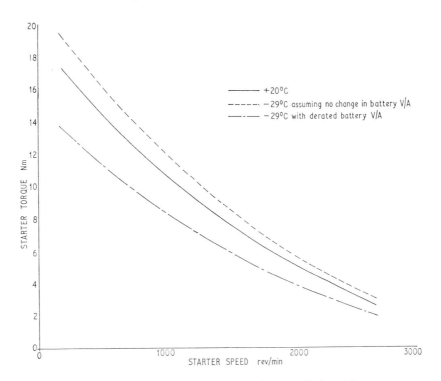

Fig. 65.2. Variation in starter torque–speed characteristic with temperature and with change in battery performance due to temperature

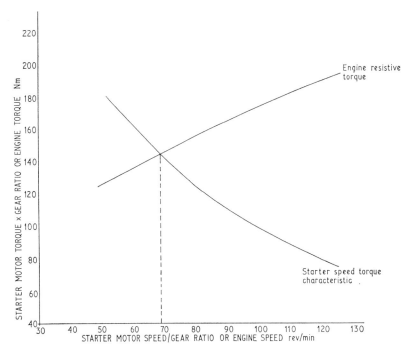

Fig. 65.3. Typical cranking speed prediction curve

3 BATTERY

Since battery performance tends to appreciate during the first part of its working life, batteries for cold testing are given three conditioning cycles consisting of a discharge at the 10-h rate until the voltage on load reaches 1·8 V/cell, followed by a charge at approximately $1\frac{1}{4}$ times the 10-h rate. Batteries are normally prepared to either a 70 or 80 per cent state of charge, depending on the specified charging system. They are prepared by discharging for 1 h/10 per cent required reduction in state of charge at the 10-h rate.

A principal problem in cold starting is the reduction in the available power from the battery. This reduction in power is mainly because the viscosity of the electrolyte increases with decreasing temperature, causing the diffusion of the electrolyte at the active material to be retarded. Also, most chemical reactions proceed more slowly at low temperatures, therefore both the on-load and off-load voltages will be lower under these conditions. In addition, the ohmic resistance of the electrolyte rises with decreasing temperature, whereas the opposite is true of the resistance of the metallic conducting material within the battery.

However, the resistance of the electrolyte is much larger and the overall effect is an increase in the internal resistance of the battery, with decreasing temperature. For a given battery, the reduction in available power with a temperature change from 20°C to −18°C is approximately 40 per cent. It therefore follows that for low-temperature

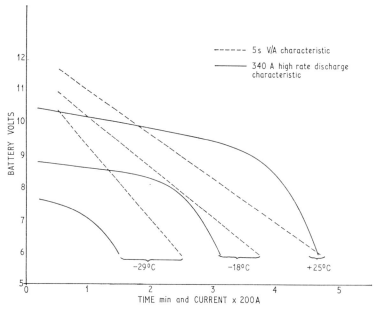

Fig. 65.4. Volt–ampere and high-rate discharge characteristics of fully charged 68-A h batteries at various temperatures

applications the only way of providing sufficient power is to either ensure that the battery temperature does not fall excessively or to increase the size of the battery. This should be considered when space for the battery is allocated in the original vehicle design.

Fig. 65.4 shows the change in volt–ampere and high-rate discharge characteristic with reduction in temperature for a typical car battery. Only in exceptional circumstances will the battery be in a fully charged condition. Surveys have shown that on cars used for regular commuter journeys, the average state of charge of the battery prior to the introduction of the alternator was 70 per cent; more recent spot checks show that this figure is now 80 per cent. These figures influence the choice of battery state for cold chamber testing.

The accurate preparation of a battery is useless if its original performance is above or below the normally expected standard. Therefore all batteries used for cold chamber tests are checked for conformance to this standard by means of volt–ampere and high-rate discharge testing, these two characteristics being the ones that have the most influence on cranking performance. These tests are carried out in the laboratory. The volt–ampere test is by the application of fixed resistive loads at increments appropriate to the ampere hour capacity of the battery on test. The high-rate discharge test is by applying a suitable constant load and measuring the time for the terminal voltage to fall to half the battery nominal voltage.

During cold testing, a battery is subjected to a particularly arduous life. Therefore, since its performance is critical to the accuracy of the test, a method of continually monitoring its condition must be used. This is achieved by reference to the ultraviolet chart recorder traces of battery voltage and starter current taken during cranking tests. By plotting the maximum voltage against minimum current and maximum current against minimum voltage, two points on a volt–ampere line are obtained.

This line will differ from the one obtained in the laboratory test, outlined above, due to the cyclic nature of the cranking load. It will also vary with cranking frequency, thus different battery volt–ampere lines will be obtained, with identical batteries, at either different cranking speeds on engines with the same number of cylinders, or at the same cranking speed on engines with a different number of cylinders. Care must therefore be taken to ensure that comparisons are valid before rejecting results due to alleged battery deterioration. Slight deterioration in the high-rate discharge characteristic has little effect on the 5-s cranking speed and influences only the cranking stamina of the system—a factor of much more importance when starting diesel engines.

To evaluate the stamina of a system, 'run-down' tests are carried out. These determine whether or not the battery has adequate storage capacity to maintain the required cranking speed for sufficient time to ensure a satisfactory start. This test will also evaluate the ability of the starter motor to discharge the applied battery without incurring damage due to overheating.

4 ENGINE RESISTANCE

Where possible, engines are tested with ancillary equipment, including a complete cooling system. If no cooling system is used, the engine is drained of coolant and the fan belt removed. For each day's test, fresh oil is used irrespective of whether or not the grade or type of oil is changed. If there is a grade change, the engine is first flushed with the new grade and then, after draining, refilled with the test oil. The normal, minimum, cold soak period for engines is 15 h.

In order to provide a measure by which engines may be compared, and to establish a datum to ensure that day-to-day testing is consistent, the 'engine resistance' must be measured. For the purpose of cold cranking, the engine resistance is defined as the resistive torque presented to the starter motor at its pinion and includes the gear losses.

The curve of mean torque required to turn the engine at mean speed is obtained over the range 50–150 rev/min for petrol engines and 50–200 rev/min for diesel engines. However, it may be necessary to extend this range to include speeds that actually occur during cranking tests on a particular engine. To obtain this curve the following method is used.

The engine is prepared and then soaked for the normal 15 h, fitted with a calibrated starter motor. It is then cranked at various speeds, over the required range, by applying the appropriate voltages. The mean current over two consecutive revolutions of the engine is obtained by analysis of the ultraviolet recorder trace of the starter current.

The starter torque corresponding to this mean current can be obtained by reference to the characteristics of the calibrated starter and, if multiplied by the starter pinion-to-flywheel gear ratio, the mean resistive torque for the particular mean cranking speed is obtained. These figures make no allowance for gear efficiency and therefore include a component due to gear losses. This value, being higher than the true resistance, is that torque which has to be met by the starter motor.

The resistive torque of a given engine will vary with temperature and oil grade. Engine resistance variation with temperature for a typical four-cylinder, 3500-cm^3 diesel engine is shown in Fig. 65.5. The variation in N m/°C is much greater at low temperatures, due mainly to oil viscosity changes below freezing point. The total resistance is the cumulative effect of all moving parts, but the main components of engine resistance are the crankshaft bearings, the pistons, the valve gear and the compression.

Fig. 65.6 shows the effect of each of these components on the resistance of a typical four-cylinder, 1500-cm^3 petrol engine at two temperatures. It will be seen that the contribution to the total made by the bearings and pistons increases dramatically with a decrease in temperature. This is true of all components influenced by oil viscosity. The compression element remains approximately constant with temperature and its effect on the total resistance at lower temperatures is therefore minimized.

It follows, therefore, that there will be considerable variation in resistance, not only for engines of different configuration in terms of number of cylinders, type of valve gear and compression ratio but between engines of identical design. The difference in resistance between engines of the same make and type will depend largely on the manufacturing tolerances and the build of each individual unit. These differences can be small for four-cylinder engines (up to 10 per cent) and large for eight- and 12-cylinder engines (up to 50 per cent). Fig. 65.7 shows typical resistance curves for a range of engines at −29°C.

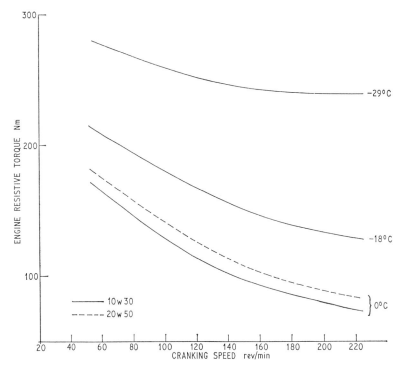

Fig. 65.5. Engine resistive curves for a 3·5-litre diesel engine

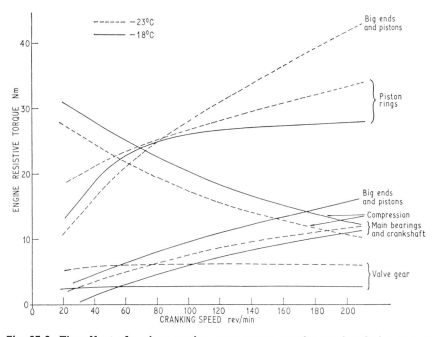

Fig. 65.6. The effect of various engine components on the total resistive torque of a 1500-cm³ petrol engine at two temperatures using 10W oil

The spread of resistance on one engine type is shown in Fig. 65.8, and this illustrates the problem facing the engineer who is responsible for specifying the starter motor–battery combination for this type of engine. To provide the increase in torque requirement over the range shown could necessitate a change of both starter and battery. This emphasizes the need to test as many engines as possible before a viable starting combination can be specified.

An important contribution to the total resistance is made by the transmission; with manual transmission there is normally a cross-over point when the drag of the gearbox components, which rotate in neutral, exceeds the drag of the clutch withdrawal mechanism. This is particularly evident on units where an 80 or 90 E.P. oil is specified for the gearbox. Beyond the cross-over point, better cranking speeds are obtained by disengaging the clutch. Fig. 65.9 shows a comparison of engine resistance, with a manual gearbox in both clutch engaged and disengaged positions, compared with that of an automatic transmission.

4.1 Effect of oil on engine resistance

The choice of a suitable oil specification for any engine is

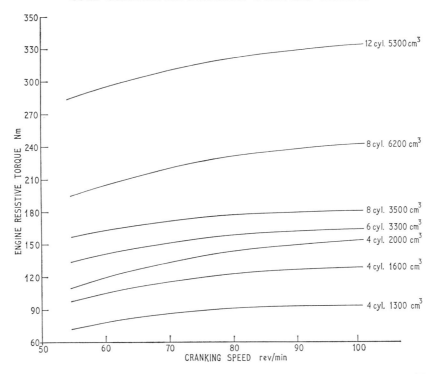

Fig. 65.7. Typical resistive torque curves of various petrol engines at −29°C using SAE 5W oil

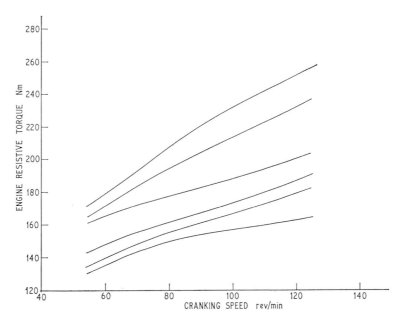

Fig. 65.8. Engine resistance variation of six different eight-cylinder 3·5-litre petrol engines of the same type at −29°C using 5W20 oil

always a compromise between engine wear, oil consumption and good startability. It has been shown that the main components of engine resistance are those produced by engine friction; therefore variation in oil viscosity has a considerable effect on the cranking speed. Fig. 65.5 shows the change in cranking torque at 0°C with a change in oil grade from 10W/30 to 20W/50.

So far the variation discussed has been between oil grades, but in addition to this a significant source of variation in cold cranking tests is due to differences between oils of the same nominal SAE grade. This is particularly evident with SAE 20W, because of the wide range of vis-

cosity in this grade. Table 65.1 shows the range of −18°C viscosities of the three oil grades normally used in cold room tests.

The range in the SAE 5W grade is small but variation does exist between manufacturers. This variation is illustrated in Fig. 65.10, which shows the difference in cranking torque on the same engine under identical conditions for two oils of this nominal grade from different manufacturers. Variation between barrels of oil from different production batches of the same grade by the same manufacturer is normally small. The problem of variation in oil viscosity can be minimized as a source of error by carrying

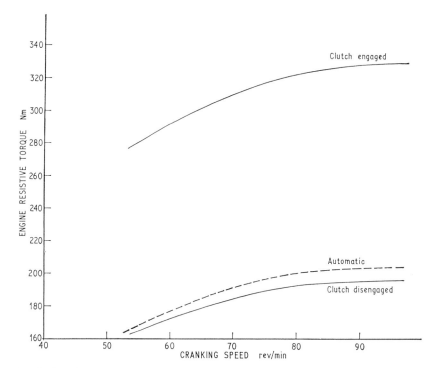

Fig. 65.9. Change in engine resistive torque with operation of clutch and for automatic transmission

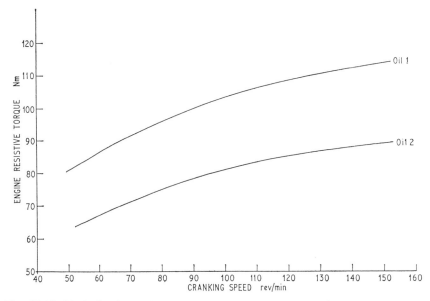

Fig. 65.10. Variation in engine resistive torque of a 1600-cm³ petrol engine due to difference in oil viscosity between 5W oils of different manufacture

out viscosity checks on all supplies of oil and the result of these checks taken into account when cranking results are analysed.

Table 65.1. Comparison of viscosity ranges of 5, 10 and 20W oils

SAE viscosity number	Viscosity range in centipoises at −18°C	
	Min.	Max.
SAE 5W		Less than 1200
SAE 10W	1200	Less than 2400
SAE 20W	2400	Less than 9600

The importance of oil viscosity in cold starting is much greater than just its effect on cranking speed. It is possible to provide a starting system that will start an engine satisfactorily in very depressed temperatures and high oil viscosity conditions. However, if the engine does not develop sufficient power to overcome its own viscous traction, it will stall as soon as the starter motor is disengaged. In this case, increasing the power of the starting system makes little difference to the startability of the engine.

It is important to observe the engine manufacturer's oil specifications in regard to oil change temperatures and to test at the lowest specified temperature for each oil. When testing is carried out on one engine using various oil grades, it is essential that the oil used for the previous test is thoroughly flushed, using the new grade, before refilling the engine with the test oil.

In service, oil viscosity will vary with use, particularly if the vehicle owner does not adhere to the manufacturer's oil change recommendations or uses the vehicle on a particularly severe operating regime, for instance, many journeys of short duration with a cold engine. In general, engine lubricating oil will become significantly more viscous due to a build-up of insolubles, particularly in diesel engines, under these conditions, and cold starting could well become a problem if the starting system specification is borderline.

5 COLD CRANKING

Dead cranking (i.e. with the carburettor dry and the ignition off, for petrol engines, or the fuel cut-off lever in the OFF position for diesel engines) is used to establish the mean cranking speed attainable with a particular battery-starter combination for the conditions obtaining. The mean speeds measured give an accurate comparison between various configurations without the variables encountered during starting tests.

The prepared engine, together with batteries at the required state of charge, is soaked at the test temperature for a minimum of 15 h. The engine is cranked 'dry' (no fuel) for 5 s during which time the battery voltage, starter voltage and current are monitored with an ultraviolet recorder. The mean cranking speed is calculated by reference to the current trace and the chart speed markers.

The flywheel is of vital importance in cold starting and normally the higher the flywheel inertia the better the cranking characteristics of the engine. The flywheel stores energy between compressions, which is used by the system on compression, thus raising the mean cranking speed. Reduction in flywheel inertia can cause stalling on compression. With four-cylinder engines using light flywheels, the use of an inertia starter drive is impractical at low temperatures, since one weak fire is sufficient to accelerate the flywheel to the speed necessary to eject the pinion. Therefore, unless this first fire produces sufficient energy to take the next piston over compression, with subsequent firing on all four cylinders, it will not be possible to start the engine.

The pre-engaged type of drive is normally specified at low temperatures, and this will allow the starter motor to assist the engine during the first, weak, firing sequence of starting because the drive is held in mesh by the solenoid-operated engaging mechanism.

6 COLD STARTING

Following cranking tests, the engine is primed with the appropriate fuel and the normal cold start procedure specified by the manufacturer is carried out. Starting aids are used when recommended and their effectiveness observed. The time to first fire, engine run and starter off are noted from the chart record of the start. The pattern of the start can also be observed on the trace, including premature pinion ejection, intermittent firing and firing against the starter. Satisfactory starts for temperate climates (down to −12°C) should be achieved in 15 s for petrol and 30 s for diesel engines. For cold climates the times are extended to 30 and 60 s respectively. The starting characteristics of engines vary considerably and have a direct influence on the selection of a suitable starting system. For clarity, the two fundamental engine types will be discussed separately.

6.1 Petrol engines

In order to start a petrol engine a suitable mixture of petrol and air must be placed in the combustion chamber. To ignite this charge, heat must be applied to a mass of gas, so that its temperature is brought to the spontaneous ignition temperature. This mass must be large enough to provide sufficient energy at its surface to bring the adjacent layers of the mixture to the spontaneous ignition temperature; the flame will then proceed through the gas.

When cold starting, the important factor is not the air/fuel ratio but the air/vapour ratio, since only a small fraction of the liquid carburant will take part in the combustion.

The amount of petrol that will evaporate in air is governed by the distillation curve, the vapour pressure of the fuel and the air pressure. It is important, therefore, that during cold room testing the correct fuel specified for the test environment is used. The two fuels normally used in the Lucas cold rooms are British winter grade (10 R.V.P.) and Canadian winter grade (13 R.V.P.); the former is used down to −12°C and the latter for all tests below this temperature.

Since cranking speeds are relatively low during cold starting conditions, the manifold depression will be low (0–5 inHg) and the control of the flow of fuel difficult. On engines where the fuel has to be drawn upwards, higher cranking speeds may be required for satisfactory filling of the manifold. It follows, therefore, that down-draught carburettors with a strangler-type choke have an advantage over the side-draught C.D. type. Another disadvantage of C.D. carburettors in these conditions is that the piston may become inoperative, due to frozen moisture forming in the suction chamber, and some form of heating may be necessary to obviate this difficulty.

Petrol injection is particularly suitable for cold starting conditions because automatic temperature–fuel control can be arranged to give the exact requirements for a particular temperature and fuel. However, unless the use of petrol injection is necessary for other reasons, the cost of such a system would negate its technical advantage if the engine can be started down to −29°C with a simpler carburettor system. The ignition requirement under these conditions will be high because there will be little ionization at the plug electrodes, thus increasing the plug breakdown voltage. For example, the plug breakdown voltage at 20°C would normally be 10–12 kV compared to 14–16 kV at −29°C. The standard ignition coil is well capable of supplying this voltage, providing that the system voltage is maintained at a reasonable level. Unfortunately this is not always so, because of the high current drain during cranking.

If the voltage drops below 7 V, it is necessary to use a ballasted system. This consists of a 7-V coil with a suitable resistor in series for 12-V operation and additional contacts on the starter solenoid to short out this resistor during cranking. This allows the coil to operate on its normal full-rated voltage.

The starting characteristics of the Wankel engine are entirely different to those of normal petrol reciprocating engines. They approximate to the D.I. (direct-injection) diesel engine in that a relatively lengthy period of assisted cranking is required, during which time the engine is firing weakly. The use of a pre-engaged starter is thus essential for this type of engine. Cranking speeds in the order of 200 rev/min (output shaft) are necessary, and engine resistive torques approximate to those of reciprocating engines of similar theoretical capacity.

6.2 Diesel engines

Diesel engine starting characteristics are entirely different from those of petrol engines. Whereas in the petrol engine a premixed gaseous charge is burned, in the diesel engine, liquid fuel burns at the surface of droplets. Therefore a system is used that supplies an air stream to present fresh oxygen at the surface of the fuel, and a spray characteristic that gives a large surface area in relation to the volume of fuel. The charge is ignited by a gradual build-up of temperature during cranking.

Starting is usually a three-stage process: (1) cranking up to first fire, (2) assisted cranking, and (3) run up to governed speed. The starting system must therefore be capable of cranking the engine at not only the necessary speed but for sufficient time to raise the temperature of the charge to the spontaneous ignition temperature, and then to assist the engine until it is developing sufficient power to be self-sustaining.

The starting characteristics of the two basic diesel engine types differ in that the I.D.I. (indirect-injection) engine, in unaided form, will normally require a higher cranking speed to start than an otherwise similar D.I. engine. In practice, this means that the D.I. engine will start unaided down to a much lower temperature than the I.D.I. engine. It is normally necessary to specify heater plugs for the I.D.I. engine, which completely changes their starting characteristics to provide startability at least comparable to that of the D.I. unit.

There are various methods employed to assist the engine during cold starting.

6.3 Ignition aids

The 'heater' plug is a device for igniting the fuel not, as its name suggests, for heating the combustion chamber. It is used most effectively on engines with a precombustion chamber and is normally specified for the I.D.I. engine. One shortcoming of this device is that with a reduction in voltage during cranking the efficiency of the heater is reduced.

6.4 Heating aids

There are two main methods of increasing the combustion chamber temperature.

Ki-gas

This method utilizes a small hand-pump to pump fuel into the manifold where it is heated by an electrically heated plug. Although some burning takes place, the main function of this system is to warm the fuel and hence the manifold combustion chamber. Its main drawback is that good starting depends on correct operator technique.

Thermostart

With the thermostart, fuel is gravity fed from a small container into the manifold via an automatically valved system.

The tubular valve body is surrounded by an electrically heated coil with an extension that forms an igniter. When cold the valve is closed until heat from the coil expands the body, opening the valve and allowing the entry of fuel. The fuel is vaporized by the heat of the valve body and ignited by the coil extension, the subsequent burning heats the inlet air. On switching off the heating coil, the valve body cools and the valve closes.

6.5 Auxiliary fuel aid

The introduction of ether into the inlet manifold is possibly the most effective cold starting aid. However, the burning is extremely rapid, causing high loads in the engine and hence possible damage.

7 INSTRUMENTATION

The instrumentation used during cold chamber testing has changed over the years as superior techniques have been developed. At an early stage it became obvious that there were many advantages in the continuous recording of cranking and starting tests. The main advantage being that it is very difficult, if not impossible, to read the maximum and minimum voltage and current using normal moving-coil instruments; also, of course, a permanent record is made of each test.

The first instrument used in the Lucas facility was an oscillograph, which utilized a tungsten light source and photographic paper that required developing and fixing, a process that was both time consuming and untidy. The later development of oscillographs with an ultraviolet light source and suitably sensitive paper provided the ideal instrument for this application. The oscillographs that are now used have galvanometers with good frequency response and minimum overshoot.

Typical traces for cranking and starting tests are shown in Figs 65.11 and 65.12. The instrument is calibrated before each day's work using a constant-voltage source. The parameters normally monitored are the starter current via a suitable shunt, the starter voltage and the battery voltage; the difference between the two latter measurements gives the voltage drop in the system due to cable resistance. In addition to the instrumentation used during actual tests a cold crank simulator is available to check the viscosity of each barrel of oil used in the cold room.

8 CONCLUSIONS

The results obtained from cold chamber tests are only valid if the utmost care has been taken in controlling the many variables encountered. The most important variable is the engine, and before any starting system is specified each engine type should be fully investigated by measuring the spread of engine resistance on as many engines as possible. Without this knowledge large errors may be incurred.

It has been shown that the starter motor torque–speed characteristic improves with decreasing temperature and that the battery volt–ampere characteristic deteriorates. Fig. 65.2 shows the overall loss in cranking performance for a typical starter motor–battery combination with a reduction in temperature from 20°C to −29°C. This loss in cranking performance is mainly due to a reduction in battery output, which, although reduced, is not offset by the improvement in starter performance.

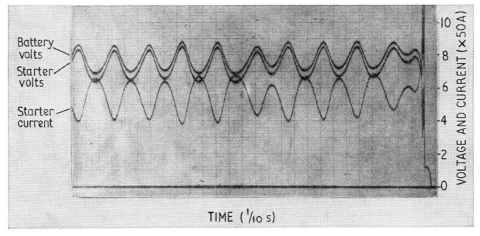

Fig. 65.11. Typical ultraviolet recorder trace of a dead crank at −29°C on a six-cylinder petrol engine

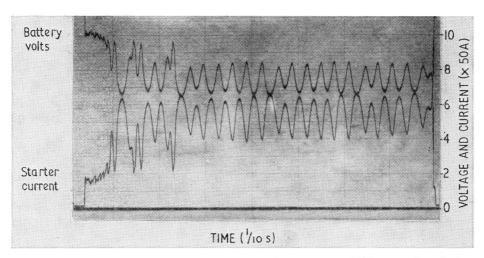

Fig. 65.12. Typical ultraviolet recorder trace of a start at −29°C on a six-cylinder petrol engine

The problem is worsened on petrol engines and diesel engines with heating aids, where the combined effect of increased engine resistance, mainly due to increase in oil viscosity, and reduction in battery power reduces the voltage available to either the ignition system (petrol engines) or to the heater plugs (diesel engines) during cranking. In practice, any measures taken to insulate the battery in order that any heat absorbed during running time can be retained while the vehicle is stationary will be of great benefit, because not only will the battery give greater output but it will be more capable of accepting charge.

The length and cross-section of the starter feed cable should be designed to give minimum voltage drop at the starter terminals, particularly at lower temperatures where cranking currents are high and hence voltage drops at a maximum.

It has been shown that it is possible—despite specifying a starting system that provides adequate cranking speed to start the engine and an adequate fueling system—the engine is incapable of developing sufficient power to overcome the oil drag. In this case the problem can only be solved by either specifying a less viscous oil or providing heating for the sump.

C72/72 LOW-TENSION ELECTRICAL DISTRIBUTION

C. H. HARTOP*   W. F. GREENSTREET†

The history of vehicle wiring goes back over 60 years and parallels the gradual but continual development of the electrical equipment of which it is an integral part. One can define the wiring as the nerves of the vehicle electrical system, controlling and distributing power throughout the vehicle to the function, safety and convenience items that are provided. Such equipment as the engine starter, ignition system, lighting, windscreen wiper and heater are examples from a limitless list, all of which are dependent on wiring in some form or other. A brief history covering major changes in design philosophy is included together with the basic requirements of theoretical circuitry in relation to the type of vehicle involved and its operations. The criteria discussed cover the physical design for economic manufacture, ease of installation and ability to withstand the environmental conditions to which it is subjected. Problems of making connections in a fool-proof manner, and of corrosion, are noted and some solutions suggested. Mention is made also of the use of printed circuits and strip wiring.

1 INTRODUCTION

THE WIRING in today's vehicles is in many respects comparable with the nervous system of the human body. For example, both facilitate control of operating mechanisms, both provide the necessary links between sensing elements and control areas, and a failure in either can often result in complete immobility.

An average vehicle uses about 400 ft of cable in various sizes, operating up to 50 or so circuits. Each cable must be terminated at both ends, requiring the use of an extensive range of terminals designed to carry a wide range of electrical currents. Nowadays, the cables are preformed into a harness or loom, for inclusion as units in the vehicle during its manufacture.

After briefly tracing the evolutionary development of the modern wiring loom, the physical features and properties required for today's vehicle wiring systems will be examined.

2 HISTORICAL

At the turn of the century, wiring was required to supply power to the ignition, lights and horn only. Twin cables were used, rubber insulated and covered in cotton braid. Where protection against chafing was necessary, the cables were either inserted in a galvanized metal tube or had a half-round section of steel, brass or aluminium wrapped round them. The cables were individually wired and routed between the components they linked, either using ring terminals or by connecting the bared cable ends to terminal posts on the components.

In general, this procedure was followed for the next 30 years or so. During this period, a wide variety of electrically operated components were introduced, including the electrical starter, dual-bulb headlamps, windscreen wipers,

stoplights, turn indicators, courtesy lights, radio and various types of instrumentation. All these items greatly increased the complexity of the wiring.

Use of the vehicle's chassis as an electrical return eliminated the need for twin cables (although they are still used on special vehicles for safety reasons). Even so, the number of cables used made it necessary for vehicle manufacturers to employ skilled electricians to wire the circuits. For both installation and servicing purposes it was essential to identify each circuit. This was done by fitting coloured sleeves over the cable ends.

However, the increasing complexity of the wiring made it ever more difficult for the electricians to cope with the increasing speed of the production lines. It was at this stage that the first tentative steps were taken toward a wiring loom.

The first looms were assembled on wooden jigs, marked to show the various branches and leads, and fitted with pegs to facilitate cable location and shaping. The cables were rubber insulated, black-cotton braided and lacquered. Circuit identification was accomplished either by coloured sleeves or by tape. The looms were cotton braided overall by special machines, the braiding having tracers for identification, a cross-tracer indicating a left-drive vehicle loom.

Ring-type connectors or terminal posts on the components continued to be used. In-line connections, between cables, were invariably made by 'male' bullet-type terminals, which were inserted into insulated 'female' metal sleeves.

Around the middle thirties the number of circuits required outstripped the number of single colours available. To overcome this problem the sleeve system was abandoned and the cables themselves were braided in each of the basic colours, with a second tracer colour incorporated in the braiding. This was a major step forward and of great assistance to the service engineers, as well as to the vehicle and loom manufacturers.

There was little change in the general pattern of loom

The MS. of this paper was received at the Institution on 16th February 1972 and accepted for publication on 9th May 1972. 24
* Electrical Engineer, Vauxhall Motors Ltd, Luton, Beds.
† Works Director (Retired), 6 Copse Road, Bexhill-on-Sea, Sussex.

manufacture until the late forties. The limitations of braiding cables together—fungus growths grew in tropical conditions, for example—caused manufacturers to seek an alternative binding material; p.v.c. (polyvinyl chloride) tape was chosen. This was wrapped round the cables spirally to provide a measure of abrasion protection, in addition to forming the physical shape required for installation.

In the early fifties p.v.c. insulation came into general use for the cables themselves, and this had the advantage that plain copper conductors could be used. Hitherto, it had been necessary to tin the conductors to prevent the chemical reaction between the sulphur content in the rubber insulation and the copper of the conductors. The p.v.c. was in basic colours, and had tracer colours embodied.

The difficulties of preventing incorrect connections during installation into a vehicle led to the development of multiway terminations. The $\frac{1}{4}$-in blade terminal and receptacle had been in use in the U.S.A. from the early forties, and from about 1953–54, for many vehicle manufacturers in this country, this equipment became the accepted standard. These terminations were often fitted into rigid mouldings so designed to inhibit wrong connections and incorporating a pressure or latching device to prevent accidental disconnection.

It was possible to use blade terminations either in-line or plugged directly into the various types of component. Eventually the range was extended to cover from $\frac{3}{16}$ in to $\frac{1}{2}$ in blade sizes, with receptacles to match. This catered for practically all the loadings required from panel lamps to generators. An advantage of this type of termination was that it could be produced in strip form and crimped to the cable at high application speeds.

The increasing variations in vehicle ranges, together with the availability of these new forms of connectors, led to the first attempt to create modular wiring assemblies. Initially, this was done mainly on commercial vehicles, where frames, engines and cabs were wired with individual looms, which were then joined through multiway connectors to produce the complete vehicle electrical system. This fundamental design philosophy is shown diagrammatically in Fig. 72.1.

This major step showed the way to breaking down the size of the loom, which as the years went by began to reach unmanageable proportions. A module, or separate loom section, could be constructed for a specific circuit or vehicle area; and although the number of terminations increased, manufacture and installation were greatly simpli-

fied. It meant also that replacement of a damaged section could be achieved more easily and at a much reduced cost.

The potentiality of using the junction between the module looms as an inspection point for checking the correct electrical installation and function of components has not been overlooked.

3 FUTURE TRENDS

Today one can notice some further changes taking place in loom design. For example, the trend towards miniaturization is leading to the adoption of connectors based on a 3-mm pin and receptacle, contained in rigid mouldings and available in many configurations for in-line or plug-in connections. Typical examples are shown in Fig. 72.2. The use of fusible links and flat-strip wiring techniques is also being explored; further details about these developments are given later.

A modern loom is manufactured using conveyer belt and mass-production techniques. A variety of special tools are used to cut the cables to length and bare the ends, to crimp on the solderless connectors and to bind the cables into the final loom shape.

So much for the historic background. Before discussing the physical design requirements and features of the modern loom, the circuits that have to be catered for will be considered.

4 THEORETICAL CIRCUITRY

The theoretical circuitry required by a motor vehicle has been developed in concert with other vehicle components, and is, generally, to a near identical pattern, differing only to meet legal requirements and the dictates of a particular company's design philosophies. By virtue of the overall requirements there is an automatic breakdown into major circuit blocks; these are, obviously, interdependent to a large degree.

The first block covers the 'heart' of the electrical system —the battery and its charging circuits—and is supplementary to the starter motor circuit and its controls. Then there is the block covering the horn and interior lamps, which may be required for warning or convenience usage at any time, whether the ignition is switched on or off. Akin to this there is a block controlled by the main lighting switches, covering the parking and driving lamps. Finally,

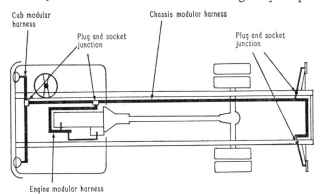

Cab modular harness
Chassis modular harness
Plug and socket junction
Plug and socket junction
Engine modular harness

Fig. 72.1. Fundamental design philosophy shown diagrammatically

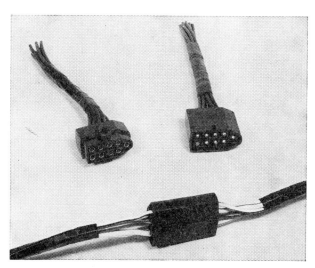

Fig. 72.2. Typical connectors

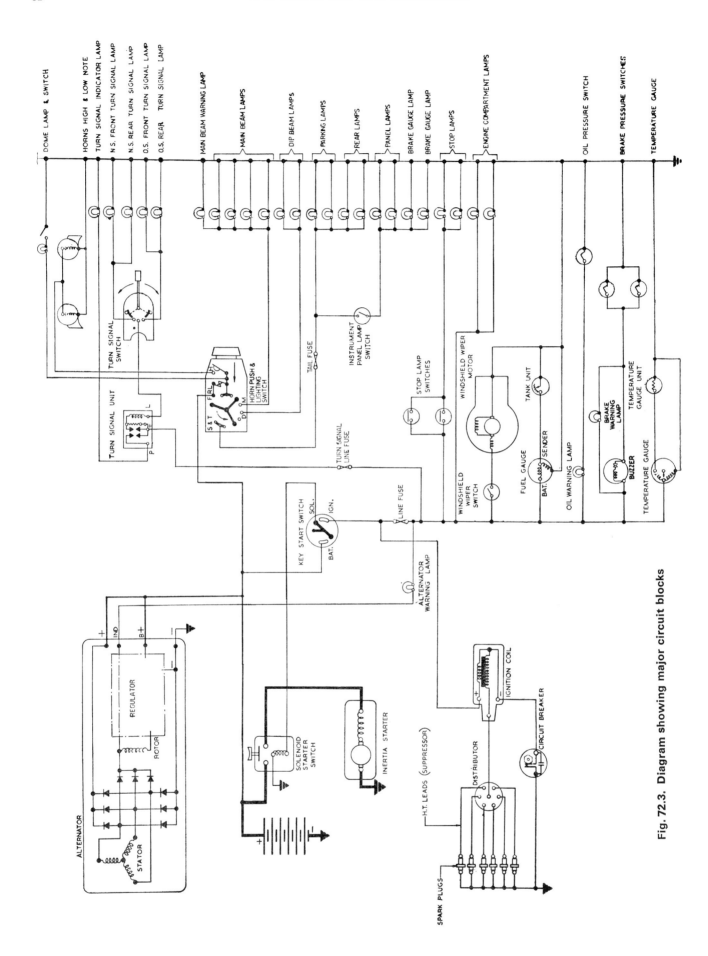

Fig. 72.3. Diagram showing major circuit blocks

there is a major block, controlled by the ignition switch and covering all the circuits required when the engine is running—the ignition system, instrumentation, direction indicators, stop lamps, wipers, accessories and driver convenience items. These blocks of circuits can clearly be seen in the diagram shown in Fig. 72.3.

5 CIRCUIT PROTECTION

Protection of the wiring system against damage from short circuits is an important feature, and thermal interruptors or fuses are widely used. However, the additional protection of fusible-links connected in the feedwire from the battery is now coming into use in this country, although such links have been fitted to vehicles in the U.S.A. for several years.

The fusible-link is the result of considerable research into protection techniques. An inadvertent short in an unfused circuit causes the p.v.c. insulation to flow on the cable involved. The heat generated can destroy the insulation on adjacent cables, as well as damaging components in the close vicinity.

Invariably, this means that the loom must be replaced from the point of shorting to the power source, because of the destruction of the intermediate and adjacent cables. Initial investigations showed that exotic insulations failed to give adequate protection to the adjacent cables. Since it was apparent that short-circuit heat could not be contained adequately, the solution seemed to lay in holding the heat to a safe value by a circuit-breaking system.

The fusible-link has been developed to function at the same 'normal' temperatures as the main feed, to permit transient overloads, and to have an expected life equal to the other wiring used (wire fuses tend to become destroyed by oxidation). Furthermore, it can cost less than a conventional fuse or circuit breaker.

In a typical application, the fusible-link would consist of a 13 s.w.g. (standard wire gauge) main feed protected by a short 6-in length of 16 s.w.g. thermosetting insulated wire as the safety link; this being connected in the loom main feed in a suitable position, as close to the battery as possible. Under overload conditions, the p.v.c. insulation on the main cabling tends to soften while the thermosetting insulation of the fusible-link tends to harden. However, before the short-circuit current is high enough to melt the p.v.c. insulation the copper of the fusible-link melts, so breaking the circuit without damage to the p.v.c.-covered cables.

Where it is desirable to remake a circuit immediately after an overload occurs, a mechanical circuit-breaker device can be used. This can be of the automatic reset, remote reset or manual reset type. In the interests of safety whilst driving, headlamp circuits would be protected by the automatic reset type; but it must be remembered that the faulty condition causing the headlamps to flick off and on should be located and eliminated immediately if permanent damage is to be avoided. A typical automatic reset circuit breaker is shown in Fig. 72.4.

6 PHYSICAL DESIGN

The physical design of a loom depends on a number of factors. It must cater for all the theoretical circuits previously outlined, and must also be capable of ready, and economic, adaptation to all the variants of a particular vehicle range. Coupled with this is the necessity for the

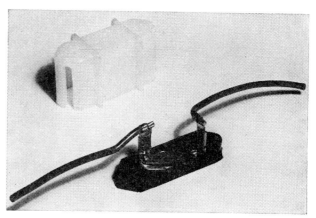

Fig. 72.4. Typical automatic reset circuit breaker

loom to be easily modified to meet subsequent vehicle changes, which may involve alterations in layout and circuitry. Naturally the loom must be planned to suit the vehicle's design, as far as layout is concerned, and it should be of such a nature that it will permit easy installation on the vehicle production line. This means avoiding, as far as possible: the need for threading long lengths of the loom through grommet holes, the possibility of making incorrect connections and, in fact, any operation that is time-consuming.

Once fitted and being used for the purposes for which it was designed, the loom must be capable of withstanding the wide variety of environmental conditions to which it can be subjected. These include metallic and electrolytic corrosion aggravated by road salt and by temperature extremes due to climatic conditions ranging from the arctic to the tropics; to the latter can be added the proximity of hot components such as exhaust pipes. The loom must also provide adequate resistance to damage during assembly, and to abrasion damage caused by vibration during the life of the vehicle. Last, but by no means least, the loom must be easy to service and economic to manufacture.

The benefits resulting from the introduction of modular loom techniques when related to the foregoing design principles are now quite apparent. First, the modular loom enables many vehicle variations to be accommodated within a single fundamental design concept, without overstepping the acceptable limits of voltage drop throughout the loom assemblies. At no time during normal running conditions should the voltage at a component be less than that for which the unit is designed to function effectively. Second, modifications to suit vehicle design changes are made easier, since it may be necessary to change only one or two of the loom sections. Third, although they increase the number of terminations, modular looms greatly ease installation problems and make full use of the variety of types of plug and socket now available. Finally, servicing the electrical system is greatly simplified—and repairs can be more economically effected—by the use of easily replaceable loom sections.

However, because of the increased number of terminations, it is even more important that incorrect assembly be inhibited. When a multiway connector is used it is common practice to use terminations of different diameters, the terminal diameter relating to the current loading of its associated circuit. The unique pattern of all multiway connectors thus makes it impossible for incorrect assembly to occur. The difficulties of ensuring that

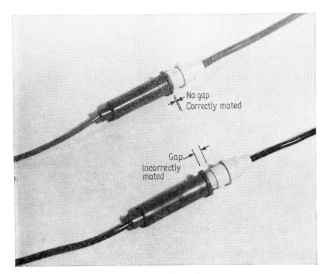

Fig. 72.5. Male and female connectors

these connectors are fully mated when assembled on the production line are being studied, and methods for resolving them are being suggested.

One technique could be to include an additional circuit that passes through each connector, purely for test purposes. If the test circuit checks out, it can be assumed that all the connectors are correctly and fully mated. This solution may appear 'way out', and it could be that it would be more practical to provide connector designs that are easy to assemble and visually inspect.

The inspection of the correct mating of the male and female connectors shown in Fig. 72.5 is greatly assisted by observing the position of the dissimilar colours on each half of the connector, where a gap would be clearly visible on an incorrectly mated connector.

7 TERMINATIONS

As previously mentioned, flat blades are currently being used in the connectors, although the 3-mm circular pin is generally gaining favour. Whatever blades or other terminals are used, however, it is certain that they have been subjected to exhaustive tests before adoption, in which the relationship of volt drop and heat rise will have been assessed, together with the mechanical strength, corrosion resistance, ease of assembly and permanency of the electrical joint.

Similarly, the colour coding of vehicle circuits has been the subject of vigorous examination, resulting in a common code agreed by the United Kingdom manufacturers. This code is available through the British Standards Institution, as British Standard A.U.7, and it is in general use throughout the industry. Cable sizes have also been agreed and standardized, and recently these have been metricated; British Standard 6862, 'Cables for vehicles', gives the latest details.

Another method by which the wiring designer can ease the installation of a loom into a vehicle is by fitting plastic location clips into the loom's outer protective casing. The clips are located at predetermined points on the loom, for attaching to specific positions on the chassis or body of the vehicle, and so greatly help in positioning the loom as well as providing a built-in means of anchorage. Illustrations of some different types are shown in Fig. 72.6.

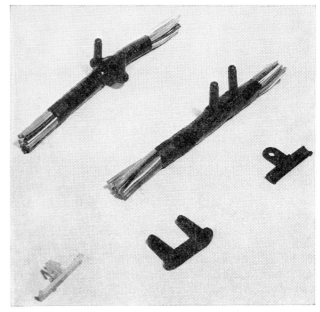

Fig. 72.6. Different types of plastic location clip

8 CORROSION PROTECTION

The environmental conditions that a wiring loom must withstand will now be examined, the problems of corrosion being dealt with first.

The increased use of rocksalts on our roads over the past few years, while helping to overcome icy conditions by lowering the freezing point of water, has aggravated the problem of corrosion of metal parts through chemical and electro-chemical reactions. The problem has been made worse by the recent change to a negative earth system on British motor vehicles.

The use of inhibitors by many vehicle manufacturers has been fairly successful, although these have introduced contamination problems on the assembly lines. Where connector terminations are concerned, it is possible on passenger cars to provide protection by ensuring that these parts are not located in the danger, or splash, areas. However, this is not always possible on commercial vehicles; therefore, to eliminate the problem, special weatherproof plug and socket connectors have been designed.

Fig. 72.7 shows typical weatherproof multiway and single connectors. In these the terminals are fully moulded in position after the cable has been connected and the

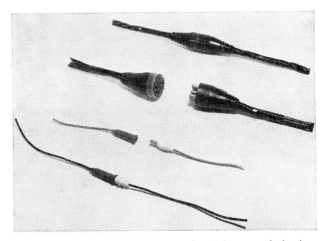

Fig. 72.7. Typical weatherproof multiway and single connectors

assembled cables have been taped together, in position. When the multiway plug and socket are connected, a flexible band effectively seals the joint at the mating faces. These designs have been successful in preventing both metallic and electrolytic corrosion.

Weatherproof connectors are intended for use outside the cab on commercial vehicles, but can of course be used on passenger cars if the location is such that protection is needed. Protective boots, shields and sealing compounds can also be used advantageously to retard the effects of corrosion. As far as the cables themselves are concerned, the p.v.c. covering is quite adequate.

9 TEMPERATURE

Turning now to temperature conditions, this is one of the features resulting from vehicle design that is constantly posing a problem as far as the wiring is concerned. Previously, it was agreed that under-bonnet temperatures were sufficiently low for a general-purpose p.v.c. cable insulation to satisfy adequately all requirements up to a temperature of approximately 80°C. This figure is, of course, the cable temperature and is the summation of the ambient and current heat rise temperatures.

However, many factors, including exhaust emission control, tend to increase the ambient temperature of the engine compartment; consequently, cables with heat-resistant insulants are under continual investigation. This problem is particularly prevalent on rear-engined coaches where the enclosures tend to increase the ambient temperature well above the working temperature of p.v.c. insulation.

Commercial vehicle manufacturers, particularly of heavy duty vehicles, have shown an interest in a synthetic rubber cable covering, with the trade name Hypalon. Although more expensive than the usual insulating materials, Hypalon has some interesting properties, and in particular will withstand the excessive heat of a short circuit without melting. Indeed, it is considered so reliable that in the U.S.A. commercial vehicles wired with Hypalon-covered cables receive a special reduction in insurance terms.

10 VIBRATION AND ABRASION

On the subject of vibration and abrasion, this is of particular importance where connections need to be made to an 'isolated' unit, e.g. the engine. Careful attention must be paid to the loom branches and cables that lead across to such units, to ensure that they are sufficiently flexible to provide the necessary free movement, without strain or whip. In addition, careful attention must be given to the anchorages at each end of the free swinging section, for it is at these points that chafing can cause damage and subsequent failure.

Determining the amount of slack that should be allowed is a problem during installation, but this can be eliminated by the use of the built-in location clips previously mentioned. Vibration should not be a problem as far as multiway connectors are concerned, for these are designed to ensure that the two parts are always held firmly in contact.

Developments aimed at providing a greater degree of protection against abrasion damage caused by rubbing against parts of the vehicle are under way. These include heavy-duty coverings, which should also help to eliminate, or at least substantially reduce, assembly damage.

11 SERVICEABILITY AND RELIABILITY

Serviceability and more economic manufacture of the loom are desirable features that can profitably result from close co-operation between the wiring manufacturer and the vehicle manufacturer. First, serviceability; this is closely linked with reliability, but it must be recognized that no matter how carefully the wiring system has been designed, or how strong and secure when installed, it is not indestructible. An inadvertent short circuit or an unfortunate accident, however minor, can damage a part of the cable network. A short circuit can result from a simple thing like a dislodged grommet; chafing of the cables against the comparatively sharp metal can eventually cause a break through the insulation.

The design of the loom and its routing must be such as to facilitate maintenance and replacement. The wiring therefore must be so located that mechanics can check the circuits and cable routings at strategic points during preventive maintenance. In addition, it must be possible to gain access to any section of the loom with reasonable ease and speed. With regard to actual replacement, it has been noted above that this is helped considerably by the use of the modular loom; but ready access to the loom section is obviously of equal importance.

Economic manufacture is not achieved by the cutting down of cable sizes, nor by planning the cables to run via the shortest possible routes. The use of smaller cables could seriously impair the life of the loom, as well as increase the heating effect along the cable runs. The resistance of a cable to current flow increases as the diameter decreases, so that not only does a smaller cable get hotter for the same current, it also produces a greater voltage drop and so reduces the component's efficiency. Hence, what is gained in terms of cost by reducing the cable size can be more than lost in reliability and performance.

Therefore, for economy the cable sizes should be the smallest *commensurate* with providing the component with not less than its minimum design voltage.

Similarly, while routing cables by the shortest possible distance is obviously the most desirable and the least expensive as far as quantities are concerned, by so doing they could be made inaccessible for maintenance or replacement purposes; or they could be located close to potential danger areas, e.g. hot manifolds or moving foot-pedal levers, and this is clearly unacceptable. For these reasons, close co-operation between the loom manufacturer and the vehicle manufacturer during the design stage is the best way to economy. In this way, the wiring can be planned properly to suit the vehicle (and its variants) without being over- or underdesigned.

With regard to the actual materials used, including the connectors, etc., naturally the loom manufacturer and vehicle manufacturer are each constantly testing and watching the latest developments, in an effort to provide a reliable product.

Nothing has yet been said about the fairly recent use of printed circuits for instrument panel wiring. These circuits comprise flat, copper conductors bonded to an insulating panel. The name derives from one of the methods of manufacture, whereby the circuit pattern is printed, either by conventional methods or photographically, on to a copper sheet prebonded to the insulating panel. Special inks are used so that when dipped into an etching bath all the unwanted copper areas are dissolved, leaving only the required copper paths. Die stamping and hand stripping of the unwanted copper are also used extensively to produce printed circuits in both rigid and flexible types. Obviously it is not possible to cross conductors using this technique, so where crossing is needed either a jumper wire must be connected or copper conductors applied to both sides of the panel.

Printed circuits can be extremely cheap to manufacture; the design techniques and production methods are now well established. However, they do take *time* to design, prove and are costly to tool, and the numerous changes to wiring layouts that take place can make life difficult for the manufacturer if sufficient time is not allowed.

There are a variety of connectors available for linking the printed circuit panels to conventional wiring systems. Typical examples of connectors suitable for flexible and rigid printed circuits are shown in Fig. 72.8 and their application in Fig. 72.9.

It is possible to print the circuits on a flexible base, so that the unit can be curved to fit into an awkward space. Because they are inexpensive to produce in quantity and easy to instal, printed circuits can save both time and money. However, their use is strictly limited to low-current circuits and to positions where mechanical damage is practically impossible.

This means they cannot be used for battery, starter and headlamp circuits, for example, since the thin copper conductors are not capable of carrying the current loads. The idea of printed circuitry is nevertheless so attractive that many experimental types have been produced for installation in various areas of a vehicle. However, all have been found to present many different problems, the major areas being current-carrying capacity and handling ability. It is for these reasons that printed circuits are mainly restricted to instrument panels; but development continues, and as the various problems are solved an increasing usage can be envisaged.

Perhaps it is the attraction of printed circuits that has led to the development of flat-strip wiring, and it is possible that this form of wiring could eventually provide a solution to the problem of packing more wiring into less space. Flat-strip wiring can be produced by a variety of methods: welding, with or without a plastic base; adhesive applied by continuous dipping or brush application; or even extrusion through special dies.

In flat wiring, as the name implies, the copper conductor

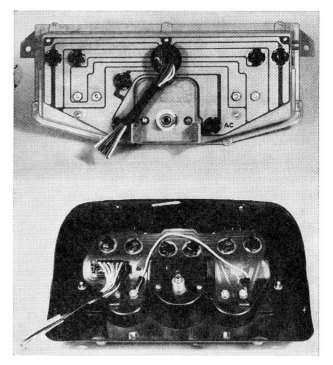

Fig. 72.9. Application of connectors suitable for flexible and rigid printed circuits

is a flat strip in its ultimate form rather than a group of copper strands twisted together, although these are currently used. Its main advantage is that it can be unrolled and laid on the open floor of a vehicle body, saving space by lying flat under the floor covering—and not needing to be routed along channels.

It can be made in multiconductor configurations, and can follow the contours of the vehicle. However, there are disadvantages. It cannot be bent as easily in all directions as round cable, and neither is it as easy to handle. Machinery to produce flat-strip cable does not lend itself so easily to changes, and could therefore mean considerable capital outlay, which would be reflected in its cost. Even so, this form of wiring has been used on certain vehicles in the U.S.A. A variety of connectors are available to join flat-strip wiring to flat-strip wiring, to conventional 'round' wiring and to components.

To sum up, it has been shown that the modern wiring loom is a sophisticated development of the original individually wired system. The decision to modularize the looms has proved to be correct, not only because it simplifies manufacturing procedures and loom dimensions but also because it makes installation and maintenance much easier and more reliable. Looms are built to stringent specifications, using the most economic components and layouts commensurate with reliability and safety. The vehicle manufacturers would not ask for more—nor expect less.

It has also been seen that the modular loom technique currently used is ideally suited to (and perfectly capable of) modification to accommodate vehicle variants and design changes. It is perhaps pertinent at this juncture to point out that the changes that occur to wiring layouts during a vehicle's manufacturing lifetime do not present any great problem to the wiring assembly manufacturer, *provided* that sufficient lead time is given. This lead time problem would be particularly aggravated where the newer, more

Fig. 72.8. Connectors suitable for flexible and rigid printed circuits

sophisticated techniques of printed circuitry and flat-strip wiring are concerned.

Wiring is still regarded as the poor relation during a vehicle design and therefore it is essential to establish the parameters at an early stage so that the many requirements can be fully considered. Only then can the most effective practical and economic loom design be developed that will take full advantage of the many different techniques available. In some ways it is rather like building a house, then calling in the electrician to plan and instal the wiring. Had he been called in during the design stages the wiring could have been planned and routed as an integral part of the structure; it would never be the electrician's intention to redesign the house but merely to suggest how economic routing can be effected.

What does the future hold for vehicle wiring systems ? The immediate future will undoubtedly see further investigation into the use of fusible-links, printed circuitry and flat-strip wiring. The potentiality of a ring main with components switched by pulse or frequency electronic systems is also a matter for study. As will have been noted, new development must depend on the trend in vehicle design and on the continual evolution of new techniques in low-tension electrical distribution and wiring components.

C75/72

SUMMARY OF PRESENT-DAY AUTOMOBILE LIGHTING

P. CIBIÉ*

This paper is concerned with vehicle lighting, and does not deal with allied subjects, such as sign-posting, or street lighting. Discussion is restricted to headlights mounted on vehicles, giving the driver, on his own vehicle, the means of making a night journey in the best possible conditions of visibility. The main characteristics of the sealed beam and the European headlamp are examined, and developments in the vehicle lighting industry considered.

1 INTRODUCTION

WE DO NOT NEED to go into the evolution of the vehicle headlamp. It should merely be observed that all vehicle manufacturers, and all countries with an active vehicle industry, felt very early on the need for lighting regulations. 'Regulations' is used in the most positive sense of the word, as their object is to put at the disposal of users a device ensuring the best possible visibility, taking into account industrial circumstances and vehicle performance at a particular time.

As a result of the evolution of various national specifications, the regulations have been studied on an international scale, bringing about the co-existence of the two principal sets of regulations currently in use. These are, first, the United States specification, known as 'The Sealed Beam', currently used in various countries (e.g. the U.K., South America, Canada and Japan). The second is the European specification, which permits several different constructions and is obligatory in the principal Continental countries; it is equally recognized with the sealed beam in the U.K., South America, Canada and Japan. The main characteristics of the two specifications in their present state of development will now be examined.

2 THE SEALED BEAM

The sealed beam was designed and produced in its present form in 1942. Since then it has not developed significantly. Physically, the sealed beam is essentially a single unit performing at the same time the two functions of light source and optical unit; the light distribution being adapted to the traffic conditions. The U.S. standard has fixed dimensions (initially two 7-in diameter light units per vehicle, then later four $5\frac{3}{4}$-in diameter units).

This system has three definite inherent advantages:

(1) Perfect sealing.
(2) Interchangeability.
(3) Low cost due to mass production.

The MS. of this paper was received at the Institution on 27th March 1972 and accepted for publication on 12th May 1972. 32
* *Chairman, Projecteurs Cibié, 17 Rue Henri Gautier, 93 Bobigny/ Seine, France.*

In contrast, it has three inherent disadvantages:

(1) The difficulty of manufacturing accurately a single device that must perform two functions.
(2) The necessity of replacing the entire unit each time a filament fails.
(3) The difficulty of further development resulting from its inherently rigid design parameters.

In the vertical plane of illumination, the sealed beam is characterized by a dip beam directed towards the near-side, so as not to cause glare to on-coming traffic, but without the sharp cut-off beam pattern that would permit precise alignment.

3 THE EUROPEAN HEADLAMP

Born in 1957 from the fusion and development of existing European national specifications, the European headlamp is characterized primarily by the presence of a removable bulb (to provide the light source) and an optical unit (providing the light distribution). This headlamp having been defined in terms of its function (i.e. its photometric performance) and not in terms of its method of construction, several versions of the bulb, and several versions of the light unit, have emerged. These variants will be examined later.

The advantages of the European specification are:

(1) The possibility of development resulting from new techniques.
(2) The precision possible in the manufacture of two discrete components.
(3) The facility of replacing the bulb alone, in the event of a blown filament.

The disadvantages are:

(1) The large number of variants.
(2) The problems of sealing.

In the vertical plane of its illumination, the European headlamp is characterized by a dip beam with a sharp cut-off, providing a precise delineation between the illuminated zone and the non-dazzle zone.

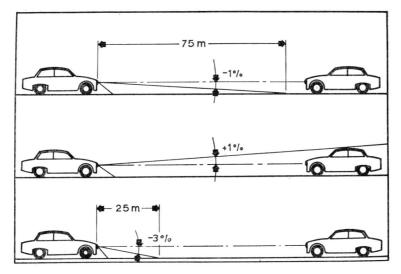

Fig. 75.1

4 DEVELOPMENT OF LIGHT UNIT SHAPES

The European light unit is not restricted in its construction or shape, and by experimenting with these factors manufacturers have been able to improve its performance. Thus it was that from the classical light unit the rectangular light unit was developed. Assuming the same location on the car body, this has the following advantages:

(1) A larger usable surface, improving the main beam illumination.

(2) A greater horizontal dimension ensuring improved performance beneath the cut-off on the dip beam.

5 DEVELOPMENT OF LIGHT SOURCES

The greatest development of light sources has taken place in recent years with the advent of the halogen bulb. Initially in single filament form (types H.1, H.2 and H.3), then, more recently, with two filaments (type H.4), they give a higher output and have a longer life.

It must not be ignored, however, that although this development has enabled more efficient techniques with greater styling flexibility, it has also brought higher cost. Nevertheless, this is not the sole consideration, as is readily shown by the use on recent vehicles of rectangular headlamps with increasingly lower height-to-width aspect ratios.

6 HEADLAMP ALIGNMENT

The two types of headlamp must be correctly aligned. Misalignment is more noticeable on European headlamps with their sharp cut-off. Methods by which this alignment can be effected have changed with developments in vehicle suspension, acceleration and braking.

Although an occasional adjustment of the headlamps was adequate twenty years ago, it has now become necessary to allow for the different horizontal attitudes a vehicle can adopt. Changes in horizontal attitude have two main causes:

(1) Weight distribution, where the effect can be corrected by a static control, as required.

(2) Accelerative and decelerative forces, which are constantly changing.

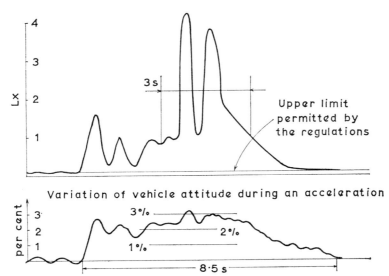

Fig. 75.2. Plot of intensity at 50 m in the direction of point B.50 for two headlamps

Although the vehicle attitude varies, the headlamp position should remain constant relative to the road, i.e. with respect to the vehicle's wheels, in order that the light beams may be most effective, as much in terms of road illumination as in terms of not causing glare to other traffic.

7 ATTITUDE VARIATIONS DUE TO WEIGHT DISTRIBUTION

For existing vehicles, variations of attitude due to weight distribution, between the two extremes, are rarely less than 0·5 per cent (expressed as the tangent of the angle of inclination). A variation of 0·5 per cent in headlamp aim is considered acceptable under all regulations.

In the worst cases, however, this variation can be as much as 10 per cent and thus renders the headlamps useless. Fig. 75.1 shows the effect of a change in headlamp aim of ±2 per cent in relation to the normal level of the dip beam, and clearly shows the danger of such a variation.

8 CORRECTION OF ATTITUDE CHANGES DUE TO WEIGHT DISTRIBUTION

Some simple devices have been used on numerous vehicles to ensure the correction of headlamp aim. They comprise manual devices at the disposal of the driver, the control being either on the headlight itself or on the vehicle's dash-board. Some systems permit a multi-position control of the headlamp aim, the optimum setting being decided by the driver, with the inherent risk of error.

Another system has two positions, giving a control for laden or unladen, but these two positions can only be a rough approximation since they do not allow for all the intermediate conditions. In both cases these devices require the conscious action of the driver, with the risk of being forgotten or neglected.

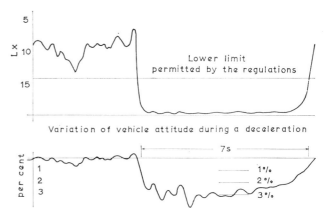

Fig. 75.3. Plot of the intensity at 50 m of a dip beam in the direction of the point R.50 for two headlamps

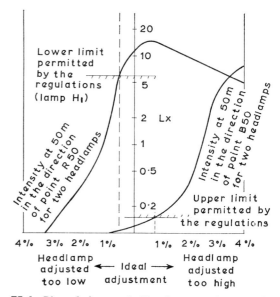

Fig. 75.4. Plot of glare and effectiveness of a pair of headlamps, as a function of vehicle attitude

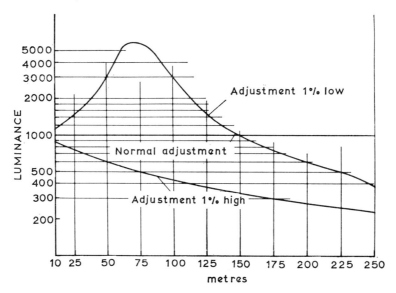

Fig. 75.5. Luminance of the main beam in front of the driver. Theoretical beam with uniform illumination from 10 to 250 m

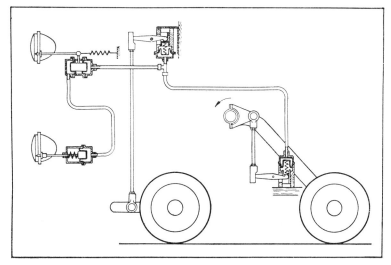

Fig. 75.6

9 ATTITUDE VARIATIONS CAUSED BY ACCELERATION OR DECELERATION

Dynamic oscillations of the vehicle produce the same effect as variations of load, but the dynamic as opposed to static movement of the headlamp aim adds further to driver fatigue, since the eyes must constantly adapt to a varying light level. During acceleration, the pitching effect causes an average change of vehicle attitude of the order of 2–3 per cent and can reach 4 per cent over 5–9 s. Fig. 75.2 shows an example of the glare graph resulting from a burst of acceleration in third gear.

Braking can also cause a lowering of the headlamp beams of the order of 3 per cent, and can reach 5 per cent over 4–7 s. Fig. 75.3 shows the graph of effective illumination as a result of braking.

Figs 75.2 and 75.3 were derived from Fig. 75.4, which shows the variation of glare and illumination of a good quality halogen dip beam as a function of the variation of the vehicle's horizontal attitude. It can be seen from this graph that the headlamp beam remains within the limits of the alignment specification for an upward pitch of less than 0·75 per cent and for a downward pitch of less than 0·6 per cent.

In both cases, the main beam is badly affected. Since the illumination from a main beam should be as homogeneous as possible, the illumination of the road should be constant, and represented as a straight line. A variation of 1 per cent upwards or downwards varies the light output, as represented in Fig. 75.5. The driver can then see greatly varying levels of illumination, giving the impression of intense high spots constantly appearing before his eyes. The same phenomenon can also occur as a result of the road surface. In this case it is much less annoying, since the amplitude is smaller.

10 THE DESIGN OF A DYNAMIC HEADLAMP LEVELLER

The first requirement of a dynamic headlamp levelling device is to be entirely automatic. It should consist of sensors on the front and rear wheels, measuring the amplitude of the movement of the car body with respect to these. This information should be transmitted to an integrator, which co-ordinates the two displacements. The resultant displacement is then transmitted to the

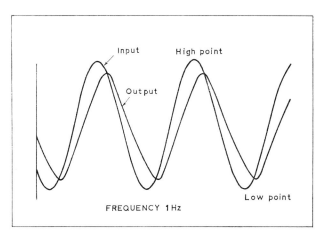

Fig. 75.7

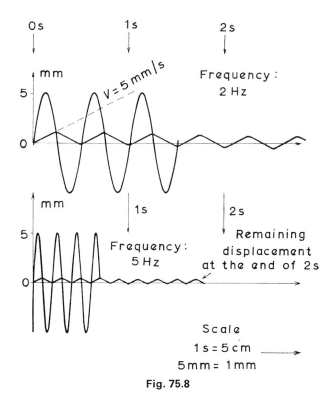

Fig. 75.8

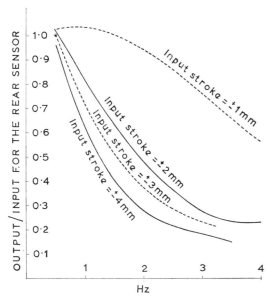

Fig. 75.9. Diagram representing the reduction of the hydraulic corrector as a result of the input stroke and the frequency

headlamp and the aim corrected. Such devices have been designed in various forms: mechanical, hydraulic, pneumatic, electrical and electronic. Fig. 75.6 shows the principle of an existing hydraulic device.

The input parameters of the movement are its amplitude and frequency. The output parameters (i.e. headlamp movement) are equally its amplitude and frequency, and also its dephasing with respect to the input movement. Figs 75.7 and 75.8 represent the input and output motions of a hydraulic device currently being tested. The conclusions are:

(1) Attenuation of the vehicular displacement amplitude (to give a virtually constant headlamp aim).
(2) Conservation of frequency (headlamp motion follows that of the vehicle body).
(3) Dephasing of the two motions (owing to the device's response time).

These tests have shown that, on present-day vehicles, the frequency of the displacement due to the effect on the suspension of ground irregularities is in practice between the limits of 10 Hz and 15 Hz. It is in this high range of frequencies that the device has to attenuate the suspension amplitude. On the other hand, lower frequencies should equally be transmitted since they are similar in their effect to those caused by acceleration and braking, and to the frequency of the vehicle body itself.

Fig. 75.9 shows the reduction due to the above-mentioned hydraulic correcter with respect to the input displacement stroke. It can be seen from these curves that for low frequencies the signal is integrally transmitted, and for high frequencies is greatly attenuated. For this particular hydraulic circuit, this can be achieved by adapting the liquid's speed of circulation to the frequency of the vehicle body.

It can also be seen that, in a hydraulic device such as this, the dephasing between input and output signals is not the same for upward and downward pitching (the liquid's motion not being the same under depression and compression). This dephasing is in fact of the order of $\frac{1}{10}$ s.

In Fig. 75.10 are shown the results currently obtained in practice. The headlamp motion follows the body motion reasonably faithfully. The lower curve represents the difference in the motions of the body and headlights, i.e. the remaining oscillations (due to dephasing, or high amplitudes). The amplitude of these oscillations stays lower than 0.5 per cent, which is extremely reasonable.

It should be remembered that devices should be able to function correctly whatever the ambient temperature conditions, and equally under any localized temperature changes throughout the device itself. Research on these systems is sufficiently advanced for it to be predicted that in a few years' time they will be used extensively.

11 POLARIZED LIGHT

The application of polarized light to vehicle lighting at present comes up against some practical difficulties. These are:

(1) The need for the extra power to increase the light

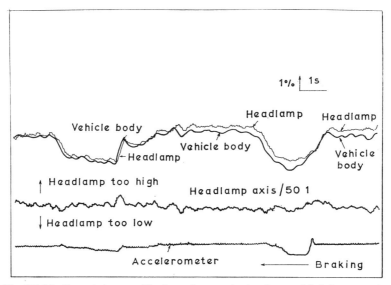

Fig. 75.10. Remaining oscillations due to dephasing or high frequencies

output by a factor of 2·5 to compensate for the light loss through the polarizing filters.

(2) The quality of present polarizer and analyser filters (thermal properties, resistance to ultraviolet light, effects of humidity, etc.).

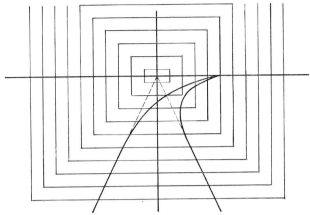

Fig. 75.11. Profile of corner

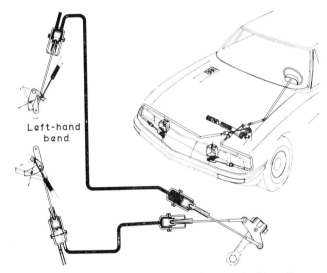

Left-hand bend

Fig. 75.12. Citroën SM—directional control of headlamps

(3) The establishing of new specifications for signalling lamps and rear reflectors.

(4) New specifications for windscreen, rear windows and rear-view mirrors.

(5) The variation of the reference axes, with regard to the total cut-off of the light (road unevenness, suspension flexibility, etc.)

(6) The determination of the conditions to be applied during the transition period.

Research is being carried out in different countries to find solutions which are acceptable in practice, and which bring about a significant increase in safety over actual conditions.

12 DIRECTIONAL CONTROL OF HEADLAMP AIM

The light output from a headlamp is applied to a rectilinear road, the profile of which is represented as a dotted line on Fig. 75.11. The profile of a road at the beginning of a bend is represented by a solid line. The light falling upon this curve gives differences in illumination creating some zones of non-visibility. If one starts with a constant illumination level of 1 on the kerbs, it can be seen that this level can be diminished by a factor of 16 at certain points on the curve.

To remedy this inconvenience there are two possibilities:

(1) A lamp may be arranged to give a light output adapted to the profile of a bend. This lamp should light up at the beginning of the bend. It would normally be a compromise, since it would be designed for a given radius of curvature.

(2) Existing headlamps may be arranged so that they can follow the road profile. In the case of a right-hand bend the rotation of the right-hand headlamp should be greater than that of the left hand. This rotation should start as soon as the steering is moved. The rotation should then slow down as the lock is increased.

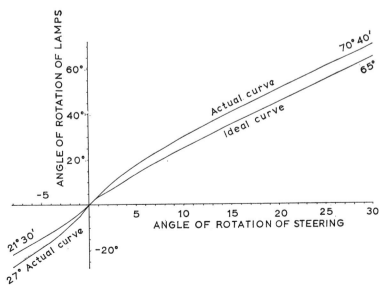

Fig. 75.13. Response curve

Fig. 75.12 represents one example currently used in production on the Citroën SM. The differential movement of the two headlamps is achieved by a system of cams. The graph in Fig. 75.13 represents the angle of rotation of the headlamps as a function of the angle of rotation of the steering.

In hydraulic systems the temperature variations can cause extraneous movement. It is necessary therefore to provide temperature variation compensators. In general, these compensators are designed so that there are iden-

tical variations in the volume of the liquid and that of the liquid-containing components.

13 CONCLUSIONS

It has been shown in this paper that the vehicle lighting industry is under constant development, and that new techniques are being constantly researched and elaborated. It is certain that these new techniques will be in use much sooner than may be thought possible today.

C79/72   ELECTRIC RETARDERS

J. REED*

Various types of electric retarders are described. Conditions of use are discussed and performances are compared. Installation and operation criteria are examined. Future trends are considered and a summary given of increased safety and reduced running costs.

1 PRINCIPLES AND CONSTRUCTION

1.1 History

THE ORIGINS of electric retarders are lost in the more general history of eddy-current devices. The principle of eddy-current operation was discovered by Faraday (1791–1867). This simple principle now has many specialized applications from electrical instruments to variable-speed drives of high power and great sophistication.

1.2 Purpose of electric retarders

The electric retarder provides a subsidiary frictionless braking system generally used for vehicles over 5 t gross vehicle weight. The increase in permitted weight, combined with regulations for higher specific horsepower and with consequent higher speeds, has produced a serious braking problem. The solution lies in improving friction brakes, which in their conventional form are nearing the limit of development, and in providing a subsidiary system, preferably with a long service life and minimal maintenance. Due to their frictionless operation, electric retarders fulfil these requirements.

1.3 Principle of operation

The eddy-current or electric retarder uses an electrically conductive rotating member in an alternating magnetic field. The effect of flux alternation is to induce a voltage in the conductive member during a change in flux density. The voltage in turn produces currents that, because the conductive member is a single piece, are free, to some extent, to wander or 'eddy' within the material; hence the generic name of the device. The magnetic flux is initially set up electrically by means of a field coil associated with the iron circuit.

A current flowing in an electric conductor gives rise to a magnetic field around the conductor. This second field tends to distort the primary alternating field, as shown in Fig. 79.1. Magnetism has the property of equalization, i.e. magnetic lines of force will always attempt to produce a uniform field. The result of this reaction is to apply force to the conductive member so that it tends to revolve and synchronize itself with the alternating field. In the case of the retarder, the alternating field is stationary so that force is applied to the conduc-

The MS. of this paper was received at the Institution on 20th December 1971 and accepted for publication on 12th May 1972. 33
* *Pye Electric Ltd, Oulton Works, Lowestoft, Suffolk.*

tive revolving member to tend to stop it. When the retarder is mounted in the transmission of a vehicle, it tends to brake the transmission when switched on. The braking power is dissipated as heat in the retarder rotor, and cooling is by self-generated airflow. It must be stressed that there is no physical contact between rotor and stator during braking.

1.4 Method of operation

Operation of the retarder may be by switch or by progressive current control. The switching method is the more popular due to its lower cost. Fig. 79.2 shows a typical switching circuit. This has been simplified by the removal of brake and warning light wiring. An actuator is mounted adjacent to the driver's hand, generally on the steering column (see also Fig. 79.8). Finger-tip operation of a lever sequentially switches on pairs of poles. Braking power is thus increased from zero by 25 per cent intervals to 100 per cent. Closure of the light-current switches in the actuator causes power to be applied to the relay coils. Relays are mounted close to the retarder to keep

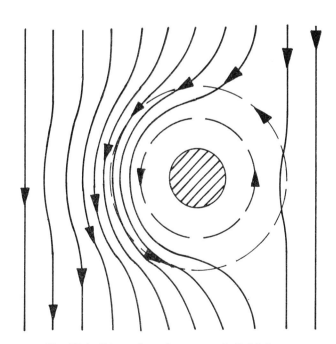

Fig. 79.1. Distortion of a magnetic field due to current flowing in a conductor

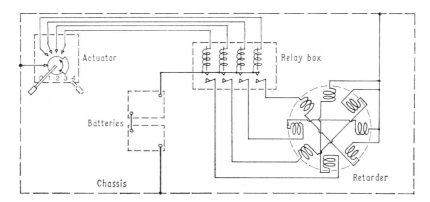

Fig. 79.2. Retarder switching system

high-current cables as short as possible. Long cables have a high resistance, which causes a voltage drop with a current flowing; this in turn reduces the retarder power. The relay box carries four relays and is mounted on the chassis within relatively easy reach of the batteries. It is advisable to fit an ignition switch in the earth lead from the actuator to avoid accidentally leaving the retarder switched on, thus draining the batteries.

1.5 Braking characteristic

Looking at Fig. 79.3, it can clearly be seen that no torque is produced when the rotatable member is stationary. Thus the electric retarder cannot, by itself, bring a vehicle to rest. However, it is also clear that, after the initial rise of torque at low speed, the braking torque remains substantially constant to very high rotational speeds, full torque being initially achieved between 600 and 1000 rev/min. When the retarder is installed between the gearbox and the differential, this is approximately equivalent to 20–30 km/h.

1.6 Types of electric retarder

There are two main classifications: (1) disc type and (2) drum type. Sub-classifications of these are: (1a) single disc and (1b) double disc, and (2a) single coil, interdigitated poles and (2b) multiple coils, straight poles. In all these types two common factors emerge. Firstly, they are all heteropolar with adjacent poles having opposite polarity. Secondly, the number of poles is fairly consistent, being dictated by considerations of braking characteristic and magnetic leakage. Generally, the number of poles falls between 6 and 16. Heteropolar operation gives full reversal of flux as the rotating member passes across adjacent poles. Fig. 79.4 shows the flux path of a pair of

poles and a section of rotor. The reversal of flux is double that provided by the flux flowing. By careful design it is possible to achieve a flux density of 2 T, which provides an alternation of 4 T. Representing the torque generation function as a proportional series:

torque $\propto$ (current)^n $\propto$ (voltage)^n

$\propto$ (change in flux density)^n

The power n is ideally 2 but generally a little lower. In the ideal condition, therefore, doubling the flux density will multiply torque by 4. As compared to the heteropolar device, the homopolar type, in which all poles are of the same polarity, will only produce some 20 per cent of the torque. The production of voltage in the rotor is expressed by

$$e = \frac{-\mathrm{d}\Phi}{\mathrm{d}t}$$

where e is the instantaneous voltage and $\mathrm{d}\Phi$ the change in flux; $\mathrm{d}t$ is the periodic time of that change. At a given rotational speed, $\mathrm{d}t$ will be small for a large number of poles. Since e is inversely proportional to $\mathrm{d}t$, it is desirable to have as large a number of poles as possible. However, considerations of flux leakage between adjacent poles and of coil space limit the number of poles to a fairly prescribed quantity. Additionally, a large number of poles would tend to reduce the rotational speed at which full torque is achieved and to cause a drop in torque at high speed; the first of these conditions is generally unnecessary and the second undesirable.

Electric retarders first made their appearance in the late 1920s, but were not generally used until after World War 2. Since then their use has increased rapidly. Compagnie Telma produce a range of double-disc retarders.

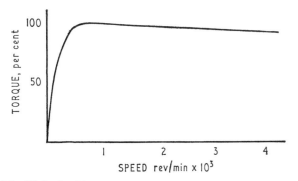

Fig. 79.3. Braking characteristic of an electric retarder

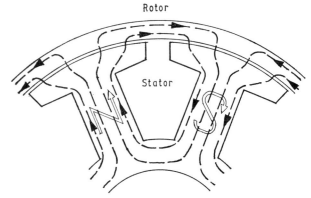

Fig. 79.4. Magnetic flux path

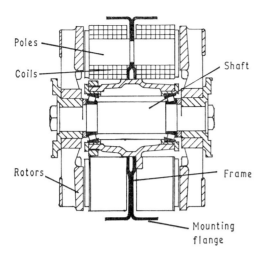

Fig. 79.5. Telma 'double-disc' retarder

A cross-section is shown in Fig. 79.5. This retarder consists of a set of eight axial poles mounted as a ring on a central frame. Each pole carries a coil either side of the frame and faces a disc at each end. The central frame also carries a bearing assembly consisting of a pair of opposed taper roller bearings. At one side of the bearing housing is an adjustment ring for bearing clearance. At each end a shim is provided for adjusting the air gaps between the discs and the pole caps. The discs, which are cast integrally with cooling fans, are carried on hubs that fit on to triangular sections of shaft to provide torque transmission. The central frame is used to mount the retarder to the vehicle chassis. The hubs at either end connect to the flanges of the propeller shafts. This company also produce a version of the retarder to fit directly to a rear axle.

Fig. 79.6 shows a retarder design by Bosch. This particular version is a double-rotor, interdigitated-pole type. The stator carries two coils either side of a central poled stator. On either side of the coils are mounted claw members that slot in between the poles of the stator. Two finned drums are carried on hubs that mate with splined extensions to a shaft, being held in place by nuts at either end. The shaft is mounted in a pair of taper roller bearings whose fit is adjusted by their housings. Central ribs on the stator serve to mount the retarder. Bosch also produce a

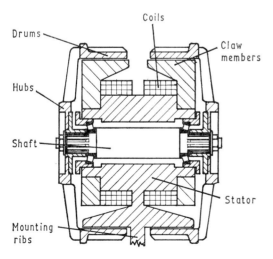

Fig. 79.6. Bosch double drum retarder with interdigitated poles

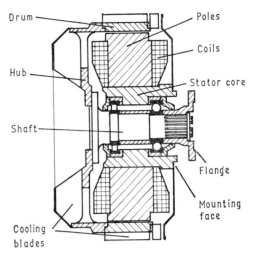

Fig. 79.7. Pye Electric retarder; single drum, multiple coils

version to mount on the gearbox or rear axle of a vehicle.

Fig. 79.7 shows a retarder design by Pye Electric Ltd. This is designed for low-cost manufacture with good reliability. The stator core carries a set of eight poles, each with an aluminium coil wound directly on it. The poles face a single finned drum with end blades for cooling both inside and outside. The drum is fixed to a hub, which attaches directly to a shaft flange. The shaft is located in the stator core by a cylindrical roller bearing and a deep-groove ball bearing. Thrust loads are accommodated by the ball bearing, which has a life expectancy of well over 150 000 km. The shaft is held by a splined flange at the other end. One complete stator face is available for mounting to the chassis or to a rear axle.

1.7 Power dissipation and cooling

Electric retarders produce braking torque by generating electric currents in a rotating drum or disc. Due to the passage of these currents in the material, heat is generated. The rate of heat generation is directly proportional to the braking power exerted. This heat must be dissipated to atmosphere, and the types of retarder previously described all have one or more fan systems to promote airflow over the heated rotating surface. Telma (Fig. 79.5) show centrifugal blades integrally cast with the disc at each end. Air is drawn in at the end annulus and ejected at the periphery. The design of the blades is carefully controlled to maintain the disc stability with varying temperatures. Bosch (Fig. 79.6) has fan blades cast into the outside of each drum. These pick up air flowing under the vehicle and draw it along the hot surface of the drum. Pye (Fig. 79.7) has a double air system. A centrifugal fan is cast integrally with the hub. This propels air through the retarder and hence cools the coils and the inner diameter of the drum. The drum itself has blades cast on its outer surface to propel air axially. A set of small blades is mounted on the end of the drum to assist in mixing the two airstreams at their junction.

The presence of air-moving blades does constitute a power absorption during normal running. Figures given (**1**)* for the Bosch and Telma retarders indicate, respectively, 6·7 kW and 2·5 kW at 300 rev/min for retarders rated at 1280 Nm and 1180 Nm.

* References are given in Appendix 79.1.

1.8 Notation

A Vehicle frontal area, m^2.
G Gradient, per cent.
P_a Horsepower of air resistance.
P_b Horsepower of brakes.
P_g Horsepower generated by descent.
P_r Horsepower of rolling resistance.
P_t Horsepower of transmission losses.
V Vehicle speed, km/h.
W Vehicle gross weight, t.

2 USE OF RETARDERS

2.1 General

All types of retarder, from exhaust brakes to hydraulic and electric retarders, are intended primarily to assist the wheel brakes in providing a safe degree of braking. There are, however, several side benefits, which include the conditions of use, the performance of the driver and, of great importance, cost reduction. As a general rule, the greater the retardation power available, the more side benefits accrue.

2.2 Conditions of use

One particular area where brakes are in prolonged use is in mountainous country on long-distance trips. On a coach tour of Swiss passes, for instance, the brakes may be applied very many times in a day, representing a high percentage of the distance involved. Such a situation creates severe wheel brake fade and even possible failure. In this situation, the use of a retarder, to supplement the brakes, reduces the fade and tends to increase the time interval for wheel brake adjustment or replacement. Tests conducted in the United States have shown that a gradient of 7 per cent (1 in 14) requires as much as 9·5 kW/t to keep the vehicle speed down to 32 km/h. On a 25-t vehicle, this means that 237 kW of heat are generated, either in the wheel brakes or in the retarder. It has been found by users that, providing the correct size of retarder has been used, the wheel brakes can, under normal conditions, be superseded by the retarder except for the final stopping from a very slow speed. On the level, the retarder, aided by the vehicle transmission friction, will actually bring a vehicle to rest. Such findings extend the use of retarders to vehicles that operate in urban conditions. A deceleration of 0·15g is quite high for a public service vehicle, except in emergency, and 0·2g is similarly adequate for a commercial vehicle. Such a level of retardation can be achieved by electric retarders without causing adverse side-effects. One other advantage of brake-fade reduction, besides increased life, is that vehicles can be run faster without incurring premature brake failure.

From the operator's point of view, therefore, retarders show several benefits. The vehicle manufacturer can also achieve gains. By virtue of the reduction of heat in the wheel brakes, wheels can be reduced in size, within the limits of load-carrying capacity. The live transmission weight being reduced, suspensions can be lightened. This, in turn, can give benefits in chassis design or in increased carrying capacity. Reduction of wheel size can also mean a lower platform and cab, a consequent reduction of frontal area and a general improvement in fuel consumption and in centres of gravity. The extra weight of the

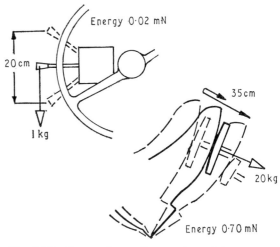

Fig. 79.8. Comparison of operation of foot- and finger-operated brakes

retarder, about 1 per cent of gross vehicle weight (see Fig. 79.12), has a negligible effect on the chassis loading.

2.3 Driver performance

There can be physical, psychological and mechanical advantages in using a retarder. The actuation of the retarder is generally by means of a switch with a gate or a sequence of switching. The switch is mounted conveniently to the driver's hand, usually on the steering column (see Fig. 79.2). The operation of this switch is much less fatiguing than the movements required to operate a brake pedal. Fig. 79.8 shows that distance moved is as little as 20 cm compared with 35 cm and force about 1 kg compared with 20 kg. In addition, the state of mind of a driver, who no longer has to contend with brake fade, is much improved. The psychological improvement will also lead to better physical conditions and the driver will remain fresher. An alert driver can cope with road difficulties much more readily than a tired one and tends to be smoother in his driving. This has a beneficial effect on wear in terms of tyres, transmission and engine.

2.4 Cost reduction

An advertisement by an electric retarder manufacturer claims that a fleet operator now using his products obtains a life of 48 000 km before replacing linings. This compares with a previous life five or six times less. Such a claim is not at all exaggerated. Intelligent use of a retarder will give great benefits in brake life and hence replacement cost. It must be borne in mind that the cost of renewing brakes involves the total vehicle-off-road costs, which include materials, labour, overheads, storage, loss of revenue and several other related factors. Figures given by operators of public service vehicles and coaches (**2**) indicate a considerable disparity in cost estimation, indicating that some operators may not allow for all the costs involved. On wheel brake life, it appears that operators without electric retarders change brakes 2·6 times a year on average; those with electric retarders change brakes once in 1·4 years on average. The advantage of using a retarder in terms of costs can readily be deduced. The cost advantage of a retarder appears to be most prominent in the case of operators running continental tours with high annual distances per vehicle.

One operator also claimed that his costs on brake drums and tyres were cut by 60 per cent by the use of retarders. Several others commented on the improvement in drums and other components. If this line of thought is taken to its logical conclusion, the manufacturers can make savings on the vehicles by incorporating electric retarders as part of the transmission; some research in this field is being carried out. This is discussed more fully in Section 5.2.

3 PERFORMANCE AND ADVANTAGES
3.1 Performance
The requirements for braking a vehicle are fulfilled in four ways: (1) rolling resistance, (2) air resistance, (3) friction losses in engine and transmission and (4) brakes. Formulae for the first three functions (3) are:

$$\text{rolling resistance } P_r = \frac{W \times V}{22 \cdot 8} \quad . \quad . \quad (79.1)$$

$$\text{air resistance } P_a = \frac{A \times V^3}{56\,000} \quad . \quad . \quad (79.2)$$

$$\text{transmission losses } P_t = \frac{W \times V(1 \cdot 2 + G)}{247} \quad (79.3)$$

The power exerted by a vehicle moving downhill is expressed by

$$P_g = \frac{W \times V \times G}{27 \cdot 4}$$

These formulae have been derived directly from the original and transposed to metric units. Now

$$P_g = P_r + P_a + P_t + P_b$$

or braking power

$$P_b = P_g - (P_r + P_a + P_t)$$

Where the performance of a vehicle is well known, it is relatively simple to obtain accurate figures for the various powers shown above. However, in the absence of test information, assumptions must be made, based on prior knowledge, of such factors as air drag coefficient, tyre rolling resistance, transmission efficiency, engine losses, auxiliary power requirements and weight-to-frontal-area ratio.

By making assumptions of this nature, it is possible to achieve a sensibly accurate figure of retarder horsepower. The basic graphs are shown in Fig. 79.9, where the known

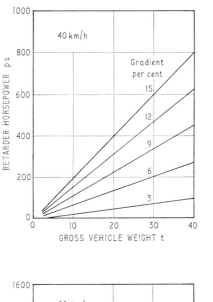

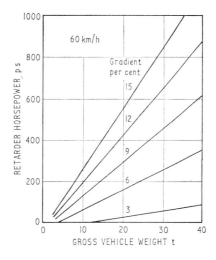

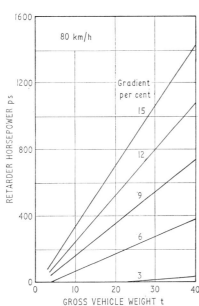

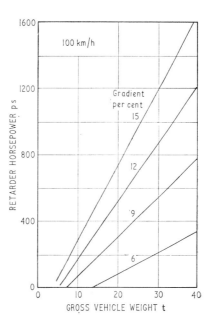

Fig. 79.9. Retarder braking powers

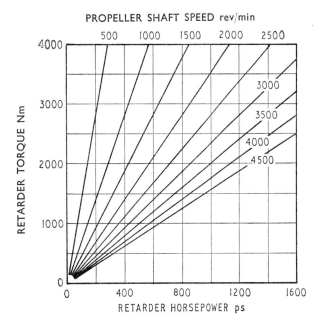

Fig. 79.10. Determination of retarder size by torque capacity

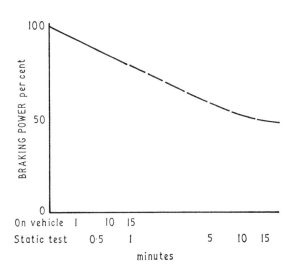

Fig. 79.11. Recoverable 'fade' of electric retarder

parameters of gradient, speed and vehicle gross weight are used to find retarder horsepower. The graphs can be extended to include wheel size and differential ratio to determine the actual size of the retarder needed (4) or, as in Fig. 79.10, use propeller shaft speed and horsepower to determine retarder size. Nearly all electromagnetic retarders are described by their braking torque.

It must be emphasized that the final selection of retarder must be subject to reappraisal of the vehicle losses, size considerations and energy ratings, since some fade will occur during operation.

3.2 Fade

All electromagnetic retarders are subject to some fade due to temperature, although this is small compared to the fade of friction brakes. Retarder fade is totally recovered after cooling down. The cause of fade is twofold: (*a*) increase in air gaps when the rotating member expands away from the stator and (*b*) reduction of magnetic permeability in the material of the rotating member. This is known as the Curie effect, and all magnetic materials have a temperature at which permeability is reduced to that of free space. This temperature, the Curie point, generally lies between 450°C and 900°C, with the exception of certain exotic alloys. The fade due to Curie effect is self-limiting in that, as permeability reduces, torque reduces and the heat generated is lower, hence limiting the temperature rise. In the limit a balance is achieved that produces a minimum of 45–50 per cent of the braking power at ambient temperature. Thus the fade limit still provides a significant power, and such ultimate conditions would not be reached until after many minutes of full operation.

It is difficult to generalize in a case like this, where layouts and cooling media are so various. Specific tests on the Pye Electric retarder type R.5 are shown in Fig. 79.11. These fade curves taken at 45 km/h are shown on a double scale of time. The first scale shows time in the operating condition under a vehicle with air flowing into the re-

tarder air inlet. The second scale shows time in the test condition on a static bed where air flow is only induced by the retarder itself. The operating condition gives a fade of 10 per cent in 2 min at full power, 20 per cent in 10 min. These are equivalent to 10 per cent fade in 1·5 km and 20 per cent in 7·5 km.

One outstanding difference between electromagnetic retarder fade and friction brake fade is that the former is always totally recovered on cooling down, whereas friction brake fade causes wear and subsequent reduced performance.

3.3 Comparison with hydraulic retarders

The initially lower weight of a hydraulic retarder is drastically offset by the need to provide an external heat exchanger and the associated reservoir and piping. Alternatively, the size of hydraulic retarder must be increased to obtain a satisfactory energy rating. In the final instance, weights of hydraulic retarders as installed tend to be very nearly equal to the equivalent electric retarder. In addition, the installation cost of piping and heat exchanger makes the hydraulic retarder an expensive accessory compared to the electric retarder.

3.4 Comparison with exhaust brake

In order to obtain the fullest effective use of an exhaust brake, the engine must be running at or near its maximum speed. This tends to restrict its operation in that the correct gear must be selected to achieve adequate braking power. There is some dispute over the effect of an exhaust brake on engine wear. Some users say that wear life is reduced drastically while some research indicates no change in wear life. Whatever the disputes about engine life, there are no arguments about power. The exhaust brake cannot produce more power as a brake than the engine does as a drive, since it relies for its operation on generating cylinder pressure by movement of the pistons. The engine merely acts as a compressor instead of a power source. The ratio of required braking power to engine power is a variable with performance requirements. However, as an example, a vehicle of 16 t gross weight has an engine of 210 hp and is offered with a retarder (as an optional extra), which has a braking capacity of 600 hp at full engine speed. The exhaust brake cannot generally provide as much braking power as is required for full subsidiary braking. Also, the exhaust brake stresses all the elements of a transmission—engine, gearbox and differential. The shaft-mounted or axle-mounted electric retarder stresses only the differential, bearing in mind the difference in power levels.

3.5 Use on articulated vehicles

The application of a transmission brake has an additional beneficial effect in the case of an articulated vehicle. Wheel locking depends on braking torque existing at low speed. The electric retarder torque characteristic (Fig. 79.3) is such that torque is zero speed and increases from low speed. When the wheels approach zero speed, as in locking, the retarder torque reduces and enables the wheels to keep turning. This is a major contribution to the reduction in wheel locking and subsequent loss of control.

4 INSTALLATION AND OPERATION CRITERIA

4.1 Space requirements

The electric retarder, while it has a high power-to-weight ratio, in the order of 1 kW/kg at 50 km/h, still requires space for mounting in a transmission. This is generally a matter of selecting a suitable point on the transmission or of making minor adjustments to auxiliaries.

4.2 Drive requirements

In the majority of vehicles, retarders can be fitted so that they run at propeller-shaft speed. However, trailers and vehicles with a combined gearbox and differential do not, as such, have a propeller shaft. In these cases, it is necessary to provide alternative means of driving the retarder. Attention must be paid at the design stage to the siting of the retarder. Care must be taken not to weaken the chassis by removal of cross-members, etc.

4.3 Operational considerations

These can be classified as follows:

(a) Batteries must have sufficient reserve to cater for the excitation current of the retarder.

(b) The retarder coils can become rather hot if left on for a long time when stationary. Prolonged use in the order of 20–30 min will cause the retarder to heat up. See Section 3.2.

(c) Driver education. The driver who has not previously used a retarder is likely to make mistakes that could cause damage; not to the retarder, but the transmission. Simple instructions will generally overcome the problem. As an example, a driver kept the retarder switched on while accelerating downhill against it. This did no damage to the retarder but caused the engine to overheat.

(d) Small reduction of revenue. A reduction in carrying capacity of about 2 per cent occurs when a retarder is fitted. Approximate weights of electric retarders compared to gross vehicle weights are shown in Fig. 79.12.

5 TRENDS FOR THE FUTURE

5.1 The effect of regulations

European regulations on braking systems vary widely from country to country. For instance, in Switzerland,

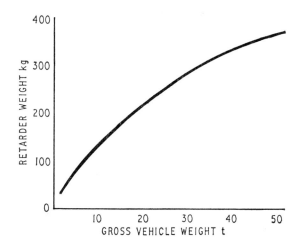

Fig. 79.12. Approximate curve of retarder weight against gross vehicle weight

regulations for public service vehicles require the use of a subsidiary braking system with stringent standards on performance. Conversely, in Great Britain no such regulation exists. However, indications are that, at the time of writing, new regulations are being considered in Great Britain and other countries. There is no doubt that many of the bad coach accidents, particularly in mountainous areas, would have been avoided by the use of a subsidiary braking system which does not rely on the wheel brakes.

Heavy vehicles are fitted with two, and sometimes three, systems for actuating wheel brakes. These certainly go a long way towards eliminating brake failure, but they do not provide any safeguard against fade. There is no doubt that fade is an important cause of accidents. The provision of a separate braking system that will leave the wheel brakes in prime condition for use in an emergency should result in a considerable decrease in such accidents.

Continental regulations require, in certain countries, that a subsidiary braking system should be fitted and that the brake should be capable of maintaining its effect down a given gradient for a given time or distance. The details vary, but a good example is that of Switzerland, where the requirement is for passenger-carrying vehicles to have such a system above 5 t gross weight, and that the system should be able to operate on a gradient of 8 per cent to keep the vehicle speed down to 30 km/h for 3 km. There are other similar regulations for parts of Germany and for the mountainous areas of France.

The importance of retarders in moulding regulations can be shown in France, where vehicles fitted with a retarder are granted a relaxation on gross weight to allow for the retarder. In the same country, certain insurance companies allow a reduction in premium for vehicles fitted with retarders.

The effect of regulations on auxiliary braking in this country would create a demand for retarders that would probably lead, in due time, to the next logical step of fitting them as prime equipment in the transmission.

5.2 Integral design of retarders

As optional equipment, the retarder can pose problems of space, stress, heat and current consumption. The effect of adding a component to a transmission is to un-balance the total design concept. If a retarder is to be fitted in the vehicle at the time of building, it is possible to improve the system in several ways. These are:

(*a*) The virtual elimination of costly support members.

(*b*) Improvement of bearing layouts to carry the extra weight and torque.

(*c*) The provision of an adequate electrical supply in the form of an alternator of sufficient power and/or batteries with an adequate capacity. The wiring loom and location of relays will also be simplified.

(*d*) The prevention of undue stress on a vehicle chassis by fitting a heavy component for which the chassis was not designed.

(*e*) The proper location of auxiliaries, such as fuel tanks, brake pipes, air reservoirs, etc., to provide adequate space.

(*f*) Satisfactory suspension geometry and stiffness to cater for extra unsprung weight where the retarder is mounted on the drive axle.

(*g*) The application of retarders to vehicles with trans-verse engines or rear engines, where available propeller-shaft space does not permit the use of the retarder as 'add-on' equipment.

(*h*) Redesign of wheel brakes having regard for their longer life and lower fade when using a retarder.

(*j*) The design of an integrated control system such that the retarder actuator is linked directly to the normal controls.

(*k*) Use with turbine-powered vehicles where engine braking is a problem and wheel brakes have problems in coping with all-up weights of 40–50 t at motorway speeds.

(*l*) The rationalization of cooling systems to reduce fan losses, whereas now both engine and retarder have individual cooling systems.

(*m*) The ready compliance with recommendations of the Department of the Environment for satisfactory air spaces of various materials from the retarder. These are:

Brake fluid	15 cm
Wood	20 cm
Rubber brake hoses . . .	33 cm
Nylon pipes and p.v.c. insulation	41 cm

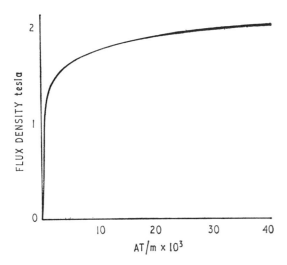

Fig. 79.13. **Magnetic saturation curve of typical ferrous material used in a retarder**

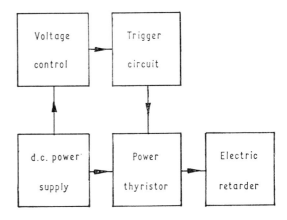

Fig. 79.14. **Block diagram of progressive braking control**

5.3 Improvements in retarder design

The main problem of weight in an electric retarder stems from the absolute necessity to use a ferrous material of high density and a limited magnetic flux density. At present, the most highly permeable irons within reason-able cost limits have a limiting flux density of 2·0–2·1 T. The high current required by a retarder is due to working

Fig. 79.15. **Pye Electric retarder, type R.5**

very close to the flux density limit. Fig. 79.13 shows a typical curve of such material where the vertical axis is flux density and the horizontal axis is magnetic motive force. Magneto-motive force is measured in ampere turns/unit length of magnetic circuit. For a given magnetic circuit, and a coil of a given number of turns, increasing current gives increasing flux density. There comes a point when virtually no gain in flux density is achieved by increasing current. The iron is then said to be saturated.

Unless new materials with higher saturation flux densities come to light, and at a viable cost, there seems to be little chance of reducing the weight of electric retarders. The main improvements are likely to be in:

(a) Lubrication, to give increased intervals between regreasing.

(b) Improved insulation, to combat the increased use of salt on roads.

(c) The increased use of progressive braking as opposed to step-function braking. This will come about with the improvement in the technology of solid-state devices, which, in turn, leads to reduced cost. A block diagram of a progressive braking control is shown in Fig. 79.14.

(d) The use of solid-state switches, instead of relays, in step-function systems, with a consequent increase in reliability.

(e) As a side effect, the increased use of electric retarders, especially when specified as prime equipment for quantity production, will tend to cause a decrease in cost.

5.4 Use of retarders in other applications

Heavy road vehicles are the major outlet for electric retarders, but there are several other areas where their use is an advantage.

(a) Trains. Particularly city transport such as tube trains, where brakes are applied at frequent intervals. A progressive application followed by a final applica-

tion of wheel brakes would give smooth braking with little wear.

(b) Cranes. Stabilization of slew movements and control of overrunning loads.

(c) Dynamometers. For absorption of power with good reliability and low installation cost.

(d) Industrial applications that require a dynamic brake.

(e) Earth-moving equipment where load dumping downhill can be a major problem.

There are many fields in which retardation is a problem, and the electric retarder is sufficiently versatile to give a sensible answer to such problems. That shown in Fig. 79.15 is the Pye Electric retarder type R.5.

6 SUMMARY

The electric retarder is a frictionless brake for use in a vehicle transmission. As such, it provides subsidiary braking, which gives increased safety and radically improves the life of wheel brakes. Selection of the correct retarder is a relatively simple procedure and installation, if properly engineered, presents no problems. The electric retarder can be mounted in the transmission line or direct to differential or gearbox casing. Apart from increased safety, the electric retarder can reduce driver fatigue and cut vehicle-off-road costs. Future trends indicate more regulations on subsidiary braking and the tendency to fit retarders as prime manufacturer's equipment, with many consequent advantages.

APPENDIX 79.1
REFERENCES

(1) AICHERT, H. 'Untersuchungen an elektrischen Wirbelstrombremsen fur Fahrzeuge', *Auto.-tech. Z.* 1969 **71**, 8.

(2) PYE ELECTRIC LTD 'Market survey on retarders', 1971, unpublished.

(3) TABOREK, J. J. Papers 5 and 6, *Mach. Des. J.* 1957 (July and August) (Penton Publishing Co.).

(4) REINBECK, H. 'Die Wirbelstrombremse fur schwere Kraftfahrzeuge', 1970 (August), Bild 6 (Bosch G.m.b.H.).

C88/72 VEHICLE HEADWAY CONTROL

A. P. IVES*   G. A. K. BRUNT*   N. B. WIDDOWSON*   J. R. THORNTON*

The paper deals with some work currently being carried out at the Lucas Group Research Centre into the control of vehicle headway using a Q-band radar system. An analogue computer simulation of a headway-controlled vehicle is briefly described. This simulation enabled the primary controlling factors and the transfer function of the control system to be identified for stable queue operating conditions. The construction of hardware based on the simulation results is described. This includes a frequency-modulated, continuous-wave radar system using a Gunn diode source operating at about 35 GHz, computing electronics containing both digital and analogue techniques and servos for the operation of the braking system and the throttle. A Ford Zodiac with automatic transmission was used as the test vehicle. The system was adjusted on this vehicle to give best drivability commensurate with the response required for queue operation. A brief comparison is made with results obtained from the computer simulation.

1 INTRODUCTION

IT IS GENERALLY ACCEPTED that road vehicles will remain the primary form of land transportation in the future. Increasing numbers of vehicles on limited road space bring problems of operation under high vehicle densities, especially in conditions of poor visibility. Total automation taking the form of both lateral and longitudinal control may therefore prove useful in the future, enabling better utilization of available road space whilst at the same time reducing driver fatigue.

The longitudinal or headway control aspect can be considered to consist of problems associated with the acquisition of headway information and the computation of control action resulting in the actuation of the controls. Microwave radar may be used as a method of acquiring headway and relative velocity information in either a completely non-co-operative mode, in which special fitments would not be required on the rear of every vehicle; or in a passively co-operative mode, utilizing corner reflectors perhaps built into rear-lamp clusters.

This paper discusses one form of longitudinal control that is suitable either as part of a totally automated system or on its own as an adaptive speed control.

2 SIMULATION

Very many papers have been published on automatic longitudinal control of vehicles, mostly in the U.S.A. (1)–(4)†, and in general a linear control law is favoured. That is, one in which the desired acceleration of the following vehicle is proportional to the headway error and relative velocity between the vehicles, and the desired or correct headway is set as a linear function of the following vehicle speed (i.e. a constant headway time).

Two main conditions should be met by a headway control system; these are:

(1) Local and asymptotic stability of queues. Local

stability suggests that any individual vehicle must be stable with respect to its leader and can be studied by considering a 'two-car' condition. Asymptotic stability suggests that small disturbances in any vehicle's position and velocity in a queue of vehicles must be attenuated as the disturbance propagates along the queue. This tends to be more restrictive.

(2) No collisions after a 'full braking' stop by any vehicle. This is a particularly difficult requirement in view of the considerable differences that are found in the braking efficiencies of vehicles, especially in commercial vehicles. Penoyre (5) discusses this problem in considerable depth and concludes that the most likely solution is to assume that by the time road vehicle automation could be introduced the present deficiencies in commercial vehicle braking systems would have been remedied. For the purposes of this paper this assumption has been adopted.

It was the purpose of the simulation work to allow experiments to be conducted in complete safety with various control laws applied to the vehicle over a range of lead vehicle manoeuvres and to arrive at a set of control parameters commensurate with the above conditions. It is not intended to discuss the simulation work in depth in this paper but only to outline the conclusions obtained from it.

Fig. 88.1 shows the effect of motorway geometry for a 'two-car' condition; Fig. 88.2 shows the basic block diagram for the controlled vehicle system in which the acceleration demand signal, ϵ, used in the simulation is given by:

$$\epsilon = A\,[(h - k_1 V_0) + kV]$$

where h is the actual headway (m), V_0 the actual vehicle speed (m s^{-1}), k_1 the desired headway constant (s), V the relative velocity (m s^{-1}), k the weighting factor (s), and A the system gain constant (s^{-2}).

Attention was paid particularly to the value of k, the weighting factor between the relative velocity and headway error terms, this value having particular importance with regard to queue stability. For a typical time spacing between vehicles of 0·7 s [headway = 3 m (10 ft) for

The MS. of this paper was received at the Institution on 14th March 1972 and accepted for publication on 3rd May 1972. 33
* *Lucas Group Research Centre, Monkspath, Shirley, Solihull, Warwickshire.*
† *References are given in Appendix 88.1.*

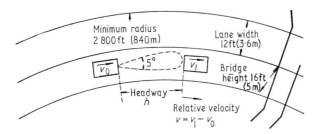

Fig. 88.1. The effect of motorway geometry

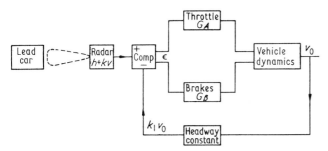

Fig. 88.2. Basic block diagram of the controlled vehicle system

every 10 mile/h of queue velocity] it was found that $1 \leqslant k \leqslant 10$ typically for best following conditions. The analogue computer simulation of the system examined the mode by which error information is transferred to vehicle control.

Initially the simulation study was carried out with a throttle actuator that gave a throttle angle setting as a linear function of error. Namely,

$$\phi = G_A \epsilon + 20 \qquad (\phi \geqslant 0)$$

where ϕ is the throttle angle in degrees, ϵ the error voltage applied to throttle servo, and G_A the throttle actuator gain in degrees per volt.

The constant $20°$ was included to give a fixed throttle effect, which compensated somewhat for the throttle setting required to maintain constant speed on a level road. It is evident that this is only an approximation.

As a result of using this type of law the effective acceleration applied to the vehicle is a non-linear function of the error voltage, since the acceleration torque applied at the road wheels is a non-linear function of the throttle angle due to the engine torque characteristics. These characteristics were built into the simulation.

On the braking side, however, the braking torque applied at the road wheels can easily be made a linear function of error voltage by controlling brake line pressure as a linear function of error. Thus,

$$P_b = G_B . \epsilon$$

where P_b is the brake line pressure in kg m^{-2} (lb in^{-2}) and G_B the brake actuator gain in kg m^{-2}/V (lb in^{-2}/V).

The results of a simulation based on these two laws were disappointing, as a unique set of operating constants could not be found that stabilized conditions for ramp and sinusoidal inputs. It was concluded at this stage that this was due to the non-linearities in the acceleration loop. The simulation was therefore changed to incorporate an acceleration feedback loop in which the vehicle acceleration was measured and compared with the acceleration

demand. In this modified system a satisfactory solution was achieved in which ramp and frequency inputs could be stabilized with one set of constants.

With the information obtained from the simulation it was then possible to consider the radar techniques employed to obtain the information on range and relative velocity, and to design hardware for the real vehicle operation.

3 HEADWAY MEASUREMENT—RADAR

Either a pulsed radar or a continuous-wave radar may be used to provide range and relative velocity information. In a pulsed system the time between transmission and reception of a radar pulse gives a measure of the range. Relative velocity information may be obtained either by differentiating the range signal or more reliably by measuring the Doppler shift in frequency of the returned pulse. However, for vehicle applications the system must measure down to a minimum range of about 3 m (10 ft), which implies pulse widths of less than 20 ns.

Fast pulse circuitry would therefore be necessary to measure the small time intervals between transmitted and received pulses at close ranges. In effect, a large bandwidth would be required to measure targets within a very few metres. In a continuous wave system, however, this large bandwidth is more easily attained within the bandwidth of the very high frequency microwave circuitry, so that measurement of small ranges is easily performed.

In a f.m.c.w. (frequency modulated, continuous-wave) radar the frequency of the continuously transmitted microwaves is changed with time. This means that the returning wave from a relatively stationary target always has a slightly different frequency to that of the transmitted wave (see Fig. 88.3). For a given frequency sweep f it can be shown that the range frequency f_R will be:

$$f_R = \frac{2 \Delta f h}{cT}$$

where c is the velocity of propagation of the radar signal, T the modulation period, h the range of the target and the difference frequency f_R between the transmitted and received waves is proportional to the range of the target. This frequency is in the audio range and is easily obtained by 'mixing' the two frequencies.

The effect of relative velocity between transmitter and target is to produce a Doppler shift in frequency of the

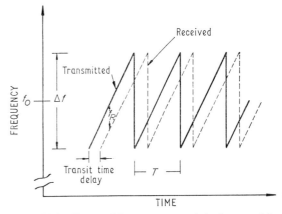

Fig. 88.3. Form of frequency modulation used in f.m.c.w. radar system

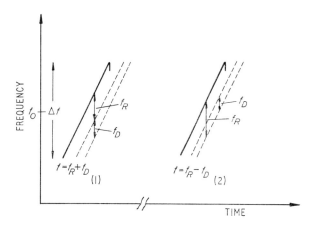

Fig. 88.4. Effect of relative velocity (Doppler frequency) on measured frequency for (1) headway increasing with time and (2) headway decreasing with time

return wave (see Fig. 88.4), this shift in frequency being proportional to the relative velocity:

$$f_D = \frac{2Vf_0}{c}$$

where V is the relative velocity and f_0 the frequency of the transmitted wave.

Thus for a two-vehicle situation in a 'follow the leader' mode in which both range and relative velocity exist the total signal frequency obtained by mixing transmitted and received waves will be:

$$f = f_R + f_D$$

$$f = \frac{2 \Delta f h}{cT} + \frac{2Vf_0}{c}$$

It was noted from work on the simulation of the control system that a control law of the form $h + kV$ is required for stable operation, and it can be seen that by rewriting the above equation an expression of the same form can be obtained, viz.:

$$f\left(\frac{cT}{2\Delta f}\right) = h + \left(\frac{f_0 T}{\Delta f}\right) V$$

whence

$$k = \frac{f_0 T}{\Delta f}$$

Clearly then, any value of k can be obtained by altering any of the three quantities f_0, T or Δf. However, a number of constraints must be met; for example, it is desirable to keep $\Delta f/f_0$ small, since this represents the frequency sweep of the microwave source, which might be difficult to make large. In addition, the Doppler frequency is low at small values of relative velocity and may be lost altogether if the period T is made too short. Within such constraints it was found that to obtain a value for $1 < k < 10$ and to give a range resolution of about 0·3 m (1 ft) it was necessary to operate in Q-band, around 30–35 GHz. The frequency sweep required was approximately 0·25 GHz (250 MHz) with a modulation period of approximately 15 ms. With this modulation period a relative velocity resolution of approximately 0·15 m/s (0·5 ft/s) is achieved and around 40 readings of combined headway and relative velocity measurements could be made every 1 s, thereby giving an opportunity for a fast reaction time to be built into the overall system.

Operation at a frequency in Q-band also has the desirable side effects that the radar equipment is small and easily mounted on a vehicle. With the relatively short-range requirement [approximately 45 m (150 ft)] the attenuation due to atmosphere and precipitation can be considered small, even with heavy rainfall giving rise to an attenuation of 10 dB/km. Narrow-beam-width antennae are easily obtained with small dimensions, and by consideration of motorway geometry, lane widths, bridge heights, etc., it became clear that a 5° beam width would be needed (Fig. 88.1). By adopting such a narrow beam width, limiting operation to motorways and, if necessary, mounting corner reflectors on lead vehicles, single-target operation may be obtained from the radar. This leads to a relatively simple radar system ideally suited to vehicle use.

4 TOTAL CONTROL SYSTEM HARDWARE

It is worth considering once again the total block diagram for the headway controller. It consists of (1) radar equipment, which provides the combined headway and relative velocity information; (2) the speed sensor, which provides information on the true speed of the controlled vehicle; (3) the computing electronics, together with the vehicle interlocks, which receives the inputs and decides on subsequent action; and (4) the actuators, with their associated controls for operation of both throttle and brakes. This section discusses these individual parts in more detail.

4.1 Radar equipment

Fig. 88.5 shows a block diagram of the system in which a Gunn diode oscillator is frequency modulated by mechanically altering the length of the cavity. A vibrator is driven from a sawtooth generator, which has a period of approximately 20 ms and an amplitude sufficient to give a frequency modulation of the oscillator of around 250 MHz.

The outgoing wave is passed through a 3-dB coupler before reaching the transmitting antenna so that part of the oscillator power is fed to the balanced mixer. The receiving antenna feeds the reflected signal back to the balanced mixer, from which the difference frequency between transmitted and received signals is extracted. It was found necessary to use a balanced mixer arrangement to overcome problems arising from the amplitude modulation also generated by the vibrating short-circuit modulation technique.

From the mixer the audio-frequency signal is amplified and passed through a voltage comparator with a certain

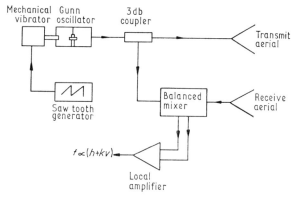

Fig. 88.5. Block diagram for f.m.c.w. radar system

amount of hysteresis. This eliminates noise below a pre-determined level and is used to prevent random signals reaching the control system when the vehicle is being operated in an open-road situation (no target vehicle). In this manner, only *relatively* large signals are processed. Under normal following conditions the output from the radar system is now a 'square' wave of varying frequency. This signal is then fed to the main controlling electronics.

4.2 Vehicle speed measurement

Several methods were available for measuring actual vehicle speed, some of which make use of the existing speedometer drive arrangement. However, it was thought at the time that a primary consideration in the choice of a speed-measurement technique must be the amount of mechanical backlash between the road wheels and take-off point for the transducer. For this reason it was decided to use the existing crown wheel in the rear axle as the 'notched wheel' for a magnetic sensor. A magneto diode (a diode whose forward characteristic is changed with a magnetic field across it) was therefore mounted inside the rear-axle housing, together with a permanent magnet by which rotation of the crown wheel caused a change of magnetic flux across the diode. These diodes are *not* dependent upon rate of change of magnetic flux; therefore it was possible to measure speeds down to zero—an obvious requirement for the system. Once again, by feeding the output of the diode to a local amplifier with hysteresis a large signal free of noise was obtained, which consists of a 'square' wave whose frequency was dependent on vehicle speed. This signal is then fed to the main controlling electronics.

4.3 Control electronics

Fig. 88.6 is a block diagram of the total control electronics accepting the two frequency signals from the speed transducer and radar unit. It is seen that a simple hold approach has been adopted in which the two frequencies are 'measured' by counting zero crossings over a period of time.

Consider first the signal entering from the radar unit. It will be recalled that the Q-band oscillator is being modulated with a sawtooth wave, which gives useful information to the control system over most of the ramp part of the wave-form. Clearly, during the flyback period, and for a settling period just afterwards, the output frequency from the radar is unusable. For this reason a period of blanking is produced from a monostable triggered from the flyback of the sawtooth. In the particular configuration this blanking occupied approximately 10 ms out of the total period of 25 ms, leaving a useful 'count' period of 15 ms.

It was also found that to achieve the required resolution from the system, both positive- and negative-going edges of the radar output were counted, this being done by a simple differentiation and subsequent full-wave rectification of the signal before reaching a counter. The output from this counter is fed to a latch (store), which holds the information between one count period and the next, updating of this latch occurring every 25 ms. Similar circuitry is used to process the vehicle speed data coming from the rear axle, and the same blanking and update pulses are used to control the speed channel counter and latch.

The outputs from the speed and headway latches are now converted to analogue voltages in the respective D–A converters, and thence to function generators. The purpose of these function generators is to scale the two signals prior to comparison and to provide operating limits for the system. In the headway function generator an adjustable limit clamps the output voltage to a predetermined level. In the total operating system this has the effect of limiting the maximum *speed* of the controlled vehicle. Similarly, in the speed function generator provision is made for limiting the minimum output voltage, and in this manner the minimum *headway* can be preset.

The two voltages, actual headway and vehicle speed, which translates to the desired headway, are now compared in the comparator stage and an error signal is produced. This error can be either positive or negative; a positive output being used to actuate the throttle system, whilst a negative output actuates the brakes.

5 SERVO ACTUATORS

Once an error voltage has been produced from the comparator, servo actuators are required to operate both throttle and brakes accordingly. It will be recalled that

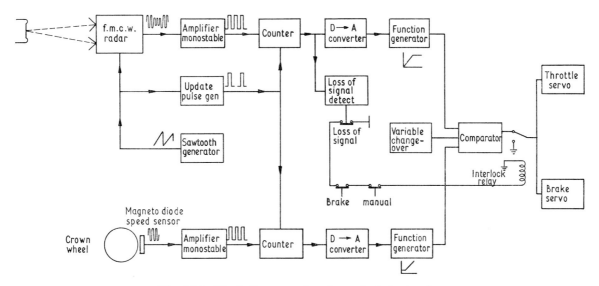

Fig. 88.6. Block diagram of main control electronics

considerable attention was paid to the translation from error voltage to vehicle motion in the simulation of the system. Two approaches were tried: one in which the error voltage produced corresponding throttle angle and brake line pressure; the other in which the error voltage produced an acceleration, which was monitored by a local acceleration feedback loop. It was decided that for the prototype vehicle the former approach would be adopted initially, and work to date has been done on the basis of this system. The latter approach has yet to be tried.

5.1 Throttle servo

The throttle servo utilizes inlet manifold vacuum as a source of power operating via bellows connected to the carburettor throttle linkage. Fig. 88.7 shows the system, in which a solenoid valve controls the degree of vacuum in the bellows by admitting air into the system. When the solenoid valve is energized, manifold depression evacuates the bellows causing them to compress and operate the throttle linkage, thus opening the throttle. The speed of response to open the throttle is governed by a constriction in the vacuum line, but a fast response is obtained for the

closure of the throttle when the solenoid valve is de-energized.

Throttle position feedback is provided by the throttle potentiometer, so that the comparator amplifier senses that the required throttle angle has been reached; the solenoid valve then oscillates to maintain a constant setting.

5.2 Brake servo

An arrangement based on the same principle as that used for the throttle was adopted for brake actuation. Fig. 88.8 shows a conventional hydraulic–vacuum servo unit that has been modified by the inclusion of a shuttle valve in the feedback pipe. Air is thus allowed to enter one side of the vacuum servo by operating the valve in one direction, this air being extracted by the vacuum system by operation of the valve in the other direction. A differential pressure

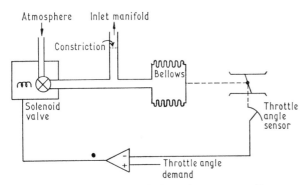

Fig. 88.7. Block diagram of throttle actuator. Response rate to open is determined by the constriction fast response to close position

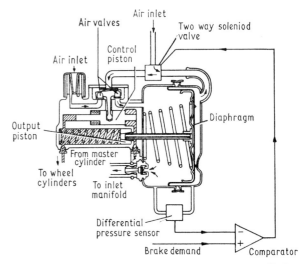

Fig. 88.8. Principles of the electrically controlled brake servo unit

Fig. 88.9. Headway-controlled vehicle. Note two radar aerials mounted in front grille

Fig. 88.10. Frequency modulated, continuous-wave radar unit, mounted under the bonnet

transducer monitors the pressure across the servo diaphragm and is therefore a measure of the brake-line pressure. Output from this transducer is compared with the demand and the valve switched accordingly. Once the required brake-line pressure has been reached, the valve oscillates to maintain a substantially constant pressure, the frequency of oscillation being determined by the rate at which pressure in the servo can rise and fall.

6 INSTALLATION AND SYSTEM INTERLOCKS

A Ford Zodiac V6 with automatic transmission was chosen for this work, the main attraction being the amount of space available under the bonnet for installation of the radar system and actuators. Fig. 88.9 shows an external view of the vehicle in which the two radar aerials are prominent in the front grille area. Fig. 88.10 shows the radar hardware mounted under the bonnet of the car so that both aerials have an unobstructed view through perspex panels covering the apertures cut in the front grille. Fig. 88.11 shows the main control electronics housed in the parcel-shelf area below the fascia. Throttle and brake servo gains could be adjusted from the front panel, and indicator lights showed the presence of a demand for braking and throttle.

A safety interlock system was included that would put the vehicle into automatic mode at the touch of a switch, yet would have safety features in that control of the vehicle could be quickly returned to the driver. Manual operation of the throttle overrides the automatic system without disengaging it, but manual application of the brakes completely de-energizes both servos and returns the system to 'standby' condition. In the event of a loss of radar signal the vehicle automatically returns to manual control, with

Fig. 88.11. Interior of headway-controlled vehicle showing main control electronics

an appropriate warning to the driver. Further attention must be given to this important area to determine the best fail-safe and self-testing approach to be adopted.

7 PERFORMANCE

At the time of writing, the testing of the vehicle and the evaluation of its performance were far from completion. At the outset of the tests it became evident that a technique by which the activities of the 'lead car' could be controlled accurately was clearly needed. It was for this reason that the testing has been broken down into two main areas: one in which the radar system was tested to determine whether the correct information on range and relative velocity was being obtained, the other to establish how the control system functioned given information on range and relative velocity.

7.1 Radar measurements

Fig. 88.12 shows a typical result of a test in which the vehicle starts from rest at a known distance from the target. Acceleration of the vehicle towards the target reduces the headway, and the true headway is thereby plotted. By accounting for the relative velocity term the quantity $h+kV$ for $k = 2$ has been plotted, and this is compared with the output of the radar unit. In this manner, the radar can be correlated with the actual conditions.

7.2 Control system

To enable controlled test conditions to be set up, a lead-vehicle simulator was built, which provided information similar to that obtained from the radar unit. This replaced

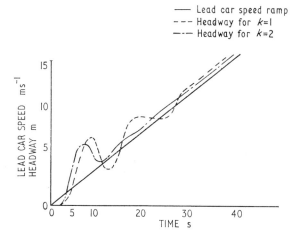

Fig. 88.13. Actual vehicle responses for a lead car accelerating from rest

the real lead car and radar system combination. Acceleration, deceleration and sinusoidal response tests could then be performed without the need for a real lead vehicle; Fig. 88.13 shows the responses obtained from some early ramp tests. It is interesting to note the effect of changing the relative velocity weighting factor k, showing increasing stiffness in the system with increasing k. Also evident is the effect of a delay in the throttle actuator, causing considerable oscillations at the start of the ramp.

Tests to date have been carried out with no acceleration feedback loop in the control system. Further work is necessary to enable direct comparisons to be made with the computer simulation results for a control system incorporating the acceleration feedback.

8 CONCLUSIONS

An approach to automatic headway control, based on the inherent information on headway and relative velocity terms contained in the output of a f.m.c.w. radar, has been proposed. The control aspects suggest that this approach is only feasible with high microwave frequencies (Q-band), to achieve a workable resolution and response time.

A computer simulation of a vehicle operating on a control law based on this combination of headway and relative velocity suggested that 'stable' operation could only be achieved by including an acceleration feedback loop, by which the headway error results in a known acceleration.

The building of hardware and the adaptation of a vehicle to verify this approach have shown that the control of headway by this method is possible. However, considerably more testing is required to confirm the results obtained from the simulation.

9 ACKNOWLEDGEMENTS

The authors wish to thank Mr J. A. Jeyes of the Engineering Product Research Department of the Lucas Group Research Centre for his work on the computer simulation and the members of the Girling Advanced Engineering Group for the assistance with the braking system used in the work. The authors also wish to thank the Directors of Joseph Lucas Limited for permission to publish this paper.

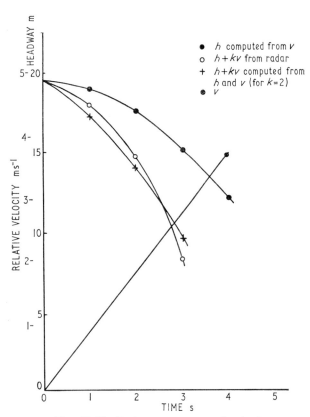

Fig. 88.12. Radar output tests for $k=2$

APPENDIX 88.1

REFERENCES
(1) BENDER, J. G. 'Experimental studies in vehicle automatic longitudinal control', *U.S. Govt. Research and Development Report PB183, 678* 1968 (July) (Ohio State Univ., Columbus, Ohio).

(2) CROW, J. W. and PARKER, R. H. 'Automatic headway control —an automatic vehicle spacing system', *S.A.E. Automotive Engineering Congr.* 1970 (12th–16th July) (Detroit, Michigan).

(3) COSGRIFF, R. L., ENGLISH, J. J. and ROECA, W. B. 'An automatic system for longitudinal control of individual vehicles', *Highway Research Record* 1966 No. 122 (Department of Elect. Engng, Ohio State University).

(4) HAROKOPUS, W. P. 'Application of radar to automobile control and sensing', *Second Int. Tech. Conf. Experimental Safety Vehicles* 1971 (26th–29th October) (Stuttgart, Germany).

(5) PENOYRE, S. 'The longitudinal control problem' (unpublished study) (Safety Division, Driver Aids and Abilities Section, T.R.R.L., Ministry of Transport).

C89/72 TRENDS IN THE DESIGN AND PERFORMANCE OF SPARK PLUGS AS RELATED TO ENGINE EXHAUST EMISSIONS

L. R. LENTZ*   R. D. MILLER*   T. E. CADMUS*

This paper discusses the conditions under which a spark plug must function and the design parameters that influence its performance. Techniques in engine evaluation of spark plugs are described. Correct functioning of the spark plug has become of even greater significance with recent developments concerning exhaust emissions. The relationship of design parameters and their effect on emission is of primary importance. Test results on the effect of gap spacing, gap configuration, gap location in the combustion chamber, and spark plug misfiring are described. Results with different percentages of exhaust gas recirculation are reported. Because of the close relationship of the ignition system spark discharge characteristics and the function of the spark plug, the effect of spark duration has also been observed. Since the effect of these variables may be influenced by engine operation they have also been examined under various operating conditions. An attempt is made to predict possible future trends.

1 INTRODUCTION

DURING THE PAST 10 YEARS the development of the spark-ignition gasoline engine in the U.S.A. has been greatly influenced by air pollution legislation enacted by the Federal Government (1)† and the State of California. As a consequence, engine design, carburation, fuels, fuel additives and ignition systems are all being carefully examined for their influence on the exhaust emission characteristics of the engine. Exhaust gas recirculation (EGR), catalytic converters and thermal reactors are currently being evaluated and can be expected on passenger cars in the near future. To predict at this time what effect all these possible modifications may have on spark plug design is beyond the scope of this paper.

The purpose of this paper is to discuss some of the parameters which influence spark plug performance and to illustrate how these parameters affect the exhaust emission and performance of the engine.

The relationship of spark plug gap spacing, gap configuration and gap location in the combustion chamber, as well as the effects of various ignition system spark discharge characteristics, is discussed. The effect of EGR on engine performance and emissions in relation to spark plug design was also investigated using a typical U.S. six-cylinder engine of approximately 4 litre displacement.

2 RELATIONSHIP OF ENGINE DESIGN TO SPARK PLUG CONFIGURATION

While the spark plug manufacturer has the responsibility of the plug design, the engine designer also has considerable influence on its final configuration. The engine designer accomplishes this by specifying the physical dimensions of the spark plug. The choice of thread dia-

The MS. of this paper was received at the Institution on 1st January 1972 and accepted for publication on 1st June 1972. 32
* Champion Spark Plug Co. Ltd, Feltham, Middx.
† References are given in Appendix 89.1.

meter, reach and type of seating is generally determined by such engine features as displacement, valve size and arrangement, combustion chamber configuration, etc. (2). Small spark plug thread diameters of 8, 10 and 12 mm would be desirable from the engine designer's viewpoint since they provide increased flexibility for valve, water passage and combustion chamber design. However, they generally are not completely satisfactory for normal automotive type of operation. These thread diameters limit the size of electrodes and the scavenging volume around the insulator firing tip, and they impose limitations on both the electrical and physical strength of the spark plug.

With the exception of one major automobile manufacturer who uses 18-mm tapered seat spark plugs, the 14-mm thread diameter is used almost exclusively. Fig. 89.1 illustrates both 14-mm and 18-mm tapered seat configurations as well as the conventional 14-mm gasket seated type. The tapered seat designs offer the engine manufacturer the advantages of a smaller hex and shell diameter for a given thread size.

3 FUNCTION OF THE SPARK PLUG

The function of the spark plug is to provide a gap in the combustion chamber for the discharge of an electrical pulse that will ignite the air–fuel mixture at the desired point in the engine cycle (3). To do this effectively, the spark plug must satisfy a number of requirements.

(1) No part of the spark plug must ever become hot enough to ignite the mixture before the spark occurs.

(2) The spark plug must provide a gap spacing and be positioned in the combustion chamber at a location that will satisfy engine operation over the range of output from idle to wide open throttle, and do it with minimum fuel consumption.

(3) The electrodes must be of such size and composition as to resist the effect of electrical erosion as well as

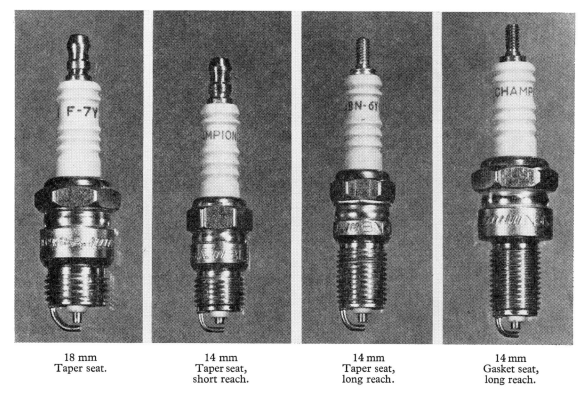

| 18 mm Taper seat. | 14 mm Taper seat, short reach. | 14 mm Taper seat, long reach. | 14 mm Gasket seat, long reach. |

Fig. 89.1. Typical spark plug thread configurations

the effect of chemical corrosion from the products of combustion.

(4) The firing end must be designed to resist fouling. This requires that the insulator tip temperature be kept fairly high at low engine outputs to avert carbon fouling. An insulator tip as long as possible and a large clearance volume are also desirable to minimize both carbon and lead fouling.

4   DETERMINATION OF PROPER SPARK PLUG HEAT RANGE

Although the methods of determining basic spark plug heat range requirements for specific engines and applications have been presented previously (4), they will be reviewed briefly. Special spark plugs, having a thermocouple embedded in the tip of the insulator nose as shown in Fig. 89.2, are used to measure the operating temperature of the spark plug in the engine. A temperature in excess of 400°C (752°F) at 30 mile/h road load is desirable to prevent cold fouling while a maximum temperature of the order of 850°C (1562°F) is necessary to prevent rapid electrode erosion. To avoid the possibility of spark plug induced pre-ignition, the maximum temperature should not exceed 950°C (1742°F).

Pre-ignition can cause severe engine damage by overheating such combustion chamber components as piston crowns and rings, valves and spark plugs. The spark plug pre-ignition safety factor is defined as the difference between the ignition timing necessary to cause spark plug induced pre-ignition and the standard timing at the particular operating condition. A minimum of 10° safety factor is normally desirable on four-stroke engines to prevent the spark plug becoming a source of pre-ignition. It is generally determined under wide open throttle operation by gradually advancing the timing of the engine

until the fuel mixture is ignited prior to the occurrence of the normal spark discharge.

Insulator tip length is the most significant design variable in controlling spark plug operating temperature or heat range. A 'cold' plug will have a short insulator tip, a short heat rejection path and a high indicated mean effective pressure (i.m.e.p.) as determined in an industry standard spark plug rating engine (5). A 'hot' plug will generally have a long insulator tip, thereby, a long heat rejection path and a low i.m.e.p. value. The relative operating temperature of two such spark plugs along with the proper heat range plug in the same engine would have the temperature characteristics shown in Fig. 89.3. Further control of these temperatures can be obtained by varying such features as insulator tip position, electrode material and the clearance volume at the firing end.

5   TEST PROCEDURE

The six-cylinder engine used in this investigation was instrumented with air and fuel flow devices while controlling engine oil, water and fuel temperatures. The effects of spark plug gap spacing, gap configuration, gap location, ignition system spark discharge characteristics and EGR on engine performance and emissions were determined under steady-state speed and load operation.

Emission data were obtained with Beckman exhaust gas analysis equipment in parts per million (p.p.m.) and per cent using continuous gas sampling. Total hydrocarbons (HC) were measured by flame ionization detection with carbon monoxide (CO), carbon dioxide (CO_2) and oxides of nitrogen (NO_x) measured by non-dispersive infrared analysis. An exhaust probe was installed in the collector portion of the exhaust manifold and the results are, therefore, an average of all cylinders.

Fig. 89.2. Thermocouple spark plug

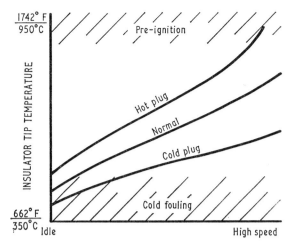

Fig. 89.3. Spark plug operating temperature

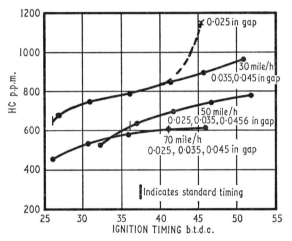

Fig. 89.4. The effect of spark plug gap spacing on hydrocarbon emissions at 30, 50 and 70 mile/h

Two basic series of tests were run during this investigation. The first was conducted with the standard carburettor giving typical air/fuel ratios for 1971–72 emission
standards. These tests were run through a range of spark
advances, generally from below standard through minimum brake specific fuel consumption (b.s.f.c.).

The second series was performed using a modified
variable main jet carburettor. These tests were run through
a wide range of air/fuel ratios at standard ignition timings
and 15° over advanced settings. Testing was concentrated
between 30 and 70 mile/h road load operating conditions.
A computer programme was used to calculate corrected
air/fuel ratio and b.s.f.c. data for each run.

6 SPARK PLUG GAP SPACING

The effect of gap spacings within the limits of 0·025 to
0·045 in with the recommended projected core nose plug
was found to be dependent upon several other variables.

The engine operating speed and load, ignition timing,
air/fuel ratio and the ignition system spark discharge
characteristics were all noted to be important when evaluating the effect of spark plug gap spacing. Fig. 89.4
illustrates that gap spacing had no appreciable effect on
HC at standard ignition timings and normal air/fuel ratios
under steady operation at 30, 50 and 70 mile/h road load.
It is only at 30 mile/h and 15° beyond standard timing that
an increase in HC is observed with the 0·025-in gap setting.
We believe that this poorer performance is related to the
reduced probability of having a combustible fuel mixture
within the smaller spark plug gap area at the time of the
spark discharge. This is probably further aggravated by
decreased turbulence in the combustion chamber at the
advanced timings and lower levels of engine power. We
calculated the air/fuel ratio to range from 14·7 to 15·6,
depending upon the test condition. No$_x$ did not appear
to be sensitive to gap spacing at the various test conditions,
and therefore these data have not been shown. The percentages of O_2, CO_2 and CO were relatively constant for
most of the test runs, except where significant amounts of
misfires were encountered. The O_2 varied from 1 to 2 per
cent, CO_2 from 14 to 15 per cent and the CO was in the
range of 0·1 to 0·3 per cent. Previous related work and
reports of other investigators (6) indicated that this
30 mile/h road load operating condition would be most
sensitive to changes in spark plug design and ignition

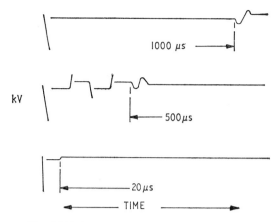

Fig. 89.5. Ignition system spark discharge characteristics

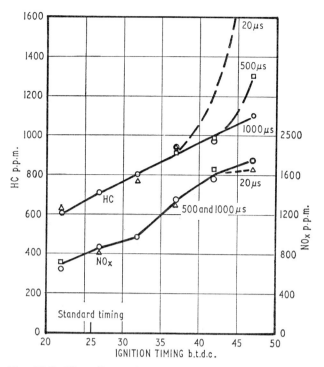

Fig. 89.6. The effect of spark discharge characteristics on the emission of hydrocarbons and oxides of nitrogen at 30 mile/h road load and a 0.025-in spark plug gap spacing

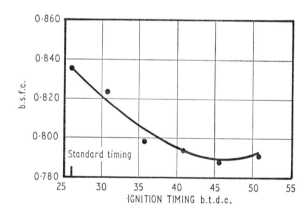

Fig. 89.7. Brake specific fuel consumption at various ignition timings with a 0.035-in gap and the standard ignition system at 30 mile/h road load

system characteristics. Therefore, much of our investigation has been confined to this area of operation.

7 IGNITION SYSTEM SPARK DISCHARGE CHARACTERISTICS

To determine the effect of spark characteristic we tested three different ignition systems, again using the recommended heat range spark plug with the gap spacing of 0.025, 0.035 and 0.045 in. The spark characteristics of these systems are shown in Fig. 89.5 and were selected because of their wide variation in arc duration. The 1000-μs system is a conventional automotive ignition system having an available voltage rise time in the order of 130 μs. The 500-μs system is a capacitor discharge (c.d.) design which used a conventional ignition coil. It has a relatively slow rise time for a c.d. system of 60 μs. The arc portion of this discharge is somewhat unusual in that it consists of several refirings of reversing polarity. Should the spark plug required voltage exceed 15 kV, the duration of this discharge will decrease to about 250 μs. However, for the purpose of this discussion we need consider only the 500-μs system. The 20-μs system is also a c.d. design but employs a special ignition coil to obtain a voltage rise time of 6 μs. Our tests indicated that the effect of the spark characteristic on emissions was related to duration and was affected by spark plug gap spacing, ignition timing and engine operating conditions.

Fig. 89.6 is a plot of HC and NO$_x$ emissions as a function of ignition timing at a spark plug gap setting of 0.025 in for each of the three ignition systems. The spark characteristics had no effect on the emissions at this 30 mile/h operating condition at the standard spark advance of 26° b.t.d.c. However, an increase in the HC emissions as a result of the shorter duration systems is noted to occur at ignition timing greater than 37°. While this takes place at approximately 11° over standard spark advance, Fig. 89.7 shows that the ignition timing for minimum b.s.f.c. is still about 5° beyond the point of deterioration. The effect of duration was minimized with a 0.035-in gap, as shown in Fig. 89.8. An increase in emissions is now observed with only the 20-μs system. This increase in HC emissions was almost entirely eliminated with a 0.045-in gap spacing.

At 50 and 70 mile/h road load operating conditions, the spark duration had no effect on the emission level regardless of the gap spacing. We attribute this to the increased turbulence in the combustion chamber at these higher power levels in providing for an ignitable mixture in the gap area regardless of the gap spacing and spark duration.

While these tests were performed using new, clean spark plugs, the results could conceivably be different if fouled spark plugs were used. High values of exhaust emission resulting from misfiring of fouled spark plugs with conventional ignition could very likely be reduced with a fast rise c.d. system. This type of system has the increased ability to fire fouled plugs, and therefore could conceivably optimize emission levels for a longer period of time by delaying the onset of spark plug misfiring.

Fig. 89.9 illustrates the increase in HC emissions resulting from various degrees of spark plug misfiring. These data were obtained by means of an electronic misfire simulator which could be programmed to eliminate any given percentage of secondary ignition discharges (7).

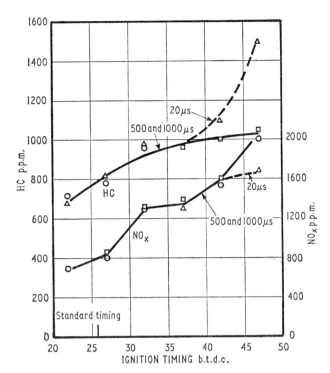

Fig. 89.8. The effect of spark discharge characteristics on the emission of hydrocarbons and oxides of nitrogen at 30 mile/h road load and a 0·035-in spark plug gap spacing

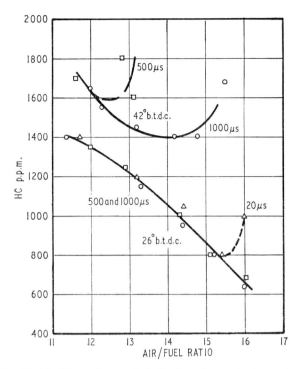

Fig. 89.10. The effect of air/fuel ratio on hydrocarbon emissions with various spark discharge characteristics at 30 mile/h road load and a 0·025-in spark plug gap spacing

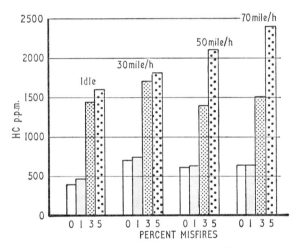

Fig. 89.9. The effect of engine misfires on hydrocarbon emissions

At 30 mile/h a 3 per cent rate of misfire results in an increase of approximately 250 per cent in HC emission levels. In view of the U.S. 50 000-mile acceptance test, this sharp increase in emission levels indicates that factors other than just the performance of new components must be considered when evaluating spark plug and ignition system designs for a given application.

8 AIR/FUEL RATIO

The effect and relationship of spark plug gap spacing and the ignition system spark discharge characteristic on exhaust emission were noted to be influenced to a considerable extent by the air/fuel ratio. The effect of the air/fuel ratio was determined at 30 mile/h for the normal 26° ignition timing for this operating condition, and also at an over-advanced ignition timing of 42°. Results with

0·025, 0·035 and 0·045-in gap spacings and the three different ignition systems were investigated. Fig. 89.10 shows the HC plotted as a function of air/fuel ratio with a 0·025-in gap setting. At the standard 26° ignition timing the emissions from the three systems are essentially the same from 11·5 to 15·4 air/fuel ratios. At ratios leaner than 15·4 there is a tendency for increased HC emissions with the 20-μs duration system. The advantage of the longer duration system is easily apparent at a 42° timing. The HC emissions from the 20-μs system are well above the 2000 p.p.m. range and, therefore, are not shown. Under such operating conditions, engine misfiring is observed as well as an increase in the b.s.f.c. of the engine, as shown in Fig. 89.11.

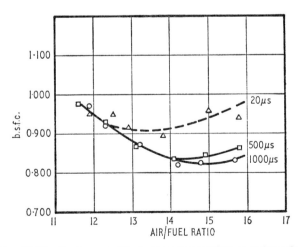

Fig. 89.11. Brake specific fuel consumption as a function of air/fuel ratio with a 0·025-in gap and 42° ignition timing at 30 mile/h road load

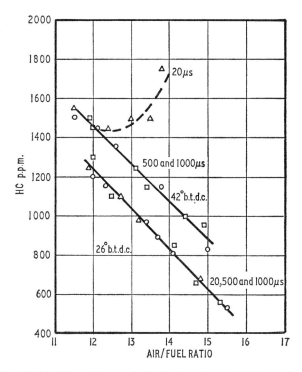

Fig. 89.12. The effect of air/fuel ratio on hydrocarbon emissions with various spark discharge characteristics at 30 mile/h road load and a 0·035-in spark plug gap spacing

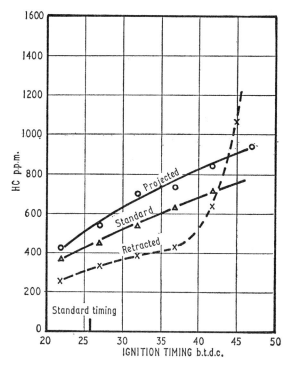

Fig. 89.14. The effect of spark plug gap location on hydrocarbon emissions at 30 mile/h road load and 14·7 air/fuel ratio

The relationship of these variables is further illustrated in Fig. 89.12 with a spark plug gap spacing of 0·035 in. There is no difference in the emissions at 26° ignition timing regardless of the ignition system. At 42° ignition timing a very significant loss in performance is still observed with the 20-μs ignition system. With spark plug gap spacings increased to 0·045 in the HC emission levels at 42° were unaffected by the ignition system characteristic.

9 SPARK PLUG GAP LOCATION

The position of the spark plug gap in the combustion chamber has been noted in previous studies to have an effect on engine performance, particularly in the areas of lean air/fuel ratios (4) (8). It was, therefore, of considerable interest to investigate the effect of this parameter on exhaust emissions. Three sets of spark plugs with the gaps located as shown in Fig. 89.13 were tested at a simulated 30 mile/h road load and 14·7 air/fuel ratio. The effect of gap location on HC emissions is illustrated in Fig. 89.14. It will be noted that there is generally an increase in HC as the gap position is projected into the combustion chamber. A similar increase in NO_x emissions was seen. The

fact that projecting the gap has a somewhat similar effect as advancing the ignition timing is only partially responsible for this change.

Other investigators have noted that at air/fuel ratios of approximately 18·6 and leaner, a projected gap will show lower HC emission levels (6). The projected gap will ignite lean mixtures more consistently because the spark is moved out of the boundary layer of gases at the combustion chamber wall to a position where the mixture is more ignitable. There will also be more burning time before any part of the flame front is quenched by the combustion chamber wall when ignition occurs in this location.

Our results with the variable air/fuel ratio carburettor at both 30 and 50 mile/h road load operating conditions also indicated this to be true. HC, as a function of air/fuel ratio, is shown in Fig. 89.15 at 30 and 50 mile/h for the projected and standard gap spark plugs at standard ignition timing. It will be observed that the HC emissions of the standard gap spark plug are less than that of the projected gap design until the air/fuel ratio is leaned into the range of 17:1 at 30 mile/h and 19:1 at 50 mile/h.

The effect of the spark plug gap location on NO_x at the various air/fuel ratios is shown in Fig. 89.16 for the 30 and 50 mile/h operating conditions. Reduced levels of NO_x are also observed with the standard gap spark plug design until the fuel mixtures are leaned out as previously noted.

A significant performance advantage of the projected gap plug design is revealed in the b.s.f.c. curves shown in Fig. 89.17 for the two operating conditions. Reductions in fuel consumption of approximately 5 per cent are realized with the projected gap spark plugs.

As previously noted, these emission readings were obtained under steady-state operating conditions with the exhaust sample collected at the common outlet of the

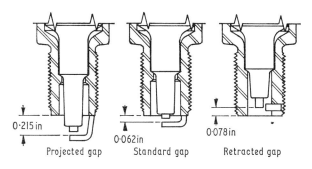

Fig. 89.13. Spark plugs with different gap locations

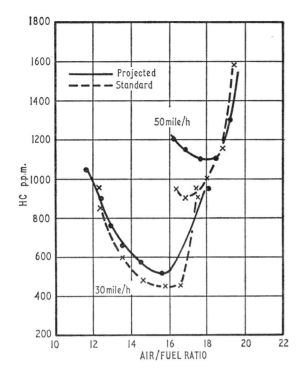

Fig. 89.15. The effect of spark plug gap position on hydrocarbon emissions at 30 and 50 mile/h road loads with various air/fuel ratios

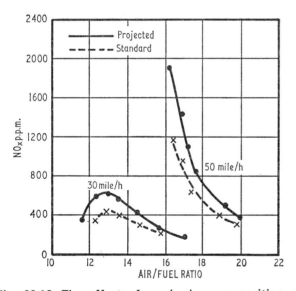

Fig. 89.16. The effect of spark plug gap position on emission of oxides of nitrogen at 30 and 50 mile/h road loads with various air/fuel ratios

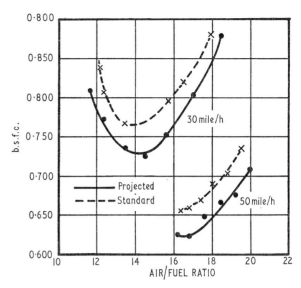

Fig. 89.17. The effect of spark plug gap position on b.s.f.c. at 30 and 50 mile/h road loads with various air/fuel ratios

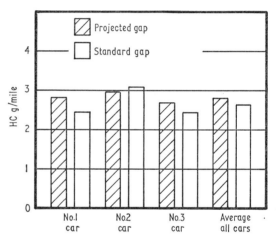

Fig. 89.18. Hydrocarbon emissions from three identical 1971 vehicles under the 1972 Federal Test Cycle

exhaust manifold. Should the exhaust sample be collected at the end of the tailpipe as specified in the Federal Test Cycle, we believe these differences in HC as a result of gap position would diminish because of a continuous chemical reaction between the manifold and end of the tailpipe. The effect of gap position during the acceleration and deceleration portions of the test cycle is unknown and would be important relative to the overall effect on the final emission value.

To further evaluate the effect of gap location on engine exhaust emission in a different engine design, we employed the services of an independent testing laboratory. In this programme we evaluated two gap positions of the proper heat range spark plug in three 1971 vehicles under the 1972 Federal Test Cycle. These cars were equipped with the same V-8 engine of approximately 6 litres and had an average of 12 000 miles of service. Slight differences in HC and NO_x values could be observed in individual plug tests, but an evaluation of the overall results showed no significant difference in emissions as a result of a 0·094-in difference in gap projection. Fig. 89.18 is a bar graph of HC emissions which is typical of these test results. It will be noted that there is a greater difference in individual cars than in plug designs. We believe the effect of gap location on emission characteristics must be established for each engine design and specific operating condition. Also, it should not be overlooked that certain features of the projected gap design provide better engine performance.

10 EFFECT OF SPARK PLUG GAP CONFIGURATION

The effect of spark plug gap configuration on exhaust emissions was also investigated. The three gap configurations shown in Fig. 89.19 were evaluated at 30 mile/h

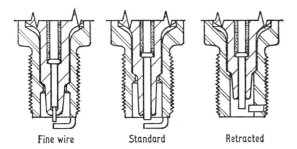

Fine wire   Standard   Retracted

Fig. 89.19. Spark plugs with different gap configurations

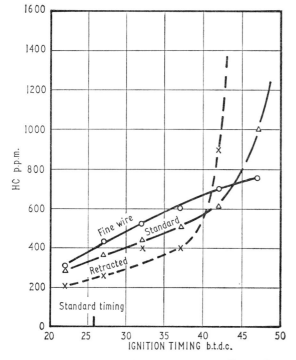

Fig. 89.20. The effect of spark gap configuration on hydrocarbon emissions with the 1000-μs duration ignition system at 30 mile/h road load

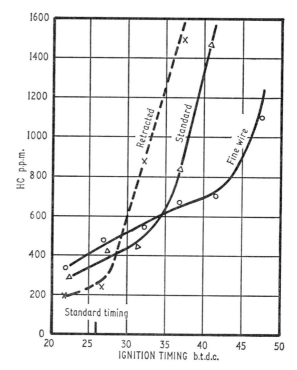

Fig. 89.21. The effect of spark plug gap configuration on hydrocarbon emissions with the 500-μs duration ignition system at 30 mile/h road load

road load, with the three ignition systems discussed previously at a 15·4 air/fuel ratio.

The HC as a function of ignition timing with the 1000-μs ignition system is plotted in Fig. 89.20. Slightly higher HC is noted with the fine wire configuration at standard timing. However, very significant reductions are observed at highly over-advanced timing, indicating the improved ability of this configuration to ignite a fuel charge under conditions of poor ignitability. The relatively low values of HC with the retracted gap had previously been shown in the 'gap location' section, and much of this reduction is believed the result of gap position rather than gap configuration.

Fig. 89.21 shows the same three spark plugs evaluated with the 500-μs ignition system. Higher emissions at standard spark advance are again noted with the fine wire gap configuration. However, the ability of the fine wire gap to ignite the fuel mixture and lower emissions at over-advanced timings is also again demonstrated.

A comparison of Figs 89.20 and 89.21 shows that the reduction of spark duration from 1000 to 500 μs had no effect on the HC emissions at standard timing. However,

the benefit of the longer duration ignition systems in providing more satisfactory combustion at over-advanced timings is evident.

11 EXHAUST GAS RECIRCULATION

Exhaust gas recirculation appears at this time to be a necessity for the engine manufacturers to control oxides of nitrogen. The theory in which EGR dilutes the incoming air–fuel mixture and lowers peak combustion temperatures is well documented (9). We do not believe spark plug design will affect EGR and its ability to control NO_x, but we are concerned about the effect of EGR on spark plug performance. Our experience to date has been with a vacuum calibrated EGR valve located between the exhaust and intake manifolds. We have externally controlled this valve and used a calibrated carburettor for EGR control. The carburettor calibration was such that recirculation was zero up to 30 mile/h road loads and at wide open throttle operating conditions.

In determining the effect of EGR on emissions we used the 1000-μs ignition system and the recommended spark plug gapped at 0·035 in. Our tests with 0, 5 and 10 per cent EGR were conducted at 30, 50 and 70 mile/h road loads and the results were noted to vary with the operating condition and the ignition timing.

Fig. 89.22 shows the relative values of NO_x with 0 per cent EGR and various ignition timings for the three speed conditions. At 50 and 70 mile/h we noted a substantial decrease in NO_x with values of 5 and 10 per cent recirculation. This is shown in Fig. 89.23 for the 70 mile/h operating condition. As expected, HC remained essentially constant. The effect of EGR on spark plug temperature with the manually controlled valve at standard timings is shown in Fig. 89.24. This was examined with only 0 and 10 per cent recirculation at 30, 50 and 60 mile/h. We

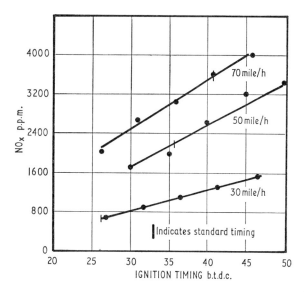

Fig. 89.22. The effect of ignition timing on oxides of nitrogen with no recirculation at 30, 50 and 70 mile/h

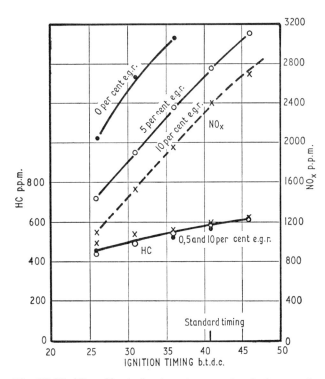

Fig. 89.23. The effect of exhaust gas recirculation on the emissions of hydrocarbons and oxides of nitrogen at 70 mile/h

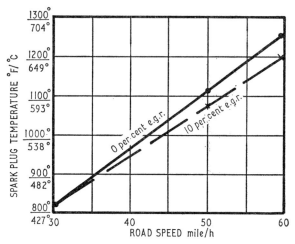

Fig. 89.24. The effect of exhaust gas recirculation on spark plug operating temperature

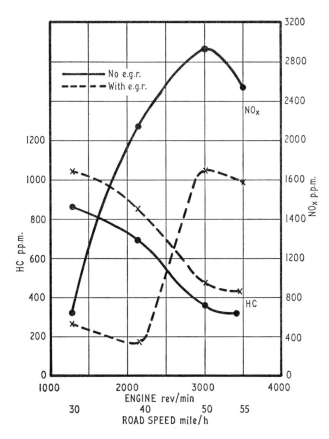

Fig. 89.25. The effect of exhaust gas recirculation on the emissions of hydrocarbons and oxides of nitrogen with a calibrated carburettor at various road loads

observed no change in temperature at 30 mile/h, but we do note a 28°C (50°F) reduction in operating temperature at 50 and 60 mile/h which correlates to reductions in NO_x.

Very similar changes in the emissions of NO_x were noted in testing the engine using the calibrated carburettor. Fig. 89.25 is a plot of emissions of NO_x and HC from 1000 to 4000 rev/min under road load operation. This is shown under normal operating conditions with the EGR valve in operation and also with no EGR by merely disconnecting and plugging the vacuum line operating the EGR valve. Significant reductions in NO_x were observed with EGR although the HC emissions increased. The

richer air/fuel ratio resulting from the use of EGR, as indicated in Fig. 89.26 is believed responsible for the higher values of HC. The decrease in NO_x above 3000 rev/min is also believed to be the result of richer air/fuel ratios in this range of operation. A slight increase in b.s.f.c. with EGR is also indicated in Fig. 89.26.

The effect of EGR with this type of installation would not be expected to influence spark plug operation or radically change the heat range recommendation. However, this is an area that will require attention if EGR is extended over a greater range of operation.

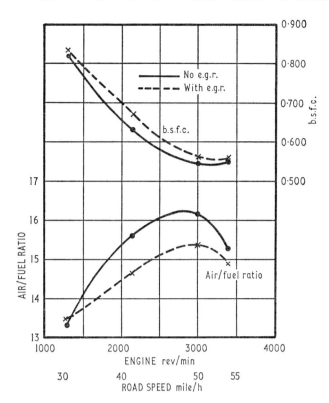

Fig. 89.26. The effect of exhaust gas recirculation on brake specific fuel consumption and air/fuel ratio with a calibrated carburettor at various road loads

12 TRENDS IN SPARK PLUG DESIGN AND DEVELOPMENT

The majority of today's new engines are being designed to use the tapered seat style spark plug illustrated in Fig. 89.1, because of their smaller overall size for a given thread diameter. U.S. manufacturers have generally standardized on the shorter reach design while the U.K. and European manufacturers appear to favour the long reach configuration. Along with the new engines, many present engine designs have been recently converted to use the short reach 14-mm taper seat plug.

A trend is also developing towards the increased suppression of radio frequency interferences (r.f.i.). In addition to the resistor high-tension spark plug cables used by most manufacturers, additional suppression is available through unit resistors in spark plug terminals or the plugs themselves. Two major U.S. vehicle manufacturers presently use both resistor plugs and resistance cable while several U.S. cable manufacturers have agreed not to market the non-resistor leads. It appears that the trend towards increased r.f.i. suppression will continue for all spark-ignited engines.

Fig. 89.27 illustrates a surface gap plug, a fine wire electrode plug and two Bantam style plugs. In two-cycle engines, the trend towards the use of surface gap spark plugs with c.d. ignition systems is well established. This combination was first adopted in the U.S. on outboard engines, but is being rapidly extended to other two-cycle applications such as motor cycles and snowmobiles. The surface gap plug has excellent life with a compatible ignition system, is not subject to the usual deposit formations and runs cool enough to eliminate it as a source of pre-ignition.

Fine wire, precious metal electrode plugs have also become popular in two-cycle engines. These plugs, although premium priced, are advantageous because of increased life and easier starting under conditions of low available voltage and cold fouling conditions present in many two-cycle engines. The Bantam style spark plugs are used in some small engine applications where the spark plug installed height must be kept to a minimum.

Fig. 89.28 shows several firing end configurations used in Wankel engines. The 14-mm N-80B is presently used as original equipment in the Japanese Mazda. The 18-mm taper seat design is the one found most successful in the NSU Ro80, while the 12-mm surface gap design is used

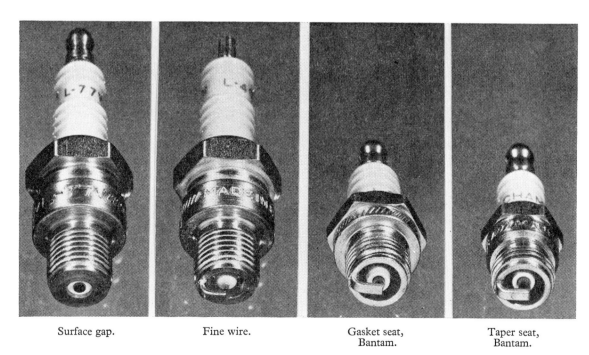

| Surface gap. | Fine wire. | Gasket seat, Bantam. | Taper seat, Bantam. |

Fig. 89.27. Typical two-cycle engine spark plug configurations

72

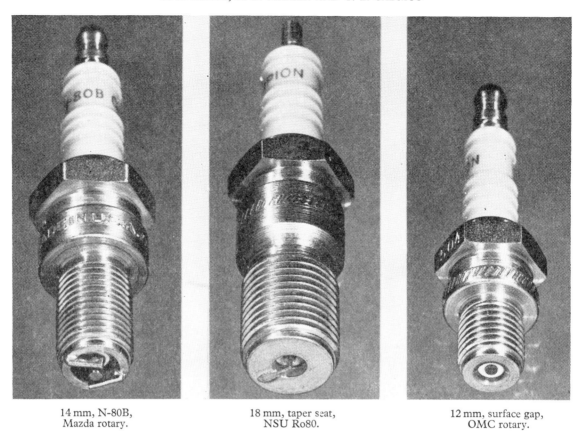

14 mm, N-80B,
Mazda rotary.

18 mm, taper seat,
NSU Ro80.

12 mm, surface gap,
OMC rotary.

Fig. 89.28. Typical rotary engine spark plug configurations

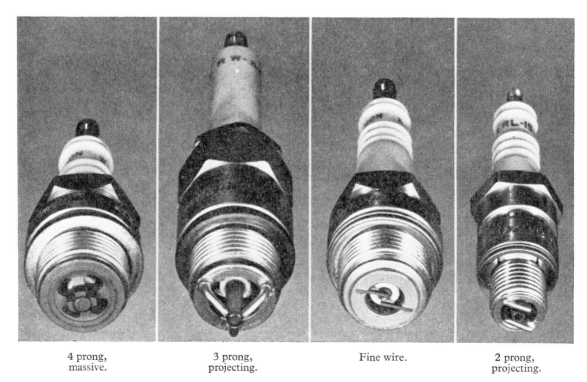

4 prong,
massive.

3 prong,
projecting.

Fine wire.

2 prong,
projecting.

Fig. 89.29. Typical stationary gas engine spark plug configurations

by Outboard Marine Corporation Wankel with a c.d. ignition system. We believe that the surface gap plug with c.d. ignition will prove to be most successful in these engines. The firing end of the spark plug can be located close to the trochoid surface, and thereby minimize blowby between chambers.

Fig. 89.29 shows a series of spark plugs used in stationary gas engines operating on natural or propane gas. Most of these fuels burn relatively clean and a spark plug can be quite cold in heat range. Primary consideration is electrode life and this figure illustrates various arrangements to give long hours of operation. Some engines must operate on gas directly from the well, and in some areas this is contaminated with impurities. These fuels are referred to as 'sour gas'. The three-prong projecting ground electrode configuration has been found helpful in these instances.

13 CONCLUSIONS

Our test results indicate that the effect of spark plug gap spacing, gap location and ignition system spark duration on engine performance and emissions becomes progressively more pronounced as fuel mixtures become leaner. Reduced emissions and fuel consumption can be realized with wide gap spacings and longer spark durations up to a certain minimum level required for consistent ignition. These two parameters must be studied together since minimum gap spacing is partially determined by spark duration and minimum spark duration depends on gap size. These minima will vary with engine design, spark advance, air/fuel ratios and engine speed and must, therefore, be determined for each application. However, our work indicates that typical U.S. gap spacings in the area of 0·035 in and spark durations approximately 1000 μs are sufficiently above the minimum levels required by the large U.S. engines.

The narrower gap settings normally used in the U.K. and Europe appear to be somewhat marginal, particularly at some of the lower engine speeds necessary in the U.S. emission tests. It is possible that wider gap settings which, in turn, may require higher voltage ignition systems will be necessary.

Smaller electrode sizes which provide increased exposure of the mixture to the spark, and less quenching of the initial flame, can also reduce emissions and fuel consumption through more consistent ignition.

The application of projected gap spark plugs in laboratory engine tests indicated a slight increase in the emissions of HC and NO_x. However, vehicle tests under the 1972 Federal Test Cycle failed to show any significant difference in either HC or NO_x between standard and projected gap plug designs. Previous investigations have also indicated that projecting the gap into the combustion chamber provides a greater ability to consistently ignite lean mixtures, and that projected core nose plugs can offer much improved fouling protection owing to better temperature characteristics.

It does not appear at this time that the application of EGR will affect either spark plug or ignition system design parameters. However, we believe that this is an area that will require continued investigation, particularly if significantly high percentages of EGR are considered.

APPENDIX 89.1

REFERENCES

(1) 'Control of air pollution from new motor vehicles and new motor vehicle engines', *Federal Register*, **35** (No. 219).

(2) EDWARDS, W. R. and ROY, G. E. 'Development of a new automotive spark plug', S.A.E. Paper No. 670148, 1967 (January).

(3) OBERT, E. F. *Internal combustion engines* 1968.

(4) TEASEL, R. C., MILLER, R. D. and ROBSON, J. V. B. 'Ignition systems and spark plug requirements', *Proc. Instn mech. Engrs* 1967–68 (Pt 2A), 15.

(5) 'Pre-ignition rating of spark plugs for ground vehicles', S.A.E. Recommended Practice J549, *S.A.E. Handbook*.

(6) BURGETT, R. R., LEPTICH, J. M. and SANGWAN, V. S. 'Measuring the effect of spark plug and ignition system design on engine performance', S.A.E. Paper No. 720007, 1972 (January).

(7) GREEN, S. J. 'Ignition misfire and tracking simulator', U.S. Patent No. 3 357 114, 1967 (December).

(8) CRAVER, R. J., PODIAK, R. S. and MILLER, R. D. 'Spark plug design factors and their effect on engine performance', S.A.E. Paper No. 700081, 1970 (January).

(9) QUADER, A. A. 'Why intake charge dilution decreases nitric oxide emission from spark ignition engines', S.A.E. Paper No. 710009, 1971 (January).

C90/72 DISPLAY SYSTEMS

T. J. L. DOBEDOE*

The information needed by the driver of a car is limited, both in quantity and quality. The requirements have been adequately met at low cost by electromechanical instruments and filament-bulb warning lights. With the development of new electro-optical display forms, no-moving-part systems may be devised which have certain advantages over traditional instruments. Two groups of electro-optical displays, active and passive, are discussed, and the implications of each system upon the electronic drive and logic circuits are considered. Electronic systems, which interface between transducer and display, are proposed and major problem areas identified.

1 INTRODUCTION

THE INFORMATION NEEDED by the driver is limited, both in quantity and quality. A simple visual indication of speed and a mileage recorder are required by law, as are certain warning and indicator lights. Indications of fuel, oil, water temperature and electrical system conditions complete the basic display requirements.

These requirements have been adequately met at a low cost by electromechanical instruments and filament bulbs. The use of electronic instruments, other than in special cases, has until recently been prohibitively expensive and, with electromechanical displays, will probably remain so for some years.

2 NEW DISPLAY POSSIBILITIES

Electro-optical display systems of various types are in development in many areas. These displays utilize a variety of physical phenomena to obtain a no-moving-part system. The display packages that result are in the form of thin panels with multi-electrode connections to the driving electronics. Such display systems offer the following advantages over traditional mechanical systems.

2.1 Packaging

The packaging problem in the area of the instrument panel is becoming more difficult. The increasing slope of the windscreen has meant placing the instrument panel further away from the driver, reducing the space behind the instruments for wiring, ducting, etc. The mechanical-drive speedometer cable presents another packaging and possible customer irritation problem (see Fig. 90.1).

2.2 Safety

The need for increased steering column collapse (9 in is suggested to achieve acceptable deceleration levels) indicates that traditional instruments may offer considerable problems in terms of space occupation and inertia. The small size of electro-optical instruments could enable them to be located more suitably to meet safety requirements.

The MS. of this paper was received at the Institution on 27th March 1972 and accepted for publication on 21st April 1972. 33
★ Ford Motor Co. Ltd, Research and Engineering Centre, Laindon, Basildon, Essex.

2.3 Display format

Present display formats are limited by the mechanical designs of the system to moving pointer or ribbon. The tendency towards increasing the use of digital information presents severe problems to the electromechanical design. The need to associate the odometer with the speedometer also imposes a design restriction. The new display systems offer a range of possibilities for novel methods of information presentation, both in type and location. With one possible exception, however, the displays must be built up in discrete areas.

2.4 Interfacing

The electro-optical systems interface well with electronic systems. Although at this time voltages are high in certain instances, the power drain is usually small. Thus, increasingly complex instrument and control systems can be used with compatible displays.

3 ACTIVE DISPLAY SYSTEMS

Most of the electro-optical display systems available are active systems, i.e. the illumination is generated within the display. A traditional example is the tungsten-filament lamp. Such display systems need a very high daylight brightness capability, and some form of brightness reduction at night. It needs no secondary illumination, with resultant cost advantages.

Experimental work at Ford has indicated that for such active displays a daylight surface brightness of up to 400 cd/m^2 may be needed for daytime driving. This has been obtained with gas-discharge systems, and has been found adequate for all daytime driving, despite a poor contrast ratio. It is possible that with some form of contrast enhancement, a figure of 200 cd/m^2 would be adequate.

Opinions on the night time requirements for an active system vary. Ford experience suggests that 100 cd/m^2 would not be obtrusive, but other authorities indicate figures of $5-10 \text{ cd/m}^2$. It seems probable that a wide range of control would be needed.

The active display systems that have been considered are: (1) gas-discharge systems, (2) electroluminescent displays and (3) light emitting diodes.

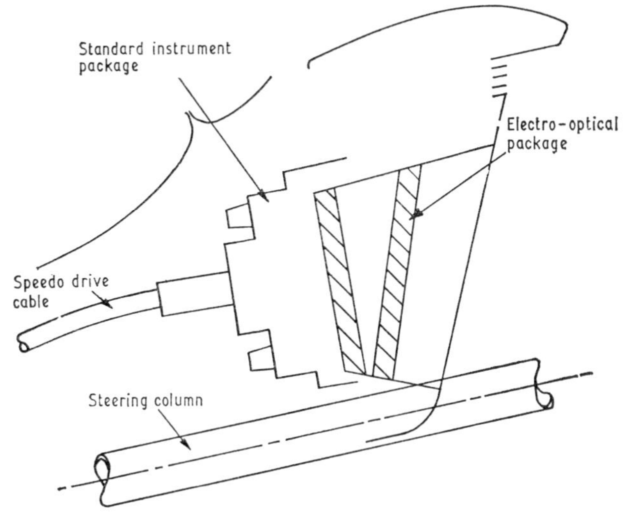

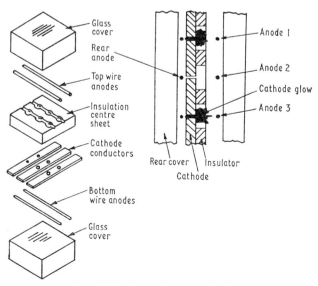

Fig. 90.1. Packaging—electro-optical versus standard instruments

3.1 Gas-discharge systems

Flat-panel gas-discharge tubes are available from a number of manufacturers. The construction of cells in such a panel is shown in Fig. 90.2. In most of these the glow discharge takes place between the wire anode and the rear cathode, and is viewed end on.

By defining the display as areas of gas-discharge panels, various formats are possible. These range from radial bars for a speed indication to the use of a matrix tube for multiple-function display (courtesy Mullard Ltd). In such a matrix system the number of connections required is reduced by cross-addressing and by multiplexing. This system also takes substantial power (80 W) at high voltage (270 V), and presents certain safety problems.

This type of display device is capable of giving more than enough light output, e.g. 3500 cd/m², and has a lifetime of 10 000 h plus. The colour range is limited at this time to neon pink.

A matrix-tube speedometer system is shown in Fig. 90.3. Here the vertical bars were scanned at a frequency of 3 kHz, and the on-time for each bar was 500 μs. With this system, the brightness of 400 cd/m² referred to above was

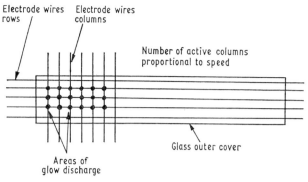

Fig. 90.3. Matrix-tube speedometer

obtained. In this display, brightness was obtained by changing mark space ratio.

3.2 Electroluminescence

These displays, based upon doped zinc sulphide materials, generate light when an electric current passes through them. Typical display construction is shown in Fig. 90.4. A typical speedometer layout for this type of system is shown in Fig. 90.5. Before such systems are possible for motor vehicle application, a substantial life, say 1000 h at 400 cd/m², needs to be established.

3.3 Light-emitting diodes

These materials are usually based on gallium arsenide or arsenide–phosphide, and are simple semiconductor diodes that emit radiation when current passes in the forward direction. As the radiation emission is a function of a gap between energy levels within the semiconductor,

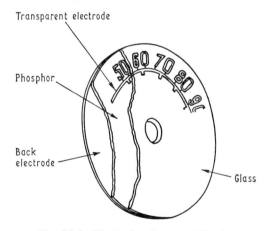

Fig. 90.4. Electroluminescent display

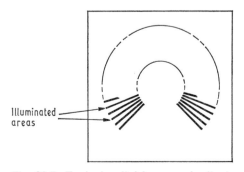

Fig. 90.5. Typical radial-bar speedo display

Fig. 90.2. Gas-discharge device

the resulting light is a narrow wavelength band. This may, however, be varied by changing the composition of the elements, and shifting the energy gap, or by anti-Stokes phosphors.

Light-emitting diodes (L.E.D.) are commercially obtainable in a range of colours from infrared to green. Unfortunately, no blue is available, and with existing materials the physics of the situation preclude its development.

Arrays of L.E.D. can be built up to give various types of alphanumeric representations (see Fig. 90.6). At the moment such arrays are expensive, particularly for large areas; unless prices fall substantially, it is only possible to see limited application. One such application would be for an odometer display where the small size makes this type of device applicable.

The performance of L.E.D. exceeds our requirements for life and for brightness. Furthermore, they interface directly with microcircuit logic systems at low voltages and powers, typically $4\frac{1}{2}$ V and 500 mW for a 7×5 alphanumeric array.

4 PASSIVE DISPLAY SYSTEMS

In these, no light is generated within the system, incident light is either reflected by, or transmitted through, the display to render the appropriate display pattern visible. The traditional moving-pointer speedometer may be considered as such a display. Such displays increase in brightness as the incident light increases, and can therefore be good in daylight. They are also easy to control to low night-light levels by means of secondary illumination, although this implies increased cost to supply wiring and bulbs.

4.1 Liquid crystals

The most interesting of the passive display systems are those using liquid crystals. A liquid crystal is not a material but a state of matter. Many materials exhibit liquid crystal properties between a crystalline solid phase and a liquid phase bounded by temperature conditions.

In the solid phase, the molecules are aligned rigidly in a crystal, and would show typical X-ray crystallographic structures. In the liquid phase, there is completely random orientation. In the liquid crystal phase, however, the molecules align themselves such that, although the phase possesses liquid properties, the material can have optical properties dependent upon the molecular orientation.

There are three types of liquid crystal state:

Smectic, in which the molecules are arranged parallel in layers.

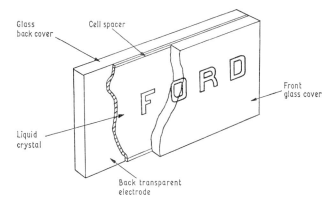

Fig. 90.7. Liquid-crystal panel construction

Nematic, in which the molecules are arranged parallel, but not in layers.

Cholesteric, in which the molecules are arranged in thin layers of common alignment.

The action of heat and voltage upon the material causes changes in the orientation of the molecules, which affect the optical properties of the system. As it is estimated that 1 in 300 of organic materials exhibits these properties to a greater or lesser extent, the development of suitable systems has a wide range of starting points and possibilities.

The system of most interest to the instrument designer is that involving nematic systems, in which the application of an electric field across a thin layer of crystal causes the molecules to rotate on their polar axes, with a resultant change of optical density. The construction of a typical panel is very similar to that for an electroluminescent panel, with the phosphor replaced by liquid-crystal material (see Fig. 90.7).

There is one important difference in the type of conductive transparent coat used in that with electroluminescence a low-resistance coating is required, whereas with liquid crystals, an electric field phenomenon, this is no longer necessary, as only low-leakage currents are carried.

Liquid-crystal systems can operate on both alternating current and direct current; typical curves obtained are shown in Fig. 90.8. Unfortunately, liquid crystals have their disadvantages. The most important of these is temperature range. Early crystals operated over a limited

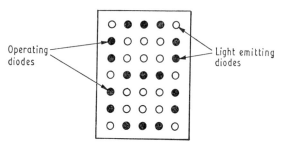

Fig. 90.6. Typical L.E.D. 35-dot, alphanumeric display

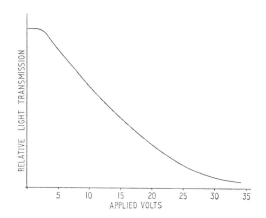

Fig. 90.8. Liquid-crystal characteristic

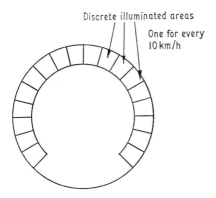

Fig. 90.9. Discrete area display

range of, say, 5–10°C. This has been extended to 50°C plus, and modern crystals will survive freezing and reliquefying. The situation with respect to temperature above the operating limit is less clear. The other problems needing resolution are (a) the increasing contrast ratios and (b) obtaining a range of colours.

Life cannot be established for our application until the crystal system with an appropriate temperature range is obtained. Liquid-crystal materials interface well with semiconductor logic as the extremely low power consumption (in the order of $\mu W/cm^2$) outweighs the slightly higher voltages (about 30 V) used. Although Ford has only considered the use of such systems in a discrete area display, such as in Fig. 90.9, work has been reported on analogue presentations with these systems.

5 DISPLAY FORMAT

Whichever systems are ultimately used, it seems likely that the discrete area display will be used in some form. The obvious suggestion is for the use of digital information for speed and engine revolutions, etc., rather than analogue. It is difficult to assess the driver acceptability of such radically differing display forms, and much human factor work needs to be done to produce an acceptable ergonomically based display design. In using discrete area displays with intercepts of, say, $2\frac{1}{2}$ km/h, it is not very probable that the driver in glancing down to his instruments will be aware of the discrete nature of the display, as he is unlikely to glance down at the instant of change.

6 ELECTRONIC SYSTEM

All the display systems discussed require electronic signal processing and driving. An ideal electronic system will have low power requirement, high packaging density, good noise immunity and will work off a 4–6 V single rail supply. The low power consumption is specially important for instruments that are permanently connected to power supplies, e.g. clocks. The ability to operate from low voltage would eliminate the need for d.c./d.c. converters, and the stabilization of logic supply would be relatively simple, even under extreme fluctuation of battery voltage.

Such an ideal solution is only applicable directly to L.E.D. displays; other displays require a compromise on one or more requirements. Thus, electroluminescence and gas discharge require high voltages, liquid crystals are lower voltage, but still too high, etc. These requirements are outlined in Table 90.1.

One can, however, divide the system in two halves: inputs and logic, address system and display (see Fig. 90.10). The input and logic system can then be considered as a universal element providing a coded output to the addressing system for the display.

Transducers for the system are unlikely to differ greatly from those in use now, with the exception of speedometer and tachometer. These will require some form of electromagnetic pick-up generating a train of pulses into the logic system.

This means that the logic will need to process both analogue and digital information. This problem can be eased if an analogue to digital converter is used on the analogue input so that all signal processing is in the digital mode. Obviously, electronic complexity can be reduced by

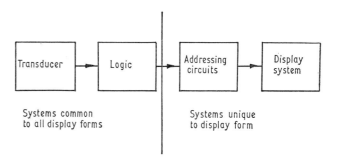

Fig. 90.10. Logic systems

Table 90.1. Summary of electro-optical properties

Display media	Potential application	Maximum brightness	Drive electronics	Temperature range	Life, hours
Gas discharge	All display functions	3500 cd/m²	Special high-voltage semi-conductor package. Scanning techniques necessary	−40°C to 150°C	10 000
Electroluminescent phosphors	All display functions	600 cd/m²	Special semiconductor package	−40°C to 75°C	Up to 2000
L.E.D.	Warning lights and numerics	3000 cd/m²	Current i/c compatible	−50°C to 100°C	10 000
Liquid crystals	All display functions	Any, depends on light source	Current i/c compatible	Limited, −15°C to 60°C	Not yet certain

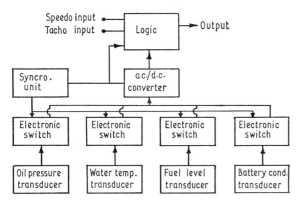

Fig. 90.11. Input multiplexing

multiplexing the input. Such a system is shown schematically in Fig. 90.11.

There are two major problems associated with the logic of the system. First, the development of a low-cost time base accurate enough for use as a clock. The use of a crystal oscillator involves not only the cost of the crystal but also an extensive dividing chain of high cost and power consumption. The second problem is the provision of a non-volatile store for the odometer. The use of a mechanical store is inelegant, expensive and creates packaging problems. Although several possibilities have been suggested, e.g. magnetic bubbles, there is as yet no obvious solution in production. A solution of this problem could be the key to the whole system. Such a logic system has greater implications than instruments alone, as it can form the basis of a more complex vehicle electronic system utilizing shared transducers, time bases, etc.

The addressing system problems are peculiar to the chosen display, but the least difficult systems are L.E.D. and liquid crystals. The major problem of the addressing system is not electronic but the number of electrical connections that need to be made to the display. In some systems, where the brightness available is high enough, these may be reduced by scanning and multiplexing techniques.

7 CONCLUSIONS

Electro-optical displays are technically feasible in the automobile, although present costs are high. A variety of such displays is possible, and there is no clear indication of a preferred system. The logic and addressing systems are complex but lend themselves to integration techniques and have potential for extension to other areas of the vehicle.

C106/72 DEVELOPMENTS IN HIGH-VOLTAGE GENERATION AND IGNITION CONTROL

N. RITTMANNSBERGER*

The paper discusses the criteria required for the development of modern ignition systems. Conventional and transistorized methods of ignition are described and contactless trigger systems, with four types of pick-up, detailed. Control of the ignition timing is considered. A summary is given of achievements possible with modern equipment, and future prospects are considered.

1 INTRODUCTION

THE BASIC REQUIREMENT of an ignition system for spark-ignited combustion engines is the dependable ignition of the air–fuel mixture in the combustion chamber at the optimum point of time and under all operating conditions. In former times the ignition timing was determined by torque, specific fuel consumption and knock limit. Nowadays there is a further criterion: the control of exhaust emissions by selection of a suitable ignition timing point. In addition, the requirements of the spark characteristics, e.g. energy, spark duration, voltage rise time, have increased. Finally, the development of modern ignition systems is influenced by demands of high accuracy and by low maintenance requirements. The questions of high-voltage generation, breakerless triggering and ignition timing control are dealt with against this background.

2 GENERATION OF HIGH VOLTAGE

The energy taken from the high-voltage sources serves to generate a spark between the electrodes of the spark plug. This spark has to be of sufficient strength and duration to ensure ignition of the mixture. With an ideal mixture, which is characterized by a homogeneous distribution of the fuel in the air and by an air/fuel ratio most suited for ignition, energy of <1 mW s would suffice to ascertain the initiation of the combustion process, and a spark duration of a few microseconds at the most would be needed.

In reality, however, circumstances are less ideal. The mixture is heterogeneous, with the consequence that the air/fuel ratio in the vicinity of the spark plug is not constant but subject to variations with time. In order to initiate combustion under these conditions either the spark energy has to be large enough for the ignition to take place, even in an unfavourable yet flammable mixture ratio, or the spark duration has to be of sufficient time to permit a flammable mixture ratio to exist in the vicinity of the spark plug as a result of mixture motion. Mixture ratios as they occur in reality are certain to be ignited

if the spark energy exceeds 50 mW s or if the spark duration is longer than 0·5 ms.

Apart from these requirements, which are determined by the mixture quality, there are others determined by the state of the spark plugs. In Europe, modern engines, with their high specific output, require spark plugs that have a high temperature range. As a consequence they tend to foul during short-distance operation, and side-tracking of the spark may occur. In addition, there are other causes of side-tracking, e.g. lead deposits on the insulator. The influence of side-tracking on spark generation decreases with a lower source impedance of the high-voltage supply, and therefore with a higher available energy. Further, side-tracking can occur due to water condensation before start-up. Its effects can be avoided if the spark energy is supplied rapidly enough for the water film to vaporize. In this case the energy rise has to be sufficiently fast.

Assuming that the high-voltage source can be sufficiently characterized by the voltage–time function for a normal capacitive load (about 50 pF) and by the internal resistance, the following requirements of a high-voltage source can be deduced from the above (I)†.

(1) High energy storage capacity.
(2) High ignition voltage.
(3) Long duration of the voltage pulse.
(4) Low source impedance or steep voltage rise.

There are several concepts that fully or at least partly satisfy the above requirements.

2.1 Conventional coil ignition

In the distributor a current flows across the breaker points through the ignition coil (Fig. 106.1). On opening of the breaker points it is interrupted, so that a voltage is induced in the coil according to the current change.

Advantages
The system is simple and reliable.

Disadvantages
The voltage decreases with higher spark rates because,

† References are given in Appendix 106.1.

The MS. of this paper was received at the Institution on 26th January 1972 and accepted for publication on 16th June 1972. 33
* Robert Bosch GmBH, Abt. KI/EJA, 7141 Schwieberdingen, Robert Bosch Str., Germany, 0711/8111.

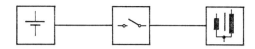

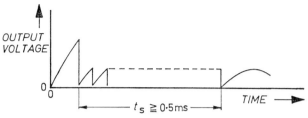

Fig. 106.1. Coil ignition system

limited by the current load of the contacts, the coil current cannot reach its final value in the short intervals between two ignitions. For the same reason spark duration is limited. Because of the high source impedance (about 500 kΩ) the system is sensitive to side-tracking. A further disadvantage is that due to the high current load the breaker points are subject to electrical wear in addition to mechanical wear. This results in short maintenance intervals.

2.2 Transistorized coil ignition

As Fig. 106.2 shows, the function of the breaker points is replaced by a transistor. The breaker contacts serve to trigger the transistor.

Advantages

More energy can be stored in the coil because the coil current is not limited by the breaker contacts. For this reason the system yields a high ignition voltage and a long spark duration. Because the current across the breaker points is significantly reduced, and because they only carry a resistive load, the electrical contact wear is negligible and contact life is improved. With such a system it is possible to replace the points by a breakerless trigger. In this manner, wear can be avoided and the ignition timing does not change during operation. This results in higher accuracy and less need for maintenance.

Disadvantages

Similarly to the conventional coil ignition, this system is susceptible to side-tracking because of the high source impedance.

2.3 High-voltage capacitive discharge ignition

With this system (Fig. 106.3) a capacitor is used as a means of energy storage. It is charged to about 500 V by means of a first transformer and at the moment of ignition discharged through a thyristor via a second transformer and the spark plug.

Advantages

The system features a high output voltage even at high spark rates. Because of the low internal resistance (about 50 kΩ) the voltage rise is very fast, which results in a high safety margin in relation to side-tracking. Similarly to the transistorized coil ignition, the breaker points serve as a trigger only. Therefore they may be replaced by a contactless pick-up.

Disadvantages

Because of the fast capacitive discharge the spark is strong but short (about 0·1 ms). This can lead to ignition difficulties at operating conditions where the air/fuel ratio is high.

2.4 Combined transistorized coil–capacitive discharge system

Comparing the advantages and disadvantages of the systems described in Sections 2.1 to 2.3 it is apparent that all the disadvantages mentioned above can be avoided with an ignition system that combines the characteristics of the transistorized coil ignition (long spark duration) with those of the high-voltage capacitive discharge ignition (low sensitivity to side-tracking).

An example of such a system is shown in Fig. 106.4. Both systems are connected on the primary side of the coil. In this manner, the voltage rise time and the spark duration are somewhat shorter than those with separate systems; however, the essential advantages of the individual systems are maintained.

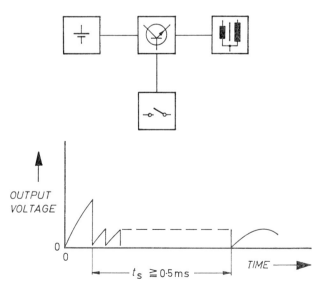

Fig. 106.2. Transistorized coil ignition system

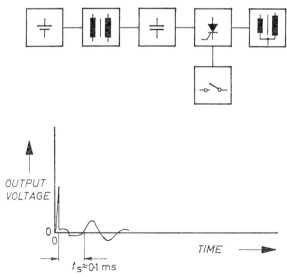

Fig. 106.3. Capacitor discharge ignition system

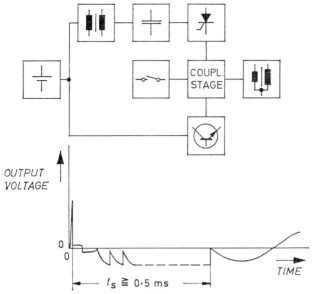

Fig. 106.4. Combination of transistorized coil and capacitor discharge ignition system

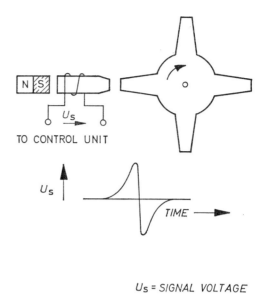

U_S = SIGNAL VOLTAGE

Fig. 106.5. Magnetic pick-up

Advantages

A fast voltage rise is combined with a long spark duration. As a consequence of this the insensitivity to side-tracking and the probability of ignition are high. Again, the high-voltage generator can be triggered by using contacts with a low electrical load or by a contactless trigger system.

Disadvantage

The only disadvantage is the comparatively high complexity.

In the Sections 2.1 to 2.4, examples were given that showed how the requirements for the high-voltage generator can be partially or completely satisfied. The systems are only shown as block diagrams because a complete description of all possible variations would exceed the scope of this article (1)–(3). It therefore seems important that the control of the high-voltage sources be discussed. It has already been mentioned that with semiconductor ignition systems the breaker points are replaced by contactless trigger systems. The resulting advantages and design possibilities are dealt with in Section 3.

3 CONTACTLESS TRIGGER SYSTEMS

Conventional breaker points with tungsten contacts require maintenance. Wear effects on the contacts and on the rubbing block result in a change of the ignition timing point and in a limited life. These disadvantages can be avoided with a contactless system. In Sections 3.1 to 3.4, four possible designs are described, all of which can be put inside the distributor.

3.1 Magnetic pick-up

The principle of a magnetic trigger is shown in Fig. 106.5. The magnetic flux is generated by a permanent magnet and conducted through a coil. The flux density in the coil is modulated by a star-shaped rotor, which is a part of the magnetic circuit and mounted on the distributor shaft. Because of the flux changes arising from this, a voltage is induced in the coil. This voltage serves

as the trigger signal for the high-voltage generator. In order to achieve the highest possible accuracy the voltage–time function must have a steep zero-crossing. This requires a large flux change at the instant where the poles of rotor and stator are precisely opposite each other. This is also important for another reason: as the voltage occurring on the terminals of the coil is dependent on the flux change with time, the voltage value is proportional to the rotational speed of the rotor. Therefore the voltage is at its minimum at low rotational speed during cranking. In order to ascertain reliable operation under even these conditions, the flux change of the coil when the poles pass each other has to be as large as possible. Since there is one spark per cylinder, the number of poles of rotor and stator has to be equal to the number of engine cylinders.

The advantages of this trigger system are mainly its simplicity and sturdiness, as well as the fact that with a rotationally symmetrical construction, wobbling motions of the distributor shaft, and therefore of the rotor, in a wide range of operating conditions do not affect the voltage signal at the coil, because all air gaps at the poles are parallel to the magnetic circuit, and thus are averaged. A further advantage is that a trigger output signal will occur only if the engine is turning. By this method, no current flows through the coil when the engine is stopped.

A certain disadvantage is the speed dependency of the output signal, which sets the lower limit of the range of rotational speed. However, it is possible to overcome this problem by means of a suitable design of the trigger and the electronic circuitry.

3.2 Field plate pick-up

As can be seen from the principle shown in Fig. 106.6, the operation of this system is such that the density of a magnetic flux generated by a permanent magnet is modulated by a star-shaped rotor mounted on the distributor shaft. However, instead of the coil the magnetic circuit incorporates a semiconductor plate the resistance of which varies with the value of the magnetic induction. Therefore a change of the rotor position results in a change of the induction of the plate, and thus its resistance. If a

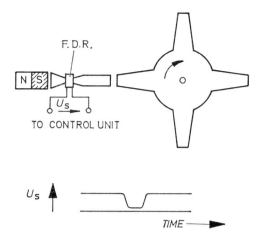

U_S = SIGNAL VOLTAGE

Fig. 106.6. Field-dependent resistor pick-up

constant current is supplied to the plate (shown in Fig. 106.6), a voltage is generated at the terminals. From the terminal voltage a trigger signal for the high-voltage generator can be developed by means of a suitable electronic circuit.

The advantage of this system is that the trigger voltage is dependent only on the position of the rotor and not on its rotational velocity. Thus a voltage is available that is constant through the entire range of the rotational speed. Since the output voltage depends on the angular position of the rotor, it is possible to use this feature to control the coil current through a suitably shaped rotor.

A disadvantage is that the resistance of the field plates is markedly dependent on temperature. This temperature dependency can be compensated by using two field plates in the form of a bridge circuit. There is, in addition, a design problem. Since rotational symmetry is difficult to achieve, wobbling of the distributor shaft influences the shape of the trigger signal.

3.3 Carrier frequency pick-up

There are several methods by which to incorporate triggers that utilize the carrier frequency principle. An example of such a system is shown in Fig. 106.7. A transmitter coil supplied by a HF generator is facing a receiver coil. Between both of them a cylinder is moving, which is shaped to shield, as much as possible, the receiver coil. Hardly any voltage will appear at its output. The circumference of the cylinder has slots, their number corresponding to that of the engine cylinders. If one of the slots is positioned precisely between the two coils, the transmitter coil will induce an alternating voltage in the receiver coil, the amplitude of which is dependent on the angular position of the cylinder but not on its rotational speed. If the cylinder is revolving, the voltage on the terminals of the receiver coil has the characteristics shown in Fig. 106.7. From this, a trigger signal for the high-voltage generator can be developed by demodulation.

The carrier frequency trigger has the same advantage as the field plate trigger (see Section 3.2). A disadvantage is that a HF generator is required, the frequency of which has to be above 0·5 MHz for reasons of accuracy. In order to eliminate noise pick-up in other electronic devices, e.g. the radio, the system has to be well shielded.

3.4 Light sensor pick-up

The light sensor pick-up operates in a manner similar to that of the carrier frequency trigger (Fig. 106.8). As in the latter case, a cylinder provided with slots rotates between a transmitter and a receiver. However, the transmitter is now a light source, e.g. a light-emitting diode, and the receiver comprises a light-sensitive element, e.g. a photo transistor.

The optical trigger has the same advantage as the field plate trigger and the carrier frequency trigger. In addition, favourable dimensional conditions exist due to the small size of the components. However, all these remarkable advantages are offset by a severe disadvantage, i.e. sensitivity to dirt. Although such systems have been investigated in various laboratories, the problem of dirt, and thus failure, has not been solved completely. Comparing the various advantages and disadvantages of all the trigger systems described, one arrives at the conclusion that at the moment the magnetic trigger is especially

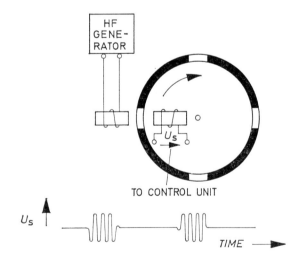

U_S = SIGNAL VOLTAGE

Fig. 106.7. Carrier frequency pick-up

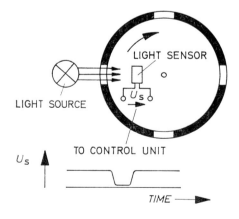

U_S = SIGNAL VOLTAGE

Fig. 106.8. Light sensor pick-up

attractive because of its simplicity. Its dependence on speed is only a minor problem. This statement is confirmed by the experience gained over many years with the ignition systems of racing cars. For the more distant future, the field plate trigger and the optical trigger represent interesting solutions. However, some technical problems remain to be solved before full-scale mass production can begin.

This section, as well as the previous ones, is intended to show ways of improving by electronic means the generation of high voltages and the triggering of the ignition spark with respect to life and functional performance. It is of further interest to consider how the ignition timing can be controlled.

4 CONTROL OF THE IGNITION TIMING

The selection of the ignition timing depends on a multitude of criteria. Sometimes it is impossible to optimize them simultaneously, and compromises between contradicting requirements have to be found over wide ranges of operation. At present, the detoxication of the exhaust gases plays a dominating role.

Because of the U.S.A. emission laws, the ignition timing at full load is determined by the maximum torque and the knock limit. At part load, and especially at idle, the ignition has to be retarded beyond the best specific fuel consumption point because of NO_x and HC emissions. If the 1976 emission laws are to be met, the ignition timing may also have to be controlled by the temperature of the exhaust reactors, to give only one example.

Whether or not, and in what manner, further parameters could influence the ignition timing in the future depends on the different concepts of emission control. Without going into details it is certain that the optimum ignition timing of future ignition systems will be determined by a multitude of criteria and engine parameters. It remains to be seen to what extent simple systems can be used to replace such basically complicated systems with sufficient accuracy. Without doubt, costs will play a decisive role.

Assuming that the known methods of controlling ignition timing by means of engine speed and manifold vacuum are inadequate, suitable new systems will have to be found. From the large number of possible solutions, two are described below: an electropneumatic system and an electronic control system.

An electropneumatic solution is shown in Fig. 106.9. In this figure the ignition timing point is represented in the usual manner through the opening of a mechanical breaker point. Obviously, it can be replaced by one of the trigger systems described in Section 3. At first a mechanical centrifugal advance control is used in the normal manner. Superimposed on this is a pneumatic control, which works additionally via an electromagnetic control valve and a vacuum-operated diaphragm. A vacuum reservoir provides sufficient servo power at all operating conditions. The control valve is actuated in a manner which ensures that the vacuum-operated diaphragm, and thus the plate carrying the breaker points, is positioned as required. In order to eliminate hysteresis, and thus increase accuracy, a position pick-up is mounted on the actuator. In this way the actual position is fed back and compared with the desired value, according to the

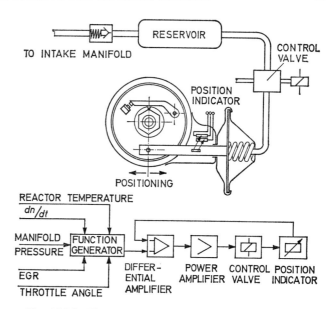

Fig. 106.9. Electropneumatic ignition timing control

requirements of a particular control system. The desired value is set up in a function generator in accordance with input variables, e.g. manifold pressure, throttle angle, exhaust gas recirculation, reactor temperature and, eventually, acceleration. With such a system all functions can be generated in principle, and even the mechanical centrifugal advance may be omitted by controlling the valve.

The disadvantage of such a system is the comparatively high cost of the electronic equipment that is required in addition to the mechanical equipment. Therefore it is obvious that all-electronic solutions must be considered. Here, so many design possibilities exist that it is prudent first to evaluate some basic considerations before describing an example of an electronic control system.

Both in the pick-ups and in the control unit it is possible to process the information using analogue, digital or hybrid technology. Fig. 106.10 shows a classification of

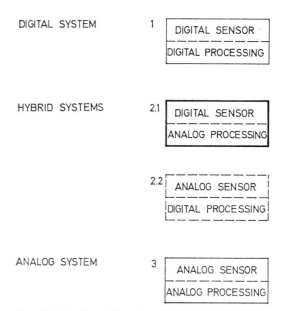

Fig. 106.10. Classification of electronic ignition timing systems

control systems according to these criteria. The classification is carried out according to the type of pick-up and the processing of information relative to crank angle and engine speed.

System 1 is digital; it presents the best solution with regard to accuracy and insensitivity to malfunction. The system is comparatively elaborate. This is especially true for the ROM (read-only-memory) which is required with such a system. It would be of great interest should ROMs of sufficient capacity, utilizing L.S.I. (large-scale integration) technology, ever become available at low prices.

At present, system 2.1 appears to be especially promising because it represents an optimum compromise with regard to accuracy and complexity. An example of such a system is given below. System 2.2, by its principle, will only be of interest should it ever become possible to develop pick-ups of sufficient accuracy to justify the precise yet expensive digital processing of the signal. With system 3, difficulties regarding the accuracy of the analogue-type pick-up exist.

The example shown in Fig. 106.11 belongs to the group represented by system 2.1. A wheel (at top in Fig. 106.11), rotating at camshaft speed, carries markings on its circumference. On passing an inductive pick-up each marking generates a pulse, which is sent to a control unit. In addition, a start-up marking is provided for each cylinder.

The parameters for engine speed, load, temperature, etc., are fed to the function generator (at bottom in Fig. 106.11). There, a pulse is formed the duration of which determines the ignition timing point. The leading edge of the pulse is defined by the ignition pulse. Gate 1 is open for the duration of the pulse of the function generator. During this time, constant frequency pulses formed in the frequency generator can travel via gate 1 to the counter, where their number is stored.

By means of the start-up pulse, gate 2 is opened so

that the pulses triggered by the markings can reach input 2 of the counter. These pulses reverse the count, starting from the previously stored value. If the count reaches zero, a pulse appears at the counter output; this triggers the high-voltage generator and the spark occurs. At the same time the ignition pulse serves to close gate 2 and to trigger again the function generator. This restarts the whole sequence, which consists of the information originating from the function generator to be read into the counter, from whence it is processed further in the above-mentioned manner at the occurrence of the next-following start-up pulse. The transformation of the information encoded in the pulse duration of the function generator into an angular function is thus effected by the forward count at constant frequency and the backward count with a frequency corresponding to the angular velocity of the camshaft. This means that the most difficult component, the function generator, only has to process a time duration, not an angle. It is clear that after a slight modification of the system a voltage can be used instead of the time duration.

Such systems, and others, can be invented in almost unlimited numbers. Which one will be put into practice depends finally on the expense necessary to reach a minimum goal.

5 SUMMARY AND PROSPECTS

It has been shown that it is possible to (1) design high-voltage generators that can satisfy every requirement, (2) utilize trigger systems that do not have the disadvantages of the common breaker points, and (3) control the ignition timing in a manner that allows the best possible technical compromise to be achieved. Questions of reliability and expense still remain to be answered. The overall reliability depends on the number of components and their individual reliability.

Therefore systems made up of few components each having high reliability will show the highest overall reliability. The number of electronic components can be significantly reduced by a high degree of integration, and the reliability of the integrated components themselves can be brought to a reasonable level if well-founded 'know-how' of component technology is allied with experience in automotive technology, with all its special functional and environmental requirements.

The cost depends on the complexity of the system and on its accuracy and reliability requirements. In some cases they can be reduced decisively if systems similar with respect to sources and processing of information can be combined, e.g. ignition and injection systems. Such systems will have greater importance if it can be assured that the design flexibility of the individual systems will not be impaired by integration.

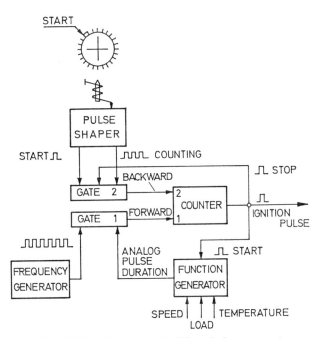

Fig. 106.11. Electronic ignition timing control

APPENDIX 106.1

REFERENCES

(1) ISSLER, J. 'Batteriegespeiste Zündenergiequellen für fremd-gezündete Motoren—heute und morgen', *Auto.-Ind.* 1965 (Heft 3).
(2) SÖHNER, G. 'Zündanlagen mit Halbleiterbauelementen', *M T Z* 1963 (Heft 9 and 12).
(3) HÖHNE, G. 'Elektronische Zündsysteme für Ottomotoren', *Auto.-tech. Z.* 1968 (Heft 3).

C107/72 SAFETY RELATED ELECTRONICS IN THE AUTOMOTIVE ENVIRONMENT

M. SLAVIN*   D. R. ELLIOTT†

Automotive control systems, using complex electronics, have been introduced in areas such as anti-skid braking and fuel injection. In such applications there are strong safety implications. Consequently, electronics reliability at aerospace levels is required at automotive cost. A Bendix-developed anti-skid system, which is described, is an example of how this objective was achieved within the hostile automotive environment. The automotive environment and the methods adopted in designing, manufacturing and testing to achieve the required reliability are reviewed. The paper discusses first-, second- and third-generation systems based on the increased use of complex integrated circuits.

1 INTRODUCTION

AUTOMOTIVE CONTROL SYSTEMS using complex electronics in areas such as anti-skid braking and fuel injection are in production. Under development are even more complex systems such as adaptive speed controls and automatic steering systems which may some day automate intercity automobile travel. Electronics have been chosen for these new systems because of the high density and flexibility available at the present state of the art. Other technologies, such as fluidics, have been considered, but at this time the state of the art of these is such that they have been found impractical for use in the near future.

In these new control systems the electronics can account for more than 50 per cent of the cost, partly because the electronic complexity is replacing mechanical complexity. In addition, strong safety implications have a significant impact on costs. The problem can be summed up by saying that aerospace reliability is required at automotive cost. The Bendix-developed anti-skid systems show how this objective was achieved within the hostile automotive environment.

2 SKID MECHANICS

Skidding of a braked wheel is the result of excessive slip between the tyre and the road surface. Slip is defined as the difference between vehicle and tyre peripheral speed as a percentage of vehicle speed. Thus, when vehicle speed and tyre speed are the same, slip is zero; when the wheel is locked, slip is 100 per cent.

In braking, slip occurs when the brake torque exceeds the road torque, producing a net decelerative force on the wheel. Road torque is the product of rolling radius and the retarding force of the slipping wheel. This retarding force is commonly normalized to an apparent frictional relationship, μ, between the tyre contact patch and the road surface. Fig. 107.1 shows μ as a function of slip.

The MS. of this paper was received at the Institution on 20th March 1972 and accepted for publication on 16th June 1972. 33
* The Bendix Corpn, Automotive Electronics Div., P.O. Box 2302, Newport News, Va. 23602, U.S.A.
† The Bendix Corpn, Automotive Control Systems Group, 401 Bendix Drive, South Bend, Indiana 46620, U.S.A.

At low slip below peak μ, an increase in brake torque decelerates the wheel, producing more slip until the equalizing road torque is achieved. However, at higher slip values, beyond the peak μ, additional brake torque increases will be countered by a decreasing road torque by virtue of a decrease in μ. Brake torque, therefore, overcomes road torque, causing the wheel to promptly lock. Tests have shown that once the peak μ is reached, a further increase in brake pressure can result, on slippery surfaces, in wheel lock within 30 ms at a road speed of 40 km/h.

3 ANTI-SKID BENEFITS

The benefits of a successful anti-skid system can be inferred from Fig. 107.1. First, since μ at 100 per cent slip is less than peak, stopping distances shorter than those attainable by locked wheels are theoretically possible. Note also that peak μ occurs at relatively low slip. Therefore, by controlling at this point, stopping distances and tyre wear in panic stops can be minimized simultaneously. Tests have shown that fewer than 10 locked wheel stops made from high speeds on dry concrete were required to blow out new tyres.

Second, by controlling slip at peak μ, the lateral force characteristic is nearly maximized. As slip approaches 100 per cent, the ability to produce or withstand lateral forces drops dramatically to almost zero. Translated to the vehicle, this means that at high slip the steering is seriously degraded and rear wheel stability is drastically reduced, i.e. yaw moments around the vehicle's vertical axis cannot be countered. The key to skid protection is to maintain slip near the peak μ, without exceeding it, when the driver provides brake pressure normally sufficient to lock the wheels.

4 ANTI-SKID CONFIGURATIONS

Two basic system configurations are produced by Bendix for automobiles (Fig. 107.2). The first, and simpler system, controls the rear wheels simultaneously. Such two-wheel systems provide basic improvement in stopping

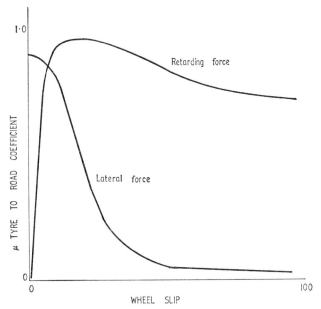

Fig. 107.1. Typical tyre-to-road characteristics

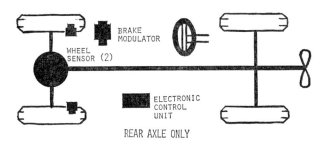

REAR AXLE ONLY

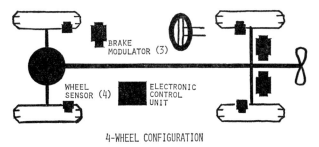

4-WHEEL CONFIGURATION

Fig. 107.2. Car production anti-skid configurations

distances and stability of the car from rear end spin-out in straight line stops.

A four-wheel system provides the same rear wheel action as the two-wheel system. In addition, each front wheel brake is modulated individually. In panic stops this complex addition provides directional control and a further improvement in stopping distances.

5 ANTI-SKID DEVELOPMENT
5.1 Vehicle characteristics
Anti-skid design required identification and detailed knowledge of the vehicle characteristics that influence skidding. Computer studies were helpful in discovering the sensitivities of those vehicle and road parameters known or hypothesized to be influential. However, detailed analytical descriptions of land vehicles were not

available. Selected vehicles were instrumented and exhaustively tested to obtain the necessary data. The important areas examined were brake characteristics, tyre–road relationships and differences between vehicles.

Tests were conducted to determine brake pressure-torque response characteristics for various types of brakes and lining conditions. Tyre–road friction coefficients were found to range from 0·05 to nearly 1·0, depending on tyre condition, inflation pressure, material and road surfaces. The effects of dynamic weight transfer and brake imbalance were also investigated.

With the types and variations in magnitudes of vehicle characteristics found, it became clear that to be successful an anti-skid system capable of significantly improving vehicle handling and braking must be extremely adaptable in its control concept. Hence, the system discussed here is known as 'adaptive braking'.

5.2 System inputs
After quantifying the parameters associated with skid control, the following system inputs were considered: (1) vehicle velocity and acceleration, (2) wheel velocity and acceleration and (3) braked wheel torque.

Wheel velocity and acceleration are the only continuous inputs considered here owing to the high cost and/or lack of feasibility for the other inputs. Wheel speed is readily monitored by variable reluctance sensors monitoring the passage of 'teeth' on the rotating wheel. This provides an a.c. signal readily converted into d.c. signals proportional to wheel velocity and/or acceleration. To assist in controlling the braked wheel over the possible 20:1 range of μ, a simple mercury switch was added to the system to sense crudely the vehicle deceleration, thereby detecting coefficient extremes.

5.3 Control scheme
From these investigations an approach to controlling the braked wheel evolved. The first element required was a 'muscle' device, which could relax and reapply brake pressure. In Bendix production systems today, the muscle device is a vacuum-powered hydraulic modulator. Since quick response is necessary, the pneumatic control is accomplished by means of electric solenoid valves. The control output had therefore to be electrical, reinforcing the decision for electronics.

From wheel speed the ECU (electronic control unit) calculates wheel acceleration. From this, together with vehicle deceleration sensed by a mercury switch, the ECU determines when the wheels are at peak μ and responds in a prearranged manner. A more detailed description of a typical system is given below.

6 ELECTRONIC CONTROL UNIT
6.1 Logic
Logic is a central problem area in anti-skid control systems. Elementary human mental processes and senses are replaced. When studied closely, the complexity of the interaction of those human characteristics required to accomplish even simple tasks becomes evident. Fig. 107.3 is a functional logic diagram for the single channel rear-wheel-only ECU operating circuitry. It represents the 'thought' process by which the system controls the brake.

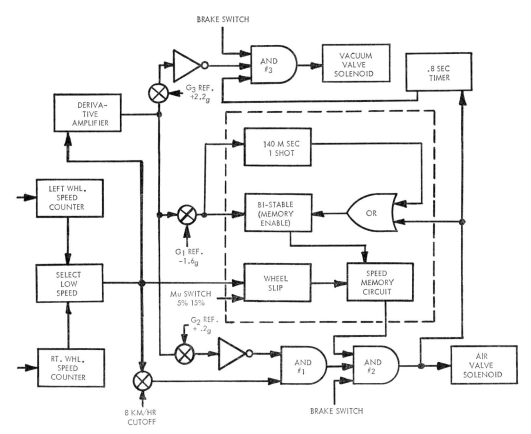

Fig. 107.3. Rear-axle-only logic diagram

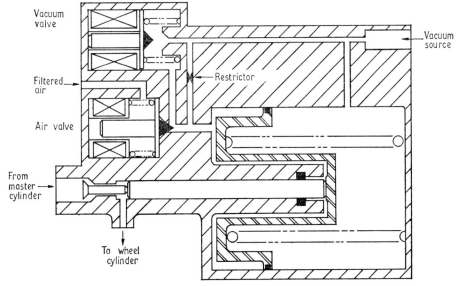

Fig. 107.4. Modulator schematic

Its output operates two valves in the brake pressure modulator, shown schematically in Fig. 107.4, which alters brake pressure by making slight changes in brake line volume.

Wheel speed signals are generated from wheel-mounted variable reluctance magnetic pickups in the form of a.c. voltage, the frequency of which is directly proportional to wheel speed. Counters convert these signals to a d.c. level proportional to the frequency. To maximize vehicle stability, the 'select low' circuit selects the signal from the

lowest speed wheel for the remaining circuits to process. The selected speed signal is used for three functions: (1) its derivative determines wheel acceleration; (2) it determines whether the vehicle is above the 8 km/h operational threshold; (3) it determines, in conjunction with vehicle deceleration, the wheel deceleration thresholds at which brake pressure should be reduced or reapplied.

If the brakes are applied when the speed is above 8 km/h and wheel acceleration is negative or less than $+0.2g$, the ECU will operate in accordance with commands from the speed memory circuit. The speed memory output is controlled by wheel deceleration as predetermined by circuit design values.

When wheel deceleration reaches 1·6g, the one-shot memory retains the instantaneous wheel speed at that time for 140 ms. If wheel speed falls by more than a given percent of the memorized value in that time, indicating that wheel deceleration is too high for existing conditions, an enabling signal is sent to AND 2 from the speed memory circuit. (The required percentage reduction in wheel speed is determined by the μ sensor and wheel slip circuit which differentiates crudely between high and low coefficient surfaces by sensing discrete levels of vehicle deceleration.) The signal from the speed memory circuit causes both air and vacuum valves to be energized by completing ANDs 2 and 3. Fig. 107.4 shows that this creates a pressure imbalance across the diaphragm, causing it to move against the spring, allowing the plunger to follow. As the plunger moves, the master cylinder port is blocked, isolating it from the wheel cylinder so that the pressure to other brake lines is not affected. The volume increase in the wheel line causes the wheel pressure to fall, relaxing the brake.

As the wheel accelerates to a slightly positive value (+0·2g), AND 2 turns off, causing the air valve to close. However, the 0·8-s timer keeps the vacuum valve energized (closed). Hence, the rate of reapplication of vacuum is limited to that which can be supplied by the restricted port. This causes the diaphragm to recover slowly with a correspondingly slow reapplication of brake pressure. The rate of reapplication or 'build rate' is determined by the brake system dynamics and is controlled by the size of the restriction. If pressure recovery is too slow, indicated by wheel acceleration exceeding +2·2g, AND 3 deactivates, de-energizing (opening) the vacuum valve and increasing the build rate substantially. In a panic stop this cycle can occur up to five times per second.

6.2 Fail-safing and failure indicating

A substantial measure of fail-safing has been accomplished. The logic is arranged so that at least two independent failures are required to create an unsafe failure (brake release or uncontrollably locked wheels). Single component failures result in a return to normal braking. Failure indication has been provided to detect failures in critical components and circuits. The brake warning light, already present in passenger cars to show brake pressure imbalance, also serves for the ECU failure indicator. Another circuit cycles the brake modulator, exercising the mechanical components when the car is started. This ensures against mechanical sticking from long periods of modulator inactivity.

At present, fail-safing and failure indication is 30–40 per cent of the total circuitry. It is easily seen that complete fail-safing in first-generation designs would add a prohibitive number of additional components which could themselves be sources of failure.

6.3 Reliability

Complexity is the enemy of reliability in several ways. First, complexity is usually accompanied by large numbers of components, which means that the reliability requirements on individual components must be extremely high. The present generation of anti-skid computers were designed before the practical availability of large-scale integration. Therefore, the number of discrete components in present systems is very large.

The two-wheel ECU contains 233 discrete components

4-WHEEL

2-WHEEL

Fig. 107.5. Anti-skid electronic control units

on two interconnected circuit boards. The four-wheel ECU contains 650 discrete components mounted on four circuit boards, interconnected by a 'mother' board which distributes the inputs, outputs and necessary interconnections among the boards (see Fig. 107.5). Methods and techniques found effective in combating these and other problems of maintaining reliability are discussed in Section 8.

7 ELECTRONICS ENVIRONMENT

Each vehicle has its own set of environmental problems. Values for the environmental factors discussed are typical for present applications of anti-skid electronics.

7.1 Temperature

Permanent damage is often a result of continued exposure to elevated temperatures and/or mechanical stress induced by repeated temperature cycling. The automotive application is such that both of these conditions exist.

ECUs must withstand temperature extremes of $-40°C$ $(-40°F)$ to $85°C$ $(185°F)$ when located in the passenger compartment. In other locations the upper temperature may be as high as $150°C$ $(300°F)$. For example, in a new system under design the electronic elements are integrated into the modulator and mounted on the rear axle next to the differential. The upper extreme temperature for this application is $120°C$ $(250°F)$.

The most common temperature-related failure is that of electrical connections opening as a result of temperature cycling. The most critical connections are those made to semiconductor elements: diodes, transistors and monolithic integrated circuit chips. For qualification purposes, all semiconductors are temperature cycled up to 800 times from $-50°C$ $(-60°F)$ to $150°C$ $(300°F)$.

Performance change with temperature change is another characteristic of many solid-state devices which must be accounted for. Either the circuit must be immune to the variations which might occur over the temperature range, or the critical part(s) must be temperature compensated, usually by the inclusion of a biasing component with an opposite temperature coefficient.

7.2 Vibration and shock

While most modern circuit components are internally immune to vibration damage they are often mounted by thin leads which are susceptible to breaking when the relatively massive component is shaken.

Most vehicle vibration is random. However, testing procedures usually employ sinusoidal resonance searches with extended testing at resonance points found. These tests are conducted with components mounted on printed circuit boards as they are in the final product.

Many low-cost components are available only in vibration-sensitive package configurations. Until sturdier configurations are available at competitive prices, vibration can be combated by the encapsulation of the circuit board, rigidly fixing the components to prevent their motion. However, with this technique the temperature aspects of the package must be carefully examined since most encapsulants are thermal as well as electrical insulators.

Typical worst-case vibration levels found in American vehicles are $5g$ from 10 to 55 Hz for automobile units mounted in the passenger or luggage compartment; up to $40g$ from 2 to 40 Hz for units mounted on the differential housing.

Because of the low weight of electronics packages and components, shock is not normally a great problem. Present design shock loads are $40g$ peak in a 20 ms sawtooth pulse.

7.3 Moisture

The anti-skid ECU employs high impedance circuits. Such circuits are sensitive to moisture, suffering severe degradation from even very high resistance conductive paths created by almost undetectable moisture films bridging across mechanical structures between circuit elements. Severe loss of operating efficiency and accuracy will ensue until the moisture is driven off.

Conformal coatings over the sensitive components and all connecting structures will usually prevent moisture from contacting the circuit, solving both problems. Encapsulation will generally provide the same protection, but at the expense of the ability of the circuitry to dissipate heat. Dry, sealed packages are another effective, if expensive, way of eliminating the problem.

Virtually all standards for electronic devices require that they will operate satisfactorily in 100 per cent relative humidity at all ambient temperatures at which the unit must operate.

7.4 Supply voltage

The ECU must be able to withstand supply line variations of at least 10–16 V with a large amount of ripple from such sources as the alternator, ignition system, d.c. motors, etc. This ripple can vary in frequency from 30 to 3000 Hz and may have an amplitude as high as 1 V or more.

A source of permanent damage to any electronic equipment is high, transient voltages pulsed (both positive and negative) into the main power lines. One source of such pulses is a factory practice of starting cars by an external source when moving them from the production line to open lot storage. When the external jumper cables are removed positive pulses as high as 120 V peak, and of considerable duration, can be generated on the open battery line. Other sources of such transients are air conditioning electric clutches and intermittent battery connections. Since the ECU is 'on' when the ignition switch is 'on', it is susceptible to damage from such transients.

Negative transient voltage spikes are easily suppressed by the use of a diode directly across the supply line. The suppression of positive spikes is much more difficult because the instantaneous power requirement is many times higher than that of negative suppression. A high current, high dissipation Zener diode across the supply line can suppress both positive and negative voltage spikes.

7.5 Electrical interferences

All ECU input and output leads are capable of conducting undesirable interference into the circuitry. Many possible sources of interference in an automobile can be coupled into the input and output lines by magnetic or capacitive or directly conductive means. Interference can also be coupled into the input and output lines by electromagnetic radiation.

Some sources of interference in the automobile are as follows: ignition system, alternator, voltage regulator and two-way radio installations. A properly designed ECU usually has electrical filtering close to the point of entry for all input and output lines.

In some cases electrical interference can be injected directly into the circuitry because of the intense electrical, magnetic or electromagnetic field surrounding the ECU. A properly designed metal case usually minimizes this problem.

7.6 Miscellaneous

Depending upon the application, it may be necessary to protect against fungus, water splash, salt spray and even total immersion.

8 DESIGN FOR RELIABILITY

8.1 Statement of problem

The reliability aim for the Bendix four-wheel passenger car system is a maximum failure rate of 2 per cent for 19 300 km (12 000 miles) or one year, whichever comes first. If one assumes an average speed of 50 km/h (30 mile/h), the expected average annual operating time for the ECU is 400 h, and the required mean time between failure (m.t.b.f.) is 20 000 h for the ECU. There are a total of 650 discrete components, making the required average m.t.b.f. per discrete component 1.3×10^7, or over 10 million hours. This m.t.b.f. is based on automotive environment, top operating temperature, stress ratio and the external connections.

The typical state-of-the-art a.m. automotive radio contains about 80 discrete parts and achieves a failure rate of approximately 2 per cent per 19 300 km or one year. The average m.t.b.f. rate for the components is therefore 1.6×10^6 h, or approximately one-eighth of that required for the four-wheel ECU. Therefore, it was apparent that design and manufacture had to be improved drastically.

8.2 Design philosophy

The circuits were designed to use the least number of discrete components while keeping the component stress ratio as low as practical, without compromising performance. Thorough design and development programmes achieved these objectives.

It was considered necessary to design the ECU for easy assembly, disassembly and servicing. This facilitated product development, leading to a more refined design, and minimized workmanship errors that can arise out of difficult assembly techniques in production, creating latent field failures.

8.3 Component reliability

Considering that a typical high-quality composition resistor, having a stress ratio of 0·2 and operating at 85°C in the vehicle environment, has an m.t.b.f. of 6.25×10^6, or approximately one-half of the required average m.t.b.f. of 13×10^6, then the problem of selecting components is indeed a major task. Fortunately, some components are better than the required system average. For instance, a high-grade mylar capacitor has an m.t.b.f. of 5.28×10^7, or approximately four times better than required. At the other extreme, conventional, non-sealed carbon potentiometers and aluminium electrolytic capacitors are extremely poor, and must be used sparingly, if at all.

Tantalum capacitors are used at a small cost penalty to fill most electrolytic applications. Aluminium electrolytics are used in only one place and in a circuit where its failure would not be catastrophic. Sealed cermet pots were used (at some cost penalty) wherever adjustments were required.

In order to come reasonably close to the cost objective, it was necessary to use plastic encapsulated small-signal transistors. As is well known, the reliability record of plastic encapsulated transistors has been very poor.

Several years ago a task force was established and charged with the responsibility of (1) determining the reliability problems of low-cost plastic encapsulated transistors, (2) devising effective accelerated life tests that correlate with field results and (3) through use of these tests, assisting the suppliers to improve their products to an acceptable level of reliability. The principal method of attack was to subject the transistors under study to temperature cycling until failure occurred. The units were then examined to determine the exact nature of the failure. Virtually all failures were found to be structural. Where consistent failures were found, structural improvements could often be devised. An arbitrary minimum temperature cycling qualification requirement of 200 cycles for 200 units without failure was established.

The net result of this programme was that an acceptable level of reliability was achieved for non-safety-related vehicle applications such as radios. However, this level was not sufficient for anti-skid systems. To achieve the required increase for the small-signal plastic transistors used in anti-skid systems, the temperature cycling requirement was increased from 200 to 800 cycles, and all transistors of this type were subjected to five temperature cycles of $-50°C$ to $150°C$ by the manufacturer. For power applications, hermetically sealed power transistors were used at some cost penalty, because the projected failure rate for plastic power transistors was not good enough.

8.4 Component and assembly qualification testing

The ultimate proof of a design is successful completion of a qualification test programme. The programme runs from the beginning of design at the component level, to the end development, when complete assemblies must pass the tests.

The exact qualification requirements for components vary as to type, performance and application. Parts are submitted to a specified programme; those that pass are recorded and the samples kept on file. Approved parts vendors may not change the composition or construction without submitting to requalification.

Complete assemblies are tested for vehicle environments and life in accordance with the customer's specifications. Often such testing reveals design weaknesses which must be corrected. The tests are repeated until a specified number of units pass without failure, demonstrating a given reliability.

Design margin evaluation is another level of testing which tests the unit to destruction (or the test equipment limit) for various environments. This indicates the margin by which the customer specification is being met. Failures found in this programme are analysed to determine whether they are random or indications of a design weakness which might result in field failures.

9 MANUFACTURING FOR RELIABILITY

The manufacturing cycle includes all processing required from the time material enters the plant until it leaves as a finished product.

9.1 Inspection of incoming material

The first step in the cycle is incoming inspection. Appropriate samples of each batch of material are inspected to key requirements for performance, durability and physical condition. Incoming inspection is very important and should not be bypassed, even when production scheduling emergencies suggest it.

Effective incoming inspection depends on sensible sampling plans, competent personnel and a determination to follow established procedures. It also requires a thoroughly proven, stable and properly documented design so that material may routinely be brought in on a schedule which allows time for adequate inspection for each batch of incoming material.

9.2 Assembly considerations

Once acceptably reliable components have been selected, the next problem is to assemble them into reliable assemblies and to test them for assurance. Experience in building automotive radios, in which a reasonable degree of reliability was required for economic reasons and customer satisfaction rather than for safety, provided a starting point.

Electronic assembly problems are almost entirely mechanical in nature. The components must be properly interconnected, mounted and protected to withstand the design environments. Printed circuit board conveniently provides the interconnections and a foundation for meeting environmental stresses. The first assembly requirement is to provide connection integrity between components and circuit board. The solution relies heavily on maximum use of automated component insertion on the p.c. board, providing consistent component placement, proper lead lengths and correct lead dress on the track side of the board, with minimum variations and error. Human error is minimized.

The condition of the copper surfaces of the etched boards and the condition of the component leads are carefully controlled to ensure good solderability when joined by the flow soldering process. Solder bath temperature is carefully controlled to prevent component damage and circuit board distortion due to excessive heat, while assuring high-quality solder joints. During the design phase the holes through which the component leads pass were specified at the minimum size consistent with the insertion methods to be employed. Good clean parts and boards, proper size holes, properly trimmed and dressed leads, soldered with proper solder bath controls, yielded assemblies with a minimum of initial defects.

The second requirement in assembly is to eliminate the potential failures existing in the newly created assemblies. Potential failure modes involve both the components and the solder joints, and were basically mechanical. Components always suffer from lead distortion when installed. This distortion can conceivably loosen the leads where they enter the component. Stresses will then be stored in the leads, which may result in the leads shifting within plastic encapsulated devices with the passage of time, par-

ticularly at higher temperatures. Solder connections, even with careful process and surface controls, can also be imperfect, including open circuits and almost invisible potential solder shorts.

9.3 Assurance through testing

To provide a practical, economical and reasonably effective means of detecting the potential open and short failures, a brutal test sequence was devised for p.c. board subassemblies and completed final assembly. Each circuit board assembly is subjected to three cycles of thermal shock between $-40°C$ and $100°C$ to precipitate failures from differential expansion. The subassemblies are then thoroughly performance tested. After passing these tests, and undergoing any necessary repair, the boards receive conformal coating or encapsulation, if required, and performance tested again to ensure that no damage has occurred during these mechanical operations.

Next, the finished boards are assembled to make a complete computer. Each computer, after a preliminary performance check, is subjected to a 6-h 'burn-in' operation to bring out 'infant mortality' component failures. Each computer then receives 30 min of $40g$ mechanical shocks at the rate of two per second to precipitate latent mechanical failures. Last, a final complete performance test is given.

The complexities of these systems and the number of test points are so great that testing by computer has been found to be the only effective way to test comprehensively at even modest production rates. The use of computer testing makes possible two substantial benefits in addition to speed. First, the human factor is minimized and the inaccuracies of subjective judgement that an operator must exert in a manually conducted test are eliminated. Second, the speed of computer testing permits additional tests to be conducted to detect marginal conditions which are often caused by a previously undetected fault within the assembly.

Fig. 107.6 shows such a computerized test station. It steps through a pre-programmed test plan, pausing at designated points to permit and to monitor adjustments. When each adjustment is correct, the computer signals the operator to continue the programme. Discrepancies found in areas where adjustments are not involved are noted automatically on the printer for correction.

Although these techniques are effective, better techniques are constantly being sought to maintain or to improve the effectiveness of the testing, and to meet the increasingly complex requirements of future systems at lower costs.

10 TECHNOLOGICAL EVOLUTION

Technology in the electronics field has been undergoing a high rate of evolution since the advent of the transistor, which represents the first generation of modern solid-state electronics. This generation is marked by electronic circuitry consisting of discrete components—i.e. transistors, resistors, capacitors and other miscellaneous solid-state devices—mounted on printed circuit boards. With the appearance of integrated circuits, the first generation is already drawing to a close.

10.1 Integrated circuits

Second and future generations of electronic devices will

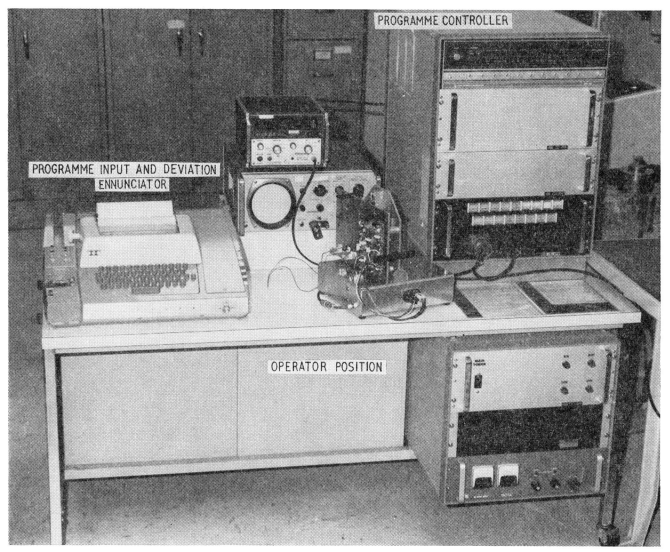

Fig. 107.6. Automated test station for anti-skid ECUs

make extensive use of integrated circuits of various types. An integrated circuit is one that is complete or carries most of the active elements of a circuit; it is contained on a substrate in a single, usually moulded, package. This construction provides a very high degree of circuit structural integrity and, therefore, reliability.

There are two classes of integrated circuit: monolithic and hybrid. The monolithic integrated circuit is a multiplicity of semiconductor devices, transistors and resistors diffused into a single piece of silicon (see Fig. 107.7). Hybrid integrated circuits are constructed on more than one substrate. In most automotive applications hybrid ICs usually consist of one or more monolithic IC's attached to a ceramic substrate having resistors and conductors printed on to it and discrete capacitors attached to it (see Fig. 107.8).

Monolithic ICs are further subdivided into 'off-the-shelf' and custom. 'Shelf' ICs are standardized circuits available from manufacturers' catalogues for general industry use. Custom ICs are designed and manufactured for specific applications of the user. They are, at present, very expensive for all but high quantity usage because of the extremely high initial costs. However, custom ICs have the advantage of requiring fewer peripheral components to complete the circuit than generalized 'shelf' ICs. Integrated circuits can be further classified as digital or linear. Digital ICs have on–off input and output; linear ICs have essentially continuous and usually linear input–output relationship.

Small-, medium- and large-scale integration are terms used in the industry to indicate the size and complexity of the circuitry on a single IC. These terms have no precise definition or limits and their history has been that the number of circuit elements per chip for each classification has grown continuously. Large-scale integration generally refers to the level of the state of the art, indicated by the size of the most complex circuit that can be produced economically. Small- and medium-scale are generally relative to the existing large-scale level.

10.2 Second-generation automotive electronics

The second generation of automotive solid-state electronics is well under way, even though it has only recently been entered. The most recent production anti-skid systems are making great use of shelf and custom linear ICs, mounted on p.c. boards along with peripheral discrete components. This technique provides approximately a 3:1

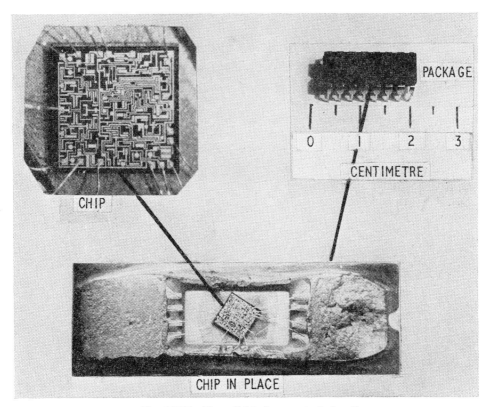

Fig. 107.7. Monolithic integrated circuit

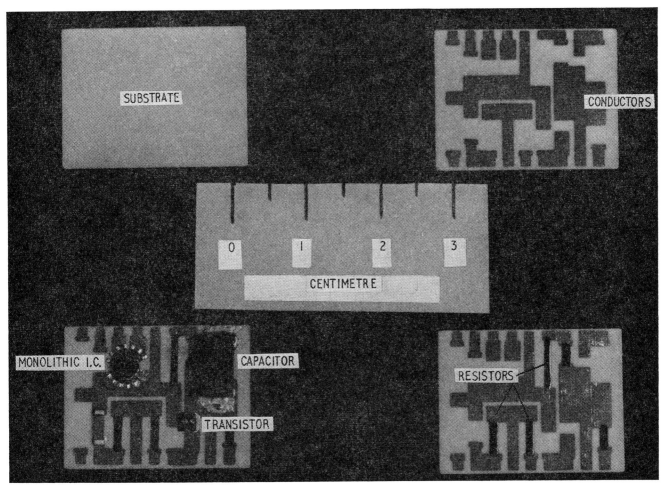

Fig. 107.8. Thick film—hybrid integrated circuit

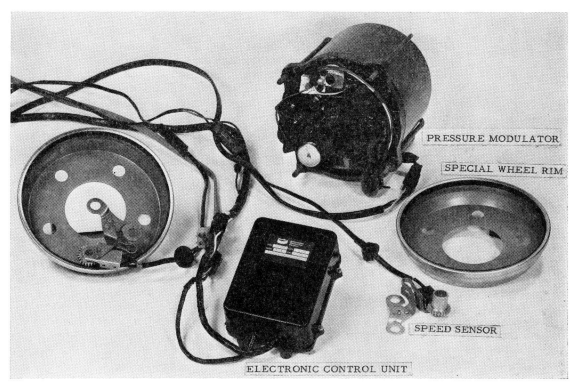

Fig. 107.9. First-generation two-wheel system

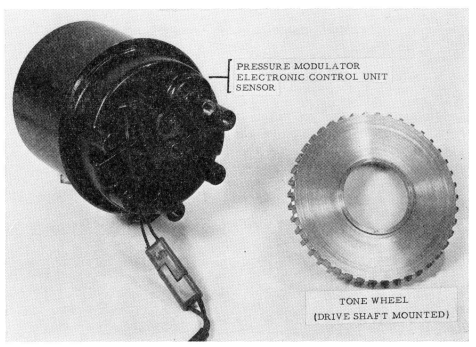

Fig. 107.10. Second-generation two-wheel system

reduction in volume and number of components, and a corresponding improvement in reliability. As the second generation advances there will be greater use of custom ICs. This trend will continue into the third generation.

As new designs evolve, another form of integration is taking place—system integration. Fig. 107.9 shows a first-generation, two-wheel, rear-axle, anti-skid system. Four separate major assemblies are located in various parts of the automobile, interconnected by a wiring har-

ness. Fig. 107.10 shows a second-generation two-wheel system, not yet in production, where all the assemblies have been integrated into a single package mounted on the rear axle, resulting in a considerable cost saving and reliability improvement.

10.3 Third-generation automotive electronics

The third generation of automotive solid-state electronics

will be marked by extensive use of hybrid ICs, with small- to large-scale monolithic chips attached to thick film substrates. In many cases this may be the entire circuit; in other cases the hybrid ICs may be assembled into p.c. boards with a very small number of external components, or other ICs. The p.c. board will act primarily as a wiring harness for the electronic modules. Third-generation systems will most likely use digital as well as linear ICs.

Size reductions from first-generation counterparts will be as much as 20:1, and reliability improvements from the first generation of approximately 10:1.

10.4 Reliability

The significant improvement in reliability for second- and third-generation electronics will be primarily due to the increased use of more complex ICs. This is because the reliability of integrated circuits is primarily a function of the number of external connections, as is true of simpler solid-state devices including resistors and capacitors. Therefore, since many devices are contained in a single integrated circuit, the need for external connections per device is minimized. Therefore, circuit reliability improves rapidly as the scale integration grows larger. For example, assume that the relative reliability between a single transistor and an integrated circuit containing 50 transistors is roughly proportional to the number of external leads, and that the integrated circuit has 10 external connections. The transistor has three connections; the integrated circuit has one-fifth of a connection per transistor junction. Hence, in the integrated circuit the chance of failure per transistor is one-fifteenth that of a single transistor, or a reliability improvement of 15:1.

Reliability also increases with system integration for much the same reason—elimination of external connections. In this case, additional benefits accrue from the elimination of cable harnesses. The danger of cable damage or failure to make connections is reduced to a minimum; electromagnetic interference channels are re- duced; testing of a complete system is made feasible, and the cost of installation, as well as the possibility of error, is reduced.

11 CONCLUSIONS

With the increasing demand for sophisticated automotive control systems, only electronic control has the high density, flexibility and speed to meet the requirements at a reasonable cost, or in some cases at any cost.

Most automotive control systems that are safety related, such as anti-skid systems, have reliability and fail-safe requirements that cannot be met by the automotive electronics that are used in radios.

The required reliability has been met in a four-wheel first-generation anti-skid system at some cost penalty. The actual field failure rate for 12 000 miles or one year is less than 2 per cent at a cost penalty of about 30 per cent.

As technology evolves, second- and third-generation systems can be produced with drastic reductions in cost and size along with a corresponding improvement in reliability, primarily due to circuit and system integration.

It is important to remember that most vehicle systems utilizing electronics have mechanical inputs and outputs, and in most cases mechanical engineers have the system responsibility. Therefore, it is essential that the mechanical system designer familiarize himself with the advantages of electronics. He may then find it possible to do economically things thought previously impossible. He must also become aware of the problem areas in electronics in order to avoid costly errors in development programmes.

Much work is required in the field of packaging. Methods and equipment are needed to reduce the cost of producing electronic component assemblies. The development of equipment to implement new techniques that will make new types of devices possible is also necessary.

In short, electronics, far from threatening mechanical engineering with extinction, actually extends over expanding opportunities.

C108/72 CONFORMITY WITH STATUTORY REGULATIONS RELATING TO RADIO INTERFERENCE FROM ROAD VEHICLES

D. W. MORRIS*

The paper is concerned with the abatement of interference in the radio-frequency spectrum caused by the high-voltage systems of road vehicles. The promotion of international agreement by the C.I.S.P.R. and the effect of international regulations are considered. The contributions made in this field by the British Standards Institution are reviewed. New legislation for the future is discussed.

1 INTRODUCTION

THE ABATEMENT of interference in the radio-frequency spectrum caused by the high-voltage ignition systems of road vehicles has been studied by engineers from many countries for a long time. In the early 1930s it was realized that the intense radiation attributed to vehicle-ignition distribution cables and associated components would be a serious problem in the development of communications and broadcasting networks.

It will be appreciated that at this time no suppression components were fitted to early vehicle designs and that the performance of radio receiving equipment was then much inferior to that of present-day standards. Therefore, investigations into the measurement of the radiated ignition interference field and observations on its subjective effects on radio networks were confined to the lower radio frequencies. Subsequently, with projected developments in the fields of television, mobile communications systems and VHF broadcasting, serious consideration was given to interference measurement and effects at higher frequencies, up to and including the VHF range.

After some years, legal standards relating to the suppression of vehicle-ignition interference were laid down in many countries, and these standards placed limits on the radiated interference field. Because of the varying protection requirements stipulated for each broadcasting network, some significant differences in the suppression methods adopted for vehicles resulted in some countries.

Fortunately, there has been general agreement among interested national and international authorities on how to deal with radio interference from its many sources. It has been realized that some uniformity in measurement methods and maximum limits proposals would be of considerable advantage to regulatory bodies, and that such uniformity could have a great bearing on the easing of international trade.

The C.I.S.P.R. (Comité International Spécial des Perturbations Radioélectriques) is an important organiza-

tion in this field. Under the sponsorship of the I.E.C. (International Electrotechnical Commission), C.I.S.P.R. member bodies comprise national committees of the I.E.C. and a number of international organizations interested in radio interference.

The purpose of the C.I.S.P.R. is to promote international agreement on all aspects of radio interference. Its prime objects are to promote satisfactory reception of sound and television broadcasting services and to facilitate international trade. In general, C.I.S.P.R. recommendations relating to radio interference are used in the technical sections of international regulations and many national standards.

In connection with standards for the suppression of interference from vehicles, valuable contributions of the C.I.S.P.R. are its Recommendations 18/1 and 18/2. These were used as the basis for the revised B.S. (British Standard) 833:1970 and also for the International Regulation No. 10 of the E.C.E. (Economic Commission for Europe) (1969). The E.E.C. (European Economic Community, i.e. the Common Market) requirements also include the recommendation in its technical standards for vehicle suppression.

Thus, the main aim in vehicle interference suppression is the reduction in radiated interference from the ignition system to levels low enough to be tolerated within the service areas of sound broadcast, television and other communications transmitters. In view of the large number of vehicles involved, it is important that the costs of suppression devices be kept to a reasonable level, and that arrangements be made with vehicle producers for the sampling of various vehicle models to ensure that the original suppression standards are being maintained.

Many other items of electrical equipment produce radio-frequency interference during their normal function on a vehicle. Examples of these items are windscreen wiper motors, alternators, regulator units, electric petrol pumps, instrument voltage stabilizers, clocks, etc. The levels of interference radiated from such ancillary devices are very low when compared with the ignition system, and they are generally disregarded in international and national standards.

The MS. of this paper was received at the Institution on 1st March 1972 and accepted for publication on 16th June 1972. 33
* Joseph Lucas (Electrical) Ltd, Great King Street, Birmingham 19.

The present U.K. standards are lower than those required for the future; they are based on limits set out in Statutory Instrument 2023 (1952) under the Wireless Telegraphy Act 1949. However, the U.K., through its representatives in the E.C.E., has supported the introduction of an international standard (E.C.E. Regulation No. 10); accordingly, B.S. 833 has been amended to comply with the requirements of this regulation.

It is fortunate that very effective suppression devices have been available for some years and that a majority of British vehicle manufacturers fit them to production vehicles as standard practice. As a result, it is probable that vehicles will meet the future standard without change.

Surveys of radiated interference from vehicles in traffic conditions have been carried out by the Electrical Research Association, Leatherhead, and by Joseph Lucas (Electrical) Limited, Birmingham. These surveys indicate that a satisfactory position has been attained with present production vehicles, with much improvement during the past 10 years, even with an increasing number of vehicles on the roads.

2 THE IGNITION INTERFERENCE PROBLEM

The basic mechanism by which radio-frequency currents are generated is illustrated in Fig. 108.1. The simplified ignition circuit shown—consisting of a high-voltage coil, two spark gaps, interconnecting leads and the associated capacitance components in the arrangement—is that for one plug circuit.

When the voltage of the system reaches the breakdown voltage of the spark gaps concerned, a rapid decay of the stored energy occurs. Normally, the distributor gap, G_D breaks down at 3–5 kV and the sparking gap at the plug, G_P at higher voltages in the range 5–20 kV, depending on conditions in the engine itself.

The voltage of each spark gap falls very rapidly to a few hundred volts, and therefore the stored energy in the distributed capacitances of the coil, C_C, the plug, C_P, and the distribution cables, C_L, is dissipated in a very short time, i.e. <1 μs. During this time the peak current in the circuit can achieve values of several hundreds of amperes.

The capacitive component of the spark function is responsible for the generation of radio-frequency currents. For a typical saloon-type vehicle of present-day design, the main interference from this source of discharge takes place in the region of 40–100 MHz, but the overall effect extends to much lower frequencies, around 0·15 MHz in the long-wave band, and also has significant values up to 500–600 MHz.

The ignition function depends mainly on the relatively low-frequency currents of the inductive discharge from the ignition coil secondary. The current associated with this

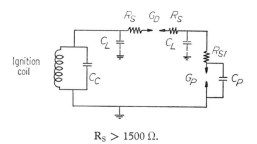

$R_S > 1500\ \Omega.$

Fig. 108.2. Simplified ignition interference suppression circuit

discharge is very much lower than the capacitive discharge and does not contribute to the radio interference problem to any great degree.

Tests carried out on practical vehicle circuits suggest that critical circuit damping can occur at about 1500 Ω; therefore it should be possible to include sufficient resistive impedance at each spark gap in order to reduce the capacitive discharge to a single undirectional impulse. The radio interference from such a suppressed circuit would be reduced considerably, and at the same time the ignition function would not be impaired (see Fig. 108.2).

Such arrangements, employing resistive damping, have been used on internal-combustion engines for many years. In practice, the suppressors take the form of composite carbon elements suitably mounted for direct connection to the spark gap concerned, distributed resistance or inductance cables and composite suppressor units using LCR filter networks. Examples of various suppression arrangements for use with ignition systems are given in Table 108.5 and Fig. 108.6 in Appendix 108.2.

To some degree, the attenuation of interference is augmented by the screening shield afforded by the metal plates of the vehicle bodywork. However, this effect is extremely unpredictable, since much depends on how well the body panels are held together to form an effective shield around the radiating interference source. Sometimes a body panel can become isolated by the inclusion of paint in hinges and locks, and if it is closely coupled to the ignition wiring, such a metal sheet can become a radiating aerial.

In general, it is not possible to calculate the attenuation of ignition interference on the very large number of varying vehicles manufactured. Therefore it has been necessary to investigate the magnitudes of the radiated field and to institute methods of measuring amplitudes over certain radio-frequency bands, and then to engineer methods for the control of such interference to levels that are considered adequate for present-day use of the many and varied radio communication systems.

3 HISTORICAL BACKGROUND

Much of the earlier work connected with radio interference was concentrated on the study of interference effects and the development of super-heterodyne and other receivers for the measurement of the radiated field. The studies gave rise to measuring-type radio receivers for the long-, medium- and short-wave bands, together with receivers for the lower frequencies of the VHF bands.

In most modern measuring sets there is provision for a detector time constant having 1 ms charge and 500 ms

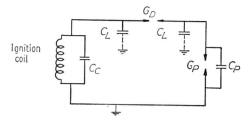

Fig. 108.1. Simplified ignition circuit

discharge characteristics. Thus, a measurement is given of the quasi-peak value of the interference level, which is used because it has been concluded that this level gives a close relation between the ignition interference field and the subjective effect on the television or broadcast receiver. Similarly, it was concluded that receivers with an intermediate frequency bandwidth of 100–120 kHz were satisfactory in view of the wave shape and pulse repetition frequencies concerned with ignition-type interference.

Much work was carried out on suitable types of portable aerials for measuring sites; these included frame, vertical rod and dipole types for the various frequency ranges under consideration. The vertical rod is now used for the frequency range 0·2–30 MHz, and the dipole for 30–250 MHz.

The work of some organizations involved in development and research in this field is worthy of note. The C.I.S.P.R. was originally formed in 1933 and carried on its work until 1939, during which time eight reports on its findings were issued. It was re-formed in 1950, its full recommendation on ignition interference being published in 1964 at its Stockholm meeting.

The Post Office and the Electrical Research Association were responsible in the U.K. for much of the work involving analysis of interference problems and the design of measuring equipment. Additional information was provided by the Society of Motor Manufacturers and Traders through the Lucas Organization in close liaison with vehicle manufacturers.

The S.M.M. & T. has maintained the manufacturer's viewpoint through its representation on the committees of the B.S.I. (British Standards Institution). The B.S.I. is also responsible for the issue of specifications in the U.K. and has circulated its B.S. 833:1953 and an amended version B.S. 833:1970 in connection with ignition interference from internal-combustion engines. The organization is also responsible for the appointment of representatives to the U.K. national committee for attendance at the meetings of the C.I.S.P.R.

4 CONFORMITY WITH PRESENT REGULATIONS AND STANDARDS

In order to decide whether or not a test sample complies with any particular standard it is necessary to establish the following items:

(1) Parameters to be measured, and the specified limits.
(2) Conditions of test applicable to the sample.
(3) Measuring equipment to be used.
(4) Conditions or arrangements for the measuring equipment.

A regulation is usually a formal adaptation of a standard or parts of a standard by a government department, and usually includes administrative detail in addition to the main technical requirements of the standard itself. Thus, in connection with interference from ignition systems, it is reasonable to examine the technical content and show how compliance can be effected in the majority of cases.

The earlier B.S. 833:1953 indicated the maximum permissible values of radiated ignition interference from vehicles over two frequency ranges; these are given in Table 108.1.

The conditions for the test sample are that it be placed

Table 108.1. Maximum permissible values to B.S. 833:1953

Frequency band	Maximum permissible field strength	Bandwidth of measuring instrument
200 kHz–30 MHz	100 μV/m	9 kHz
30 MHz–150 MHz	50 μV/m	100 kHz

on flat ground, as far as possible from any radio-wave-reflecting objects, and 10 m from the vertical dipole aerial attached to the measuring receiver. Measurements are conducted from the nearside of the vehicle only, whilst the engine is accelerated rapidly from idling to near maximum speed.

The measuring receiver is required to have a quasi-peak-type indicating meter, its main characteristics complying with B.S. 727.

In the case of this particular procedure, measurements are conducted with the dipole aerial in a vertical plane, and fixed at 2 m above ground level. This is a reasonable condition since a majority of television transmissions are vertically polarized, and it is known from earlier work that the ignition interference radiation is also predominantly of vertical polarization in the lower VHF region (see Fig. 108.3).

With reference to Statutory Instrument No. 2023 (1952), the Wireless Telegraphy (Control of Interference from Ignition Apparatus) Regulations 1952 reveal that the frequency range 40–70 MHz only is selected for measurements on vehicles. In practice, two frequencies are normally used, 45 and 65 MHz; these will give a typical interference characteristic for the sample. It is of interest to note that these measures for the control of interference still apply today. In normal practice a sample batch of six vehicles is selected at random from production and a statistical analysis is carried out to assess the probable level for the production series. For the future, it is expected that this legislation will be amended by October 1973 and will be applicable in April 1974.

Conformity with this legislation is, in fact, not difficult to achieve, bearing in mind that the most effective measure for suppression is the attachment of a suitable suppressor device directly to the interference source, i.e. to a spark gap.

A certain amount of interference suppression is normally included in the ignition distributor in the form of a composite carbon brush, having a resistance value of 10–12 kΩ, resting on the distributor rotor under a light spring pressure. In most early vehicles additional suppressors are attached to the sparking plugs; these are also of the composite carbon variety and are usually about 5–10 kΩ, and connected to the ignition distributor towers through cables having copper-core conductors.

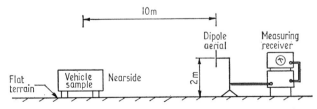

Fig. 108.3. Arrangement for measurement of vehicle ignition interference for existing regulations

Of more recent date, an ignition cable having a distributed resistance in the form of impregnated nylon fibres has become the general standard for production cars. This cable gives an improved suppression performance because of its presentation of a high resistive impedance to the spark gaps in the ignition distributor and engine spark plugs. It has a rising impedance characteristic with frequency because of distributed capacitance to the engine components. Usually the cable has a resistance value of some 15–25 kΩ/m.

Both systems were used extensively to meet the 1952 legislation, but preference has been given during recent years to the resistive cable system. The main reason for this is the proposed extension of the frequency range for measurement—up to 250 MHz and perhaps finally to 400 MHz.

In 1962, the French government issued a very stringent regulation in which the maximum permissible interference level from ignition was 30 μV/m over the frequency range 30–250 MHz. It became clear, therefore, that none of the systems used on cars manufactured in the U.K. would meet these suppression requirements. Subsequently, an improved arrangement, which added resistive inductors to the spark-gap outlets, was introduced for vehicles exported to France. The design work carried out at this stage has been of considerable importance in dealing with vehicles having fibre-glass body components, where the usual advantage of metallic screening is obviously absent.

5 CONFORMITY WITH FUTURE REGULATIONS AND STANDARDS

Reference has already been made to the introduction of an improved standard concerned with interference from ignition systems. This is based on C.I.S.P.R. Recommendation 18/1 and will eventually become an international common standard. The first steps toward this goal have already been taken by the Inland Transport Commission of the E.C.E., and its Working Party 29 has issued Regulation No. 10 on the control of ignition interference from vehicles.

The U.K. has supported the introduction of a common standard, and recently the new B.S. 833:1970 was published. It is now intended that the legislation applying under the Wireless Telegraphy Act 1949 will be amended to conform with new requirements.

B.S. 833:1970 indicates the maximum permissible values of radiated ignition interference for vehicles over a single frequency range 40–250 MHz, as in Table 108.2.

The conditions for the test sample are that it be placed on flat ground, as far as possible from any radio-wave-reflecting objects, and 10 m from the dipole aerial attached to the measuring receiver. Measurements are conducted from both sides of the vehicle, whilst the engine is run at

Table 108.2. Maximum permissible values to B.S. 833:1970

Frequency range, MHz	Limits, μV/m
40–75	50
75–250	50 at 75 MHz, then increasing linearly with frequency to 120 at 250 MHz.

1500 rev/min for multi-cylinder types and 2500 rev/min for single-cylinder units.

The measuring receiver is required to have a quasi-peak-type indicating meter, its main characteristics complying with B.S. 727.

In this procedure measurements are conducted with the dipole aerial in both the vertical and horizontal positions on each side of the vehicles. The aerial is fixed at 3 m above ground level.

The new legislation will require measurements to be made on a single sample of a production series or a prototype sample over the frequency range 40–250 MHz. Therefore measurements in this range will be made at spot frequencies of 45, 65, 90, 150, 180 and 220 MHz, each having a tolerance of $\pm$5 MHz to allow a clear measuring frequency to be selected. At each frequency four separate measurements will be made, for vertically and horizontally polarized interference at each side of the vehicle, the highest reading at each frequency being considered typical of the vehicle type. For compliance with the limits, the single prototype sample is required to have maximum interference levels 2 dB (20 per cent) below the limit, and selected samples from a production series are permitted maximum levels 2 dB (25 per cent) above the specified limit for each frequency of measurement (see Fig. 108.4).

Under the 1958 Geneva agreement, tests conducted in the country of origin will receive recognition on a reciprocal basis in other countries operating Regulation No. 10. For this purpose each vehicle will be allocated an approval number for its type by the Department of the Environment after testing under the authority of the Ministry of Posts and Telecommunications.

The measures already adopted for interference suppression by most U.K. manufacturers will, in general, be adequate for the new legislation. Minor variations in the suppression system could be required on some engine designs, because of the proximity of the ignition leads to the body panelling. It is certain that an improvement will be required for motor-cycles and other engines without metallic enclosures; this category will include motor vehicles with fibre-glass body components.

6 SURVEYS OF INTERFERENCE FROM VEHICLES IN TRAFFIC CONDITIONS

Surveys were carried out between 1957 and 1969 to

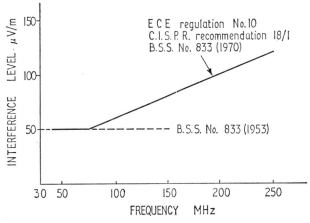

Fig. 108.4. Graphical presentation of limits of maximum permissible radiation

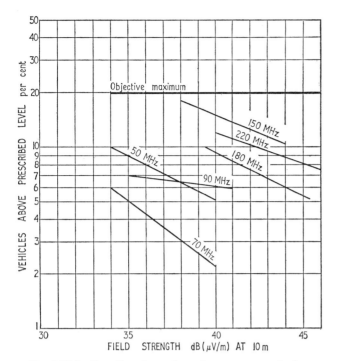

Fig. 108.5. Results of quasi-peak measurements for vertical and horizontal antenna positions

Table 108.4

Frequency	No. of vehicles	No. above limit (+6 dB)	Percentage above limit (+6 dB)
50 MHz	500	26	5·2
70 MHz	412	9	2·2
90 MHz	510	31	6·0
150 MHz	502	52	10·4
180 MHz	506	27	5·3
220 MHz	513	39	7·6

assess the effects of the suppression measures introduced on production cars. From observations made during these surveys it is concluded that some of the older type vehicles, fitted with simpler suppression systems, cause an overall interference above the expected levels. However, a notable improvement is observed for vehicles fitted with modern equipment, and a subsequent analysis of the results shows that a satisfactory position has been achieved (see Fig. 108.5).

A later exercise carried out by Joseph Lucas (Electrical) Limited accounted for measurements on 13 000 vehicles. During this exercise an assessment of the subjective effects of ignition interference on Band I (40–70 MHz) and Band III (176–216 MHz) television and Band II (88–108 MHz) VHF/FM sound broadcasting was made (see Tables 108.3 and 108.4).

Mention has been made of the C.I.S.P.R. Recommendation 18/1; the technical content of which indicates that with an 80 per cent confidence level, 80 per cent of vehicles tested will comply with the limits laid down. The results of the traffic surveys so far carried out show that this requirement is met by present-day vehicles.

7 ACKNOWLEDGEMENTS

The author wishes to thank the Directors of Joseph Lucas (Electrical) Limited for permission to publish the information contained in this Paper, and also the British Standards Institution for permission to reproduce British Standard 833:1970 referring to 'Ignition suppression arrangements' and 'Suppression devices'.

APPENDIX 108.1

Radio-frequency levels discussed in the text are sometimes expressed in the terms $\mu V/m$ or dB relative to $1\ \mu V/m$. The decibel scale is a means of expressing differences in power levels or corresponding voltage levels relative to a fixed resistance or impedance value. It has become customary to use the decibel scale in defining interference voltage or field strength values. The reference levels used are invariably $1\ \mu V$ or $1\ \mu V/m$ respectively.

The decibel notation is expressed:

$$20\log_{10}\frac{V_2}{V_1}\ \text{dB}$$

where V_1 is the reference level, say $1\ \mu V$ or $1\ \mu V/m$ for the impedance concerned, and V_2 is the level of interference voltage or field in μV or $\mu V/m$ respectively.

APPENDIX 108.2
EXAMPLES OF SUPPRESSION ARRANGEMENTS FOR IGNITION SYSTEMS

This section gives, for guidance, examples of suppression arrangements that have been found satisfactory for very many vehicles and other equipment incorporating spark-ignited, internal-combustion engines. It is not possible to specify precise methods of suppression that will be satisfactory in all cases because features in the design of a vehicle or engine have a great effect on the magnitude of

Table 108.3

Frequency	No. of vehicles	No. above limit	Percentage above limit
50 MHz	2212	231	10
70 MHz	1719	100	6
90 MHz	1000	69	7
150 MHz	2200	408	18
180 MHz	2019	197	10
220 MHz	1500	166	11

Table 108.5. Examples of suppression arrangements

Type	Engines with distributors	Engines without distributors
Engines with metallic enclosures and vehicles with metallic engine enclosures	A with 2 or 3 or 4 or B with 1 or 2 or 3 or 4 or C with 1 or 2 or 3 or 4 or D (all sparking plug leads) with 1 or 2 or D (all leads) or E (all sparking plug leads) with 1 or 2 or E (all leads)	A or B or C or D or E
Vehicles and engines without metallic enclosures, motorcycles, mopeds	B with 3 or 4 or C with 3 or 4 or B with D (all leads) or B with E (all leads) or C with D (all leads) or C with E (all leads)	B or C

The metallic screened plug suppressors (type B) must make firm contact with the metal body of the sparking plug.

A		Plug suppressor
B	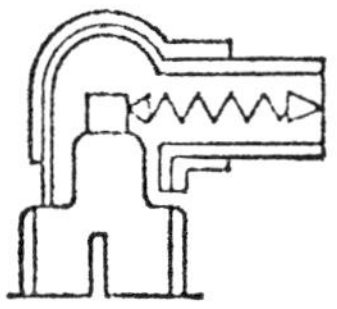	Screened plug suppressor
C	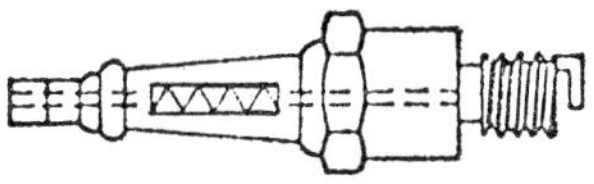	Suppressed plug or resistive plug
D	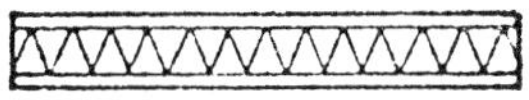	Resistive cable
E	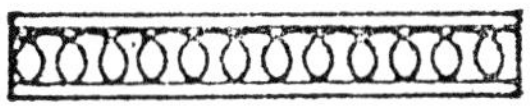	Reactive cable
1	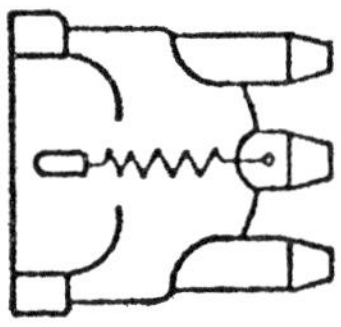	Distributor cap with inbuilt central resistor (resistive brush) or with plug-in resistor
2	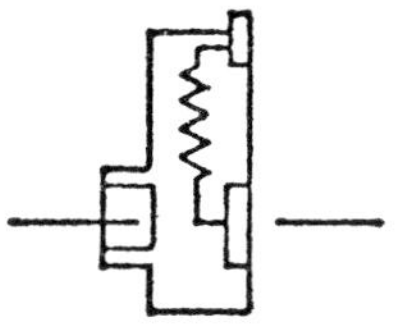	Resistive rotor
3	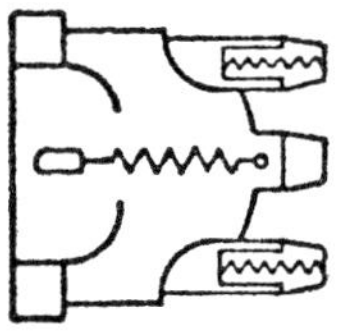	Distributor cap with inbuilt central resistor (resistive brush) or with plug-in resistor and resistors in the distributor cap outlets or in the cables near the distributor cap
4	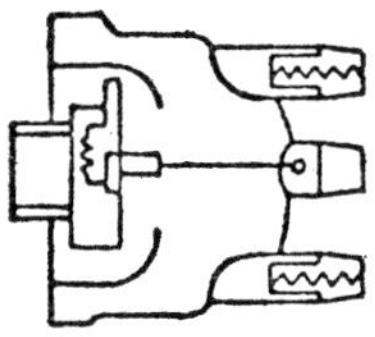	Distributor cap with resistive rotor and resistors in all sparking plug outlets

Fig. 108.6. Suppression devices

the interference generated or radiated. For example, the level of interference is dependent on the disposition of the ignition components and the lengths of the connecting cables. Such cables should not run close to a metallic bonnet in which interference currents may be induced. The cables should, as far as possible, follow paths close to the engine block.

In Table 108.5, engines and vehicles are divided into two groups for the purpose of specifying suppression methods, because some assistance in suppression is often given by the metal body of a vehicle and more suppression may be needed where no metal body exists. The type of suppressors used in the arrangements given in Table 108.5 are shown in Fig. 108.6.

C111/72

DIAGNOSTIC AND QUALITY CONTROL EQUIPMENT

J. BUSHNELL*

This paper reviews the development of individual instrumentation for electrical ignition and gas analysis, including the integration of meter-type circuitry into unified control systems and multiple harness connections. It considers present trends towards automated test equipment, and future developments, including provision by vehicle manufacturers of simplified test connections and function sensors, and the possibility of computer control of testing on a commercial basis.

1 INTRODUCTION

IN ORDER TO APPRECIATE the present trend towards the simplification and automation of vehicle diagnostic and quality control equipment, it is necessary to consider the background history of the development leading up to it.

2 ENGINE TESTING METHODS

Engine testing equipment developed slowly on a basis of proving that each individual component was satisfactory and, hence, that the complete engine performance quality was up to the required standard. These items of test equipment followed a basic pattern, and such instruments as the tachometer, vacuum gauge, compression gauge, exhaust gas analyser and basic ignition timing devices were developed first, followed by equipment for testing the coil, condenser and distributor.

At this stage no equipment was available for testing the ignition system when operating other than the simple neon, which could be used to determine the presence of a voltage at the plugs. A main disadvantage of such equipment was the complexity of connections, controls and meters inherent in their use. Fig. 111.1 shows typical units connected to an engine.

A further disadvantage of a most valuable, yet simple, piece of equipment, the vacuum gauge, was the necessity of drilling and tapping the inlet manifold to obtain a test point. With water-jacketed manifolds and the introduction of multiple carburettors the positioning of the vacuum gauge became more critical, and it has tended to fall into disuse. However, it is still an extremely valuable instrument for overall checking. One of its main facilities, that of being able to determine ignition timing to some degree, was eliminated when anti-knock fuels were introduced, as it is extremely difficult to detect the point at which knocking now occurs.

The MS. of this paper was received at the Institution on 9th May 1972 and accepted for publication on 20th June 1972. 44
* *Managing Director, Crypton-Triangle Ltd, Bristol Road, Bridgwater, Somerset.*

3 AREA TESTING OF ENGINES

It soon became apparent that the results of such tests indicated a large percentage of good components and only a very small percentage of faulty ones. To improve efficiency, a method called 'area testing' was introduced. Using this method, the engine was divided into four main areas: (1) electrical, (2) ignition, (3) compression and (4) carburation.

New instruments were devised to enable each section to be tested; only after unsatisfactory results were individual components tested. This resulted in testing time being reduced from 1–2 h to some 30 min.

Nevertheless, there was still no method of testing the ignition system under operating conditions. The first step towards this came in the late thirties with the introduction of the cathode-ray oscilloscope; however, most mechanics found it too complex to use. It remained effectively a laboratory tool until 1955, when an oscilloscope was introduced in America which enabled a semi-skilled operator to analyse satisfactorily the operation of the ignition system.

Systems were then developed incorporating overall master switching so that, with five or six basic connections to the engine system and a sampling tube in the exhaust pipe, it was possible to carry out a whole series of tests without removing components or dismantling the systems (see Fig. 111.2). Further, the switching complications were reduced in that having been initially set to the type of vehicle, i.e. four-stroke, four-cylinder, negative earth electrical system, the test could then be conducted in a routine manner that permitted all items and areas to be covered in approximately 20–30 test routines. It was necessary in many of these to vary the engine speed so that the operator became a throttle control, a switch selector, and a meter and oscilloscope trace interpreter. The confusion of having to make many connections and move many switches was thereby eliminated, enabling the operator to concentrate more fully on the diagnosis and testing being undertaken.

With the ability to display, visually, traces of the ignition system on a cathode-ray tube, it now became practical to

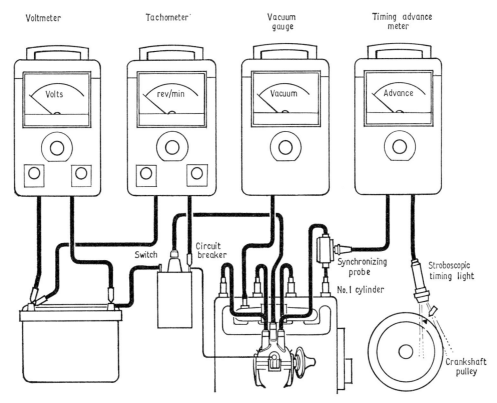

Fig. 111.1. Typical test system using individual units

examine each cylinder ignition operation individually and also to compare them collectively. However, this, in turn, led to further complications, as dependence upon the following was necessary:

(a) The degree of ignition suppression.
(b) The characteristics of the ignition circuit.
(c) The mixture strength in the cylinder.
(d) The compression ratio or actual compression of the cylinder itself.

In practice, the results would vary and the traces would change; thus, not one standard pattern but several evolved. The skilled operator could interpret the results based on the type of engine, e.g. a simple, low-compression, single-carburettor engine would have a different characteristic to a highly sophisticated, very high compression, multi-carburettor sports engine. Therefore the use of such a tool by semi-skilled and unskilled operators on anything other than routine testing was impractical and likely to produce misleading results. Training programmes were instituted, but the variety of vehicle systems made training not the easiest of tasks. Nevertheless, once an operator had assimilated the basic information, provided that he was allowed time to examine new faults on strange vehicles, his experience and skill improved rapidly as he was able to check and compare results before and after correction.

Problems can arise when an operator, familiar with a vehicle and its usual faults, tends to use his own judgement rather than the results obtained from the instruments. If these do not agree with his own fault diagnosis, he tends to reject the equipment information rather than progressing with the routine, which may be indicating a completely different fault than that anticipated.

An additional complication is that the full routine must be completed to ensure that all faults have been eliminated, or at least detected, rather than stopping short when the first fault appears to have been found. As an example of this a miss on a vehicle engine under normal conditions could be identified from the results of the first tests as being due to an excessive dwell angle, i.e. contact breaker points too close and burnt, and no further tests carried out. Completion of the tests may show that this is only part of the cause and that faulty plugs, ignition coil or distributor cap may be a contributory factor on the basic defect. To avoid this it is essential, with any form of test equipment, that a regular progressive routine should be created and utilized by the operators. Haphazard or random selections taken at will must be avoided.

4 VEHICLE TESTING

In dynamic areas of the vehicle functions, e.g. wheel balancing, brake testing, performance testing and suspension testing, equipment was developed more slowly as many items were covered by road testing rather than by dynamic testing, since this was the most convenient method of measuring the actual performance. However, crowded city conditions, and the fact that results from this form of testing were often a matter of personal opinion rather than objective data, led to the development of equipment for testing in these areas. In general, testing could be broken down in the earlier stages into the following four items.

4.1 Wheel alignment

By attaching reference points to the front wheels—for preference directly on to the rim or even on to the bearing

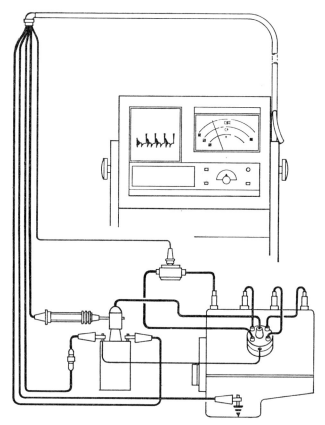

Fig. 111.2. Example of modern engine analyser

pedal pressures is also equally accurately measured, very sophisticated diagnosis can be achieved; but the skill of the operator and his experience remain a vital part.

4.3 Power performance

In measuring power performance, acceleration, etc., from the back or front wheels on a chassis dynamometer it was expected in the early stages that a test here would indicate all other areas of the vehicle either good or in need of adjustment. However, it proved difficult to achieve the maker's specified performance figures at the drive wheels for either horsepower or acceleration characteristics. Subsequent experience showed that, because of the variation in tolerances of engines and transmission systems, the results could vary very considerably from one vehicle to another. Thus faults affecting performance, e.g. incorrect timing or carburation, could be missed on a vehicle incorporating close-tolerance components, since the results obtained would be the same as those obtained from a correctly adjusted vehicle using components with wider tolerances.

The improvement on the first vehicle performance when correctly adjusted could be as high as 10 per cent or even 15 per cent compared with the other vehicle. This meant that chassis dynamometry as a means of diagnosis has a more limited use than was initially expected. Because of a high capital outlay and the lack of information generally available regarding performance standards, it has not progressed as originally anticipated, and certainly not as far as in other areas of test equipment.

4.4 Wheel balancing

This has undergone considerable development, through many devices from simple static balances to the very advanced and sophisticated electronic read-out device. However, the basic problems still remain: it is a time-consuming exercise, and schools of thought between 'on-the-car' balancing and 'off-the-car' balancing are still at variance. In theory, on-the-car balancing represents more nearly the true conditions under which difficulties are experienced. It may not be the real answer, as a combination of wheel imbalance combined with, in the case of front end, incorrect alignment, possible suspension difficulties and tyre out of true tend to be corrected by the addition of weights to the wheels. This may result in improvements at certain speeds but increased difficulties at other speeds, and balancing the wheels does not remove the basic cause or causes of the instability in other parts of the vehicle. In this respect wheel balancing is blamed, as is the engine in the performance area, for many faults not directly capable of correction by wheel balancing alone.

4.5 Other areas

All the other areas capable of diagnosis and testing—e.g. suspension, cooling systems, electrical system, exhaust system and, perhaps the most annoying of all, leaks, squeaks, rattles and groans—have been tackled in many ways. Nevertheless, there still do not exist completely satisfactory methods of dealing with all the possible variables which exist other than that master computer, a human being with adequate skill and experience in all the necessary areas.

face—optical measurements could be made, using projection systems, of the camber, castor, toe-in and king pin inclination. The main areas here were time consuming; in general, toe-in and camber were the only items capable of being readjusted without major mechanical surgery.

4.2 Brake testing

When brake testing, decelerometers used in the vehicle on road test were supplemented by roller brake testers or 'skid plate' brake testers, developed to allow tests to be made at slow speeds on each axle or all four wheels simultaneously. The initial test speeds were in the order of 0·1–0·5 mile/h. Whilst these produced good results in the hands of a diagnostician who had experience of braking systems, it was felt that with the introduction of disc brakes and very high speed motoring, satisfactory results could not be obtained at low speed. However, the difficulties in producing the power required to test braking systems at road speeds of over 100 mile/h, involving 200 hp/axle to spin up to the appropriate speed rapidly enough to make it a time-saving exercise, tended to make it not the type of equipment that a service station could use effectively, or even economically.

Subsequent extended tests to meet legislative requirements have shown that roller testing from 0·1 mile/h up to 40 mile/h gives sufficiently similar results to satisfy legislative testing procedures with no difference in accuracy between the systems. Providing (a) indication is taken of the performance of the wheels during the braking periods by accurate observation or printing out and (b) the actual performance of the braking cycle under controlled

5 AUTOMATED TEST EQUIPMENT

The present trend towards automated test equipment offers certain great advantages but requires immense thought and advanced planning. To ensure further development of automated test equipment, it is necessary to define clearly a number of questions and to reach an understanding of what is required to be established.

Obviously, it would be possible to fit all the necessary sensors to any vehicle to enable safety, performance and wear characteristics, and any other required data, to be measured. The economics of this would probably be non-commercial, and the information to set the standards for pass limits extremely difficult to determine. It will be necessary to establish tolerances from vehicles on the production line, and by testing to those tolerances to establish standards for 'go', 'no go' or tolerance testing over the anticipated life of the vehicle, which in some cases may be as long as 100 000 to 200 000 miles. Furthermore, change of components and replacement items fitted to the vehicle, combined with modification, which may not necessarily be easily identified, will result in further complications in producing the overall information.

6 BASIC AUTOMATED TESTING

There are certain clearly defined areas in which either automated tests or comparator print-out information can be readily achieved; perhaps one of the easiest examples is that of brake testing. When using brake testers it is possible, without any attachments to the vehicle, to establish the braking performance against legislative standards by using the weight of the vehicle, and testing one, two or all four wheels simultaneously. The limit of 50 per cent braking efficiency and the tolerance for left pull or right pull, front or rear wheels, are indicated, using go, no go standards.

Whilst this can be done, it is not at present possible without the use of built-in sensors to establish whether the brake linings are worn to a point at which the brakes might fail in the next 10 miles. Furthermore, there is no firmly established, completely satisfactory method of testing anti-locking braking devices or the more sophisticated electronically controlled braking systems without using built-in sensors. Legislation in many countries does not specifically call for tests on these items but requires only that the system meets certain specified performance figures.

7 EXHAUST EMISSION

If emission is to be tested to legislative standards then no problem exists, as the vehicle type can be determined and the actual standards used to ascertain the tolerances required to produce the ultimate data. There are many factors to be considered prior to making the final exhaust emission test, e.g. whether emission need only be checked at idle with the engine hot, or whether it is necessary to make a dynamic test under deceleration, acceleration or even cold choke conditions.

8 TOLERANCES FOR LIFE

It must be stressed that whilst there is no difficulty in undertaking any of the tests as a routine, they should satisfy economic considerations; and adequate information regarding satisfactory tolerances should be available for each vehicle from production line until disposal in the scrap-yard.

9 AUTOMATED ENGINE TESTING IN SERVICE

Equipment already exists that can be connected to an engine to establish the performance of many of its functions and present information within specified tolerances in an easily assimilated form. Examples of some of the parameters that can be measured are battery condition, charging system condition, dwell angle, plug operation, coil polarity and reserve, 'timing and advance, cylinder balance carburation', oil pressure and fuel flow rates.

However, if accurate measurement of overall performance is to be made, further complications ensue. For instance, the use of a low octane fuel in a high-compression engine could give misleading results, unless there was some method of determining the type of fuel being used in the vehicle on test. In addition, to programme the comparator or computer accurately some system of providing information on the modification state of the vehicle is required.

10 STANDARDS AND VEHICLE IDENTITY

To meet the above requirement, a possible method of identifying the vehicle is suggested. When on the production line a printed slug, incorporating all the necessary basic manufacturing limits for that vehicle, i.e. not for the class of vehicle but for the actual vehicle, should be inserted in the vehicle in such a manner that its engine will not operate unless the slug is present, and only if the correct slug has been fitted. When automated testing is required the slug would be removed, fitted into the computer, the circuit over-ridden by the computer connections and the slug used as the basis for the tolerances applied to the vehicle's performance.

The problem still remaining is: if modifications are incorporated or components are replaced or repaired, how is the slug altered? Examples of such modifications are the fitting of new plugs, or the replacement of a distributor, contact breaker set, battery, shock absorbers, brake linings, etc. Further, how can it be known that the items fitted are the true replacements for that vehicle; and how can they be positively identified?

11 PRESENT METHODS OF AUTOMATED TESTING

There are three areas in which testing can be carried out: safety, performance and wear tolerancing and replacement indication. Fig. 111.3 shows the simplified block diagram of a system for testing headlamps, brakes, engine and steering geometry.

The system incorporates transducers, signal conditioning units, performance standards information, comparator units, control and operator cueing units, information retrieval and print-out and a visual display of information. The safety regulations probably present the easiest areas for automated test and computer print-out because these deal with legislative requirements in total and not individual vehicle requirements in particular. Such areas are brakes, suspension, headlamp alignment, steering wear, steering alignment, tyre integrity, exhaust emission and the problematical fields of corrosion and noise. These may

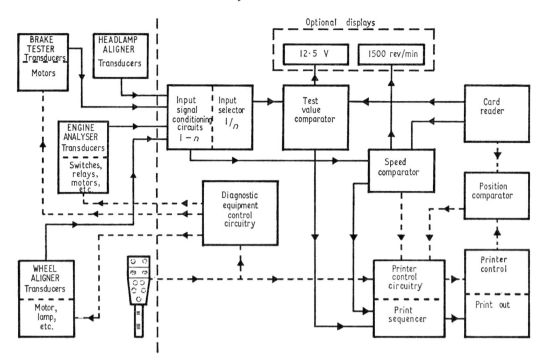

Fig. 111.3. Simplified block schematic of possible automated test system

be measured under power conditions or running light, and in a specified enclosed area or otherwise. Other items dealt with are suspension, shock absorbers and overall exhaust integrity to provide emission settings.

The probable short-term compromise will be to take those tests already being carried out effectively and to implement them in an unskilled operation by the use of equipment capable of reading into either a comparator print-out without memory stores, i.e. straight go or no go, or alternatively a computer with memory store enabling previous tests on the vehicle and information obtained therefrom to be utilized for further comparisons.

12   REQUIREMENT FOR SENSORS

As has been noted, there are areas of the vehicle that can be partially tested without the use of built-in sensors but with the limitation, particularly in the safety area, shared by all non-destructive testing methods, that there is no measure of the margin of safety remaining. Brakes are an excellent example, as the result of a test of a braking system could be perfectly satisfactory while only minute thickness of lining or pad material remained. As already stated, sensors could be built in anywhere with doubtful viability, and if those tests that can be performed without skill should be the first to have sensors, then the following are the areas to be considered.

12.1 Braking systems

In braking systems the equipment required would be:

(a) Sensors in the linings.

(b) Sensors in the master cylinder or the system itself combined with rigidly established test procedures.

(c) Sensors in the newly developed anti-locking devices to prove their dynamic operation by tests undertaken with the vehicle stationary.

12.2 Engine

The sensors here, particularly in relation to emission control and engine wear and performance, should be, in order of priority:

(a) *Ignition timing.* Here the addition of an electro-magnetic or similar type of sensor to the flywheel, with accurately indicated points on the flywheel, would enable the ignition advance timing to be checked without the need of stroboscopic checking devices, and adjustment to be made more rapidly to correct variations.

(b) *Ignition sensor.* To operate with (a) to give speed indication by connection to No. 1 plug, although there are other methods available in checking ignition timing that do not involve direct connections to No. 1 plug. The use of this, combined with a further sensor in the king lead itself, would enable an overall check of the efficiency of the ignition system to be taken without operator participation or removal of components.

(c) *Oil integrity.* That is, pressure and flow combined with oil level check from an in-built sensor.

(d) *Electrical system.* This check should include battery electrolyte level and operation of the charging system where no ammeter is fitted. This may need to be combined with voltage and current measurement points to establish effectiveness of lighting systems or safety systems, i.e. indicators, stop lights, etc.

(e) *Fuel flow.* This is perhaps an unnecessary requirement except where detailed information is readily available, which would permit its use with dynamometry to check actual consumption performance.

12.3 Suspension

If the suspension is treated in total and not the shock absorbers alone, then sensors built-in with a test rig, which would allow the suspension to be dynamically operated (as opposed to road testing), would enable the safety feature of the suspension under carrying conditions to be checked and diagnosed. Whilst it is appreciated that shock absorbers probably exercise more influence on the suspension than other items, replacement of shock absorbers alone is by no means the cure for all possible suspension problems.

12.4 Wheels

It is debatable whether a case can be made for sensors to detect tyre pressures on passenger cars, although a case could be made for this on commercial vehicles. However, some method of tyre testing is undoubtedly required to meet legislative standards. This may involve sensors being built into the tyres themselves to give rapid indication of faults, using external detection devices for indicating wall damage or tread depth. This leads, of course, into the area of wheel balance; again, it is not felt that a case can be made for sensors to detect wheel balance as a built-in device. It is considered that the vehicle should be treated as a dynamic test operation.

13 PLUG-IN DEVICES

Depending on the number of sensors and the methods by which they are integrated into the vehicle, plug-in devices become an essential part of the test routine. If such devices are to be used, then it is vital that standardization on an international basis be achieved, particularly for legislative testing areas. Multiplicity of umbilical cords with different connectors at one end leading to different types of test equipment at the other would cause innumerable problems in standards, tolerances and accuracy of results. This is quite apart from the economics of the situation and the information required on interchangeability of such umbilical cords and the standardization of international test equipment inputs on testing routines.

14 EXTENT OF EQUIPMENT

A point worth making is that many of the tests will only be required a few times in the life of the vehicle. Therefore it may be more economic in total to have test equipment capable of being connected rapidly to the vehicle at convenient points, without sensors being built-in. This might enable the tests to be taken at the expense of a few extra minutes of test time, which may be preferable to building in the sensors to the vehicles themselves, with the possible additional areas of fault conditions arising from the sensors as opposed to the vehicles.

Certainly, some sensors are essential and these could be for brake linings and systems, and ignition timing for emission control. However, it may be that standardization of other checking points on vehicle systems might be a better solution than building in an infinite number of sensors to an infinitely variable number of points on an ever-widening range of vehicles.

Whether computer control of testing as a commercial service proposition is desirable is a debatable point; the human being is still the most satisfactory computer. Therefore, although degrees of skill vary, if equipment is designed appropriately to take into account maximum unskilled operation for diagnosis, and the operator is trained as a diagnostician, this may be a better answer than the high capital expense of fully computerized testing

systems and the cost of fitting sensors to the basic vehicles. Further, it is possible that the difficulties of maintaining sensors fitted to vehicles could create as many problems as they solve. It will be extremely difficult to achieve satisfactory results in all areas if the required data are not available, including information going back to the production stage.

Finally, equipment capable of being developed to handle diagnosis must ultimately be used as a quality checking device to prove that those items diagnosed as being defective, or in need of replacement or adjustment, have been adequately corrected to the standards required. In this case speed of operation is paramount, but it is a delicate decision as to whether to recheck all areas or only those on which work has actually been carried out. The difference between the two could mean the difference between fully built-in sensors at all times and a test system of attaching various devices as and when the tests are required.

15 ADDITIONAL CONSIDERATIONS

Points which also have to be considered to enable comparator testing, computer diagnosis or quality control systems to be effective are as follows.

(1) Availability of the test information for each vehicle and its up-dating to meet manufacturers' modifications and changes as a result of experience of the vehicles since new.

(2) Storage of information and its effective replacement by new information as it is issued, which must be capable of handling not only the new vehicle with the modification but the earlier vehicle as well.

(3) Ready identification of the vehicles by those concerned with the test, and the identification from this of the test data required for that vehicle.

(4) The ability of any such equipment to be utilized as a standard piece of equipment without information on the vehicle being tested, i.e. non-franchised vehicles or vehicles for which the service station does not have basic information. This leads to whether or not the operator's skill is needed to handle such items or whether sufficient throughput of standardized vehicles can be maintained to justify continuous, or at least economically continuous, operation.

(5) The extent to which the information produced by the computer could indicate repair orders as a result of the diagnosis, and whether or not this could be used for costing (assuming standard time information was available), operator loading and ultimately invoicing.

(6) The degree of information required arising out of (5) above to be produced to be handed to the customer as an accurate report and a cost estimate, and how flexible this might have to be to cover either repeat item testing or full quality testing.

(7) The ability of any automated system to operate with up-dated requirements of either vehicles or test equipment, i.e. the replacement of internal-combustion engines by some other means of motive power.

16 CONCLUSIONS

The main problem in producing automated test equipment is not insurmountable if the manufacturer produces a vehicle to a given set of standards, or identifies the vehicle with a set of its own performance figures. From then on, the standards and tolerances required to be used and the amendment information resulting from manufacturers' modifications must be rapidly disseminated to the test areas utilizing the equipment.

Success or failure will depend on standardization of sensors, plug-in points, test routines and test equipments. At present, these vary and the routines required by car manufacturers vary as much, if not more so. The gains in removing operator opinion and replacing it with machine fact could have a marked customer reaction, but could lead to a significant increase in servicing costs by indicating a requirement for more replacements and servicing, the extent of which would be proportional to the tolerances applied.

MOTOR CYCLE ELECTRICAL EQUIPMENT

C113/72

D. W. NORTON*

This paper discusses motor cycle electrical equipment from its beginnings, and traces its development up to the present, with some comments on possible future trends. The equipment described is divided into sections following this past, present and future pattern where possible. Various diagrams are included to illustrate certain parts more clearly.

1 INTRODUCTION

THIS PAPER reviews developments in motor cycle electrical equipment, describes the items of electrical equipment in general use at the present time, and mentions possible future trends where appropriate. The main emphasis is placed on ignition and generating systems because these have been the major areas of development.

2 IGNITION

2.1 Historical

The earliest motor cycles employed a trembler coil ignition system fed from a small battery. Since the engines were slow speed and low compression, ignition timing was not critical and they worked satisfactorily on the 'shower of sparks' produced by the coil.

The introduction of the h.t. (high-tension) magneto in the early years of the century provided an ignition unit that was independent of an external source of supply, and gave the accuracy of timing necessary to cater for developing engine performances. With advances in permanent magnet materials, the original rotating wound armature designs gave way to rotating magnet machines. Magneto ignition was used universally on motor cycles until the 1950s: the principle is still employed in some flywheel generator units used on mopeds, scooters and small motor cycles.

2.2 Flywheel generators

The flywheel generator, usually a composite unit providing current for both ignition and lighting purposes, has a rotating permanent magnet field system forming an integral part of the engine flywheel. One limb of the stator is used for ignition, carrying either a complete magneto-type winding or a generating winding, which feeds an ignition coil. Because of space limitations, in the latter instance an externally mounted coil is usually preferred. A cam-operated contact breaker is incorporated.

2.3 Energy transfer ignition

The arrangement of generating coil and external ignition coil referred to above is known as an energy transfer

The MS. of this paper was received at the Institution on 19th June 1972 and accepted for publication on 23rd June 1972. 43
* J. Lucas Ltd, Chester St, Birmingham B6 4AL.

system. Fig. 113.1 shows the circuit. The generating winding is short-circuited by the contacts, closed at a maximum flux position. When the contacts open, the current flowing through them passes instead through the primary winding. This rapid build-up of current produces the flux, which gives rise to the high secondary winding voltage. It should be noted that the spark occurs at the plug with the build-up of current, not with the collapse, as in conventional coil ignition systems. Because of this the iron circuit of the ignition coil is completely closed, as in a transformer, unlike the open construction of the conventional ignition coil. The energy transfer system is used extensively on two-stroke engines, where, because of fixed ignition timing, it works extremely well.

When used on four-stroke engines, which need advance and retard, particular attention must be paid to maintaining accuracy of magnetic timing. Fig. 113.2 shows the variation of plug voltage with magnetic timing. Some larger motor cycles equipped with alternators also employ energy transfer ignition, when certain of the alternator windings are used for this purpose (Fig. 113.3).

2.4 Flywheel generators with electronic ignition

Later developments in flywheel generators have eliminated the contact breaker, replacing it with a magnetic pulse generator feeding into an electronic system. One example is shown in Fig. 113.4. A coil is used to generate current, which charges a capacitor via a rectifier. The pulse generator provides a voltage at the required instant, which, again via a rectifier, switches on a thyristor. This allows the capacitor to discharge through the primary winding of an h.t. transformer, thus producing the h.t. voltage in the secondary winding.

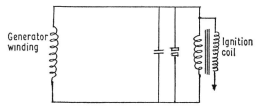

Fig. 113.1. Energy transfer circuit using a flywheel generator

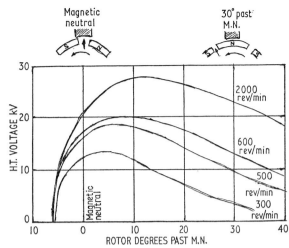

Fig. 113.2. Diagram showing h.t. voltage variation with magnetic timing

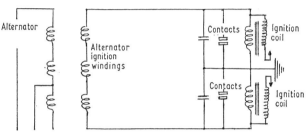

Fig. 113.3. Energy transfer circuit for twin-cylinder machine using an alternator

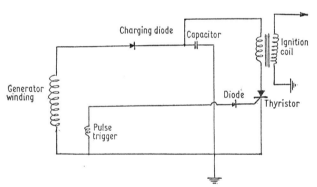

Fig. 113.4. Electronic ignition circuit (flywheel generator operated)

The electronic ignition flywheel generator is becoming increasingly popular, particularly for use on competition machines. It has the advantages of being unaffected by water and not requiring any external source of supply.

2.5 Coil ignition

While ignition systems for smaller motor cycles developed as described, larger machines have mostly changed to a conventional coil ignition system, separate contact breakers and coils being used for each cylinder. The contact breakers are carried on a baseplate usually mounted in the timing cover, the cam being carried on an auto-advance mechanism mounted in the end of a camshaft. Contact breaker designs have improved considerably over the years, progressing from phenolic resin heels to the present lightweight nylon design, capable of satisfactory performance up to 12 000 engine rev/min.

Smaller ignition coils have been developed for motor

cycle applications, space being at a premium. These are basically identical to the larger car coils, being in effect an auto-transformer with an open iron circuit.

In order to ensure adequate 'build-up' time for the primary circuit, the contact breaker closed period, controlled by the cam, is 160°. The cam forms part of the auto-advance mechanism, which is centrifugal in action. The advance curve shape is not critical: in most cases only a retard position for starting is required, the engine then running fully advanced.

Emergency starting (i.e. with the battery discharged) is, of course, a necessary requirement. With earlier 6-V alternators, this was made possible by switching four of the six alternator coils from charging to ignition purposes. Fig. 113.5 shows the arrangement for single-cylinder machines. For twin-cylinder machines the arrangement differs: the basic energy transfer circuit is applied to one cylinder, while the second relies on the battery recharging—simultaneously carried out by the remaining two alternator coils—to provide ignition.

With the advent of the 12-V Zener diode-controlled alternator system, the emergency start circuit was simplified. All six coils of the alternator are permanently connected to the battery. With the battery discharged, the six-coil output provides starting, no switching of coils being required.

Starting can be made easier still, and 'no battery running' obtained, by fitting a 5000-μF electrolytic capacitor in parallel with the battery. If the battery is discharged or has been removed, the capacitor stores the rectified pulses from the alternator, giving them back as additional energy to assist starting.

2.6 'Contact breakerless' coil ignition

As with the flywheel generator, the latest development of the coil ignition system has eliminated the contact breaker. An electromagnetic pick-up or pulse generator replaces the contact breaker, generating a voltage that is fed into an electronic switching circuit controlling the operating of a power transistor in the ignition coil primary circuit (Fig. 113.6). This electronic ignition system will doubtless become more widely used in the future.

3 GENERATING AND CHARGING SYSTEMS
3.1 Historical

An early form of generator used on motor cycles was the combined magneto-generator, employing the primary

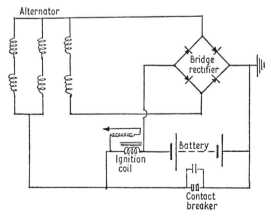

Fig. 113.5. Emergency starting circuit

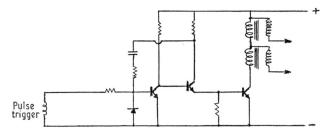

Fig. 113.6. Electronic ignition circuit (battery operated)

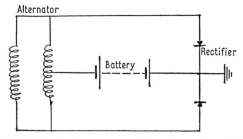

Fig. 113.7. Early alternator with push–pull rectification, 6 V

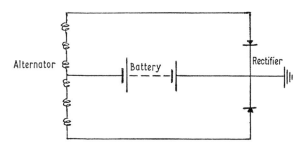

Fig. 113.8. Later alternator with push–pull rectification, 6 V

current of the magneto to provide lighting. The a.c. current was used as generated, and no battery was fitted. Bulbs were 6 V and of modest wattage. The current available was limited to a value that the contact breaker could handle without excessive sparking. Consequently, the lighting provided was not really adequate.

A step forward was made in the form of a separate d.c. dynamo, first with third brush and later with automatic voltage control of output. The yoke diameter was 3 in, and the armature was positioned eccentrically within the frame, achieved by having only one field winding on one pole piece, the other pole being formed in the yoke. The output of such a generator, as finally developed, was 60 W at 6 V.

3.2 Alternators

The next stage in generator development was the introduction of the alternator, designed in such a manner that the stator could be mounted either in the primary chaincase or the timing cover and the rotor driven on an extension of the crankshaft, so eliminating the need for an additional drive, which is necessary for d.c. dynamos. A further attraction was, as already mentioned, the inclusion of emergency starting should the battery be discharged. Although a discharged battery did not affect a magneto-ignition machine, the change from magneto to coil ignition was in progress, and this ability to start with a discharged battery was thus of prime importance.

The first design was an inductor-type alternator, having static field magnets, generating windings and a multiple-pole iron rotor, the purpose of which was to effect the flux changes necessary to generate current. The a.c. generated in the windings was converted into d.c. by selenium plate rectifiers. The windings were centre tapped and two rectifier plates used in a 'push–pull' circuit (Fig. 113.7). A 6-V system was retained, the output being about 50 W.

The inductor alternator was quickly superseded by the first of the current types of rotating-field alternator. With this design six magnets were employed, each being situated on one face of a central steel hexagon, through the centre of which was the hole to accommodate the crankshaft. The outer end of each magnet was capped with iron laminations and the whole assembly die cast in aluminium. The hexagonal-shaped stator consisted of laminations having six poles, round each of which was a generating winding. The coils were connected in series and joined to the external circuit, as shown in Fig. 113.8. 'Push–pull' rectification was still employed.

Because rectifier failures were experienced under emergency starting conditions, two coils were wound on each pole and connected in series parallel. The complica-

tion of 12 windings had now more than offset the cost saving obtained by using push–pull instead of bridge rectification (i.e. two rectifier plates as against four), and therefore the generator was redesigned to function with a bridge circuit. A return was made to six windings, these being connected two in series, three pairs in parallel (Fig. 113.9). Output of this alternator arrangement was 60–70 W at 6 V.

As the next step a smaller size, circular-frame alternator having a more efficient rotor field system was introduced, providing the same output as the previous hexagonal frame alternator. Additional increase in load demand resulted in a change to 12 V, as the easiest way of increasing output further. By this means the cable used in the harness could remain the same thickness and, more important, the same alternator could be used since, being basically a constant-current machine, it would produce almost twice the output, i.e. 120 W.

Up to this point, alternator output had been controlled by the lighting switch, which connected and disconnected the alternator windings as required. Obviously, this arrangement suffered from the same disadvantages as

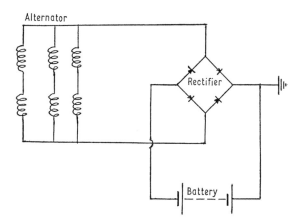

Fig. 113.9. Alternator with bridge rectification, 6 V

the third-brush dynamo, viz. that the output was not sensitive to the battery charge condition. This shortcoming had been accepted at the outset when a permanent magnet field system was chosen, since it was felt that the 'flat battery starting condition' more than compensated for this shortcoming.

With the availability of the power Zener diode, a simple yet effective method of charge control became possible. The Zener diode is a semiconductor device connected in the circuit in such a manner that current will flow through it only when the voltage applied to the diode has reached a predetermined value known as the breakdown voltage. Hence, if a Zener diode having a value of breakdown voltage similar to that of a fully charged battery (about 14·5 V) is connected across the battery, then once the latter attains its fully charged condition the diode will conduct. Excess energy is thereby dissipated as heat in the Zener diode. Provided that the Zener diode seats flat on its heat sink and there is an air flow for cooling, a reliable charge-control system results.

Zener diodes currently available, operating with the degree of cooling possible in motor cycle applications, can absorb up to 10 A, which means that, allowing for ignition current, maximum output is about 11·5 A. This limit will shortly be reached when improved alternators with higher energy magnets become available. Following the introduction of Zener charge control, the internal connections of the stator were further modified, such that there are now two sets of three coils in parallel (Fig. 113.10).

3.3 Rectifiers
Alongside the development of the alternator, improvements in rectification were made. The original selenium plate rectifiers were somewhat marginal in performance. The peak inverse voltage that they would stand was about 18 V and the reverse leakage current about 10 mA. Hence, if left connected when the machine was not in use, the battery would become discharged. Furthermore, with such a low p.i.v. (peak inverse voltage) there was danger of breakdown, particularly if the battery should accidentally become disconnected.

With the advent of the silicon diode the situation vastly improved, the p.i.v. increased to 400 V and reverse current reduced to 5 μA. With this margin in hand, even though the battery were to become disconnected, the open circuit voltage of the alternator (about 250 V maximum) could do no damage. Hence the combination of the silicon diode and an encapsulated alternator stator produced an extremely reliable system.

3.4 Flywheel generators
Reference has already been made to these generators in connection with ignition. In general they are utilized on small two-stroke engines, in many instances supplying lighting and ignition loads directly without the use of a battery. Outputs vary from about 18 W at 6 V up to 80 W at 12 V, the latter being used in conjunction with a rectifier and battery.

Dealing with the smaller sizes first, these are normally of four- or six-pole construction and carry a variety of windings. One may be used to supply the headlamp, one the ignition, one the tail-lamp and one the stop-lamp. Each winding is designed to supply a constant load, so that the headlamp bulb should have main and dip filaments of equal wattage, e.g. 18/18 W. In certain designs one or more of the generating coils is used to charge a battery, working through a single rectifier element—a system known as half-wave rectification. While being a cheap way of charging a battery, it is less efficient since it utilizes only one-half of the a.c. cycle.

Larger flywheel generators invariably employ batteries, charged through either half- or full-wave rectifiers. They are normally of six-pole design. The rectified output fed into the battery is utilized to provide current for operating the horn, tail-lamp and, if fitted, direction indicators. In most cases the headlamp is supplied directly from the generator, bulb wattages being up to 35/35 W. There are instances where the flywheel stator windings have been modified so that they are all connected via a bridge full-wave rectifier to charge a 12-V battery, the charge being controlled by a Zener diode in the same manner as for the alternators previously described.

A device for protecting headlamps from excessive voltages when they are fed directly from the generator is the clipper diode. This device, in effect, comprises two Zener diodes connected back-to-back so that current flow is opposed in both directions until the breakdown voltage of the diode is exceeded. Once the diode conducts, the voltage across it remains approximately equal to the breakdown voltage even though current may vary considerably. Thus if a clipper diode is connected across bulbs fed directly from the generator, excessive voltages will be prevented from being applied to the bulbs. Like the Zener diode, the clipper diode requires a suitable heat sink to ensure satisfactory operation (Fig. 113.11).

3.5 Batteries
Earlier 6-V batteries had containers made in a pitch-based composition, with individual cell lids sealed into position with pitch. Connections between adjacent cells were made by external lead bars on the top of the lid. Wooden separators were employed and venting was achieved through holes in the individual screw-in-type filler plugs. A cover protected the intercell connectors and terminals from accidental short-circuiting. Typical capacity was 13·5 Ah (20-h rate).

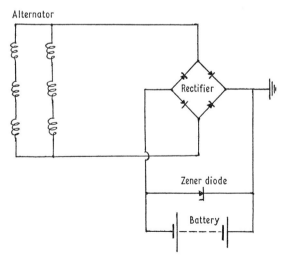

Fig. 113.10. Alternator with bridge rectification and Zener diode charge control, 12 V

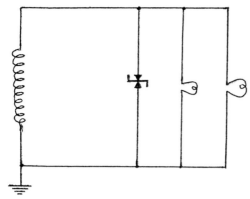

Fig. 113.11. Direct lighting circuit, clipper diode
controlled

During the early 1950s, advances in materials technology brought about significant changes in battery design. The case material became polystyrene copolymer (a translucent plastic) and the intercell links were concealed within a one-piece lid, which was sealed to the case by epoxy resin. To combat a vibration problem improved separators were introduced, made in a synthetic material. Individual filler plugs and venting were retained.

With the coming of 12-V electrical systems a new battery was introduced having a transparent container made of styrene—acrylonitrile. The lid design was improved to incorporate a one-piece manifold, which vented all six cells to atmosphere, provision being made for fitting a venting tube if required. The individual screw-in filler plugs were replaced by press-in plugs carried on a single plastic strip. A typical capacity of 10 Ah (20-h rate) represented a suitable compromise between capacity and bulk.

The use in recent years of electric starters on motor cycles brought new design considerations. For satisfactory starter performance as much plate surface area as possible is required, demanding more and thinner plates, while the internal resistance (tending to increase with the use of extra plates) must be maintained at an acceptable level. Designs have been introduced conforming to these requirements.

4 ELECTRIC STARTERS

A number of motor cycles have from time to time been equipped with electric starters, normally of manually pre-engaged pattern, but for one reason or another production of such machines has been discontinued. Other machines were fitted with a dual-purpose generating and starter unit mounted on the crankshaft, a system employed on some foreign machines. Although absolutely quiet in operation, this type of combined unit has inherent disadvantages in performance.

The picture has changed completely, however, with the Japanese 'invasion' of world motor cycle markets. Most of these machines employ a constant-mesh starter layout. A pinion on the starter motor shaft forms the sun gear of an epicyclic gearbox, mounted directly on to the drive end of the motor. The output shaft carries a gear that meshes with a second gear carried on a roller clutch attached to the engine crankshaft. Overall gearing varies with engine capacity: on machines of 250–450 cm³ the ratio is about 14·5:1.

Several starter installations are currently under development for British motor cycles, and these show successful performance at temperatures down to 0°C or below. One of these, for a 750-cm³ twin application, employs a small compact gearbox giving a reduction of 50:1 in one stage. The gearbox is mounted directly on to the end of the starter, the shaft of which carries an eccentric turning a large diameter gear. This meshes with a stationary gearring housed in the gearbox body. By means of a double slider, the eccentric motion of the gear is transferred to the output shaft, which runs concentric with the input shaft. A non-reversing clutch, mounted on the gearbox output shaft, carries a sprocket, from which is chain driven a second sprocket mounted co-axially with the half-speed pinion meshing with the crankshaft gear. Overall reduction is about 24:1. Although this may appear excessive, it should be borne in mind that the engine has a compression ratio of 10:1 and a high cranking resistance. As a relatively small battery is used (16 Ah), the nominal 12-V battery potential falls to about 7·8 V during cranking.

In order to obtain satisfactory ignition performance, a ballasted system is employed, entailing the use of a resistor in series with the supply to the two ignition coils (of nominal 6-V pattern), only one of which draws current at any given time. The value of the resistor is the same as the primary resistance of one coil. During cranking, the resistor is shorted out by additional contacts on the solenoid starter switch, and the ignition coils operate directly on the depressed battery voltage. During normal running, half the system voltage is dropped across the ballast resistor, so that, again, the coils operate at nominal voltage.

With the solenoid-operated, pre-engaged-type starter sometimes used, the solenoid operating current is too high for the starter button to handle directly, so a relay is necessary in the circuit. It seems certain that the use of starters will expand on future motor cycles.

5 LIGHTING

5.1 Headlamps

The pattern of headlighting development has, in general, been similar to that for cars, going through the stages of:

(1) separate 'silvered' reflector and fluted front glass, with bulb focusing by an adjustable bulb holder,
(2) combined aluminized reflector and front lens assembly with prefocus bulb,
(3) 'sealed beam' light unit.

As generator capacities have increased, filament ratings have risen from the 30/24-W bulbs of the d.c. dynamo era to 45/40-W filaments used in modern 12-V sealed beam units. Further improvement in headlighting will be centred on the use of quartz-halogen bulbs; these are at present optional on one machine and others will surely follow.

The introduction of sealed beam units, in 7-in and $5\frac{3}{4}$-in diameter conforming to the standard sizes specified in America, provided the main impetus to standardization. This was, perhaps, the beginning of American influence, not only on lighting but on the design of all motor cycle electrical equipment, an influence that is increasing.

5.2 Rear lamps

Similarly, changes in rear lamp design and materials have progressively resulted in larger, more powerful combined stop, tail and number plate lamps conforming to world-wide requirements. A further improvement in design is to follow shortly, to meet an American legal requirement for January 1973.

6 SIGNALLING

6.1 Direction indicators

The use of direction indicators on motor cycles began with the Ariel 'Leader', and the practice was quickly taken up by Japanese manufacturers. Already a legal requirement in America, they are now also invariably fitted in this country as original equipment. A four-lamp system (an American requirement) is used, with 21-W bulbs for 12-V systems and 18-W for 6-V systems.

6.2 Horns

Electric horns are commonly of high-frequency type, in which the note is produced by an arrangement of armature, flexible diaphragm and tone disc. When the self-interruptory, electro-magnetic horn movement is energized, the diaphragm vibrates and the impact of the armature on the core face sets the tone disc vibrating at a higher frequency. These two sets of vibrations combine with their various overtones to give the horn its characteristic note. During the process of development, such horns have been greatly reduced in size and weight, while at the same time performance has increased, in particular to meet American and Italian legal requirements.

Wind-tone horns are in limited use. In this horn, an electro-magnetically vibrated steel diaphragm sets in motion the column of air in the horn flare. The flare is of involute form, the horn note becoming lower as the involute is lengthened. Such horns are used on touring machines and very largely on police motor cycles where two horns of different pitch, in conjunction with a suitable relay, are arranged to give the familiar two-tone warning signal.

7 SWITCHGEAR AND INSTRUMENTS

7.1 Switchgear

At the time that motor cycles were equipped with a third-brush dynamo and magneto ignition, the lighting switch incorporated charge-rate control so that in the 'off' and 'pilot' positions a low output was given, the full output being obtained when the 'head' position was selected. The same switch, minus the charge rate control, remained in use when the dynamo with automatic voltage control was introduced.

The advent of alternators and the emergence of coil ignition systems necessitated the use of more complicated switching embodying separately mounted but electrically linked lighting and ignition switches. The latter was required to include the emergency start position described previously.

Introduction of Zener-diode-controlled, 12-V charging systems brought a return to more simple switching. The lighting switch controlled only lights, and the ignition switch was a simple key-operated, two-position device. Perhaps it was oversimplified, since complaints were made

of interference with parked motor cycles, lights and horns being too easily operated. As an antidote, a more complicated four-position switch was designed where, except for parking lights, nothing could be operated with the ignition key removed.

More recently, handlebar-mounted, multi-function switches were introduced, the switch-body casting being designed to carry either the clutch or front brake lever, depending on which side the switch is mounted. One switch has 'dipper', 'horn' and 'headlamp flash' functions; the other, 'direction indicators', 'emergency stop' and 'starter button'. A recent addition is the inclusion of a front brake switch inside the casting. To complete the system a two-position 'turnbuckle' switch is mounted in the headlamp body, changing from 'pilot' to 'head' and vice versa.

Further changes will be required in the near future to satisfy pending American requirements. These will include clear marking of each function and changes to the design of the emergency stop switch. Redesign will certainly be required, which may make possible the inclusion of the 'pilot' to 'head' switch in one of the handlebar clusters, and possibly the return to a simple two-position ignition switch.

With the introduction of braking lights, several designs of brake switches were produced. At first, brake switches were fitted only to the rear brake, but later, to satisfy American requirements, front brake switches were added. Current designs include, for the rear, a plastic-bodied push-on switch; for the front, a compression switch mounted in line with the front brake Bowden cable.

7.2 Ammeter

During the period that the d.c. dynamo was commonly used on motor cycles it was normal practice to mount an ammeter either in the headlamp body or, very occasionally, as part of a petrol-tank-mounted instrument panel. However, as in motor car practice, the use of an ammeter has today become out of fashion.

7.3 Warning lights

Warning lights, mounted in the headlamp and with various lens colourings, are employed to monitor the operation of headlamp main beam, charging system, direction-indicator equipment and engine oil pressure.

8 CONCLUSION

Particularly during the past 10 years, sweeping changes have been made in motor cycle electrical equipment, partly due to design changes, but even more so by additions to the specification. Apart from electric starters, which have already been mentioned, and extra warning lights, such as a neutral gear indicator, it seems probable that there will be little additional equipment on motor cycles in the coming years.

In essence, motor cycles should be light machines, easy to handle and therefore safe machines. Already their weight is really heavier than is desirable. Thus although design change and improvement are always acceptable, it would be a retrograde step to make the motor cycle any heavier or more expensive by the addition of further equipment.

C114/72

RADIO NOISE INTERFERENCE CHARACTERISTICS OF AUTOMOTIVE VEHICLES, INCLUDING ELECTRIC VEHICLES, IN JAPAN

F. MINOZUMA*

This paper reviews earlier research work carried out in Japan and quotes measured radio-frequency field strength results for production cars on frequencies between 30 and 200 MHz during the past 20 years and, during the last three years, between 200 and 1000 MHz. The effectiveness of various methods of suppression is discussed. Recent work is described and proposed methods of correction are given.

1 INTRODUCTION

FROM 1949 TO 1950 the author had been working on a theoretical approach to improve the effect of the noise measuring meter (1)† (2). Assuming the limited response of the detector, probability distribution functions were obtained as IF output. Using input functions for the detector, the output efficiency was calculated for quasi-peak, IF envelope average and r.m.s. detectors.

Fig. 114.1 shows the calculated results of the detector for recurrent pulses. The abscissa indicates a product of $gRnP$, where g is the mutual conductance of a detector diode, R the detector load resistance, n the number of pulses per second and P is twice the inverse bandwidth frequency. The product nP must be considered when comparing the characteristics of input pulses; P is a common transmission time interval or spectrum, and gives an indication of the resolution capability of the receiver. These curves are comparable with CISPR curves to a first approximation.

Fig. 114.2 shows the detection efficiency for the input of white noise; the parameter is gR and the abscissa is nP or $2n/B$, where B is the bandwidth frequency of the receiver. The figure also compares several quasi-peak detectors with IF envelope and r.m.s. detectors.

These characteristics of bandwidth limitation and resolution of input noise pulses are very important features of the RF noise meter in communications. The author also found the characteristic response curves for human ears and eyes (Fig. 114.3).

From these results, it was found that only a detector of $gR = 500$ could be used reasonably as the subjective interference meter in the case of amplitude modulated carrier waves over quite a wide range. The pulse resolving power of the meter is shown by the distinctively different slope of the curves at around 0·1 or 0·2 of the abscissa

values. This theory was accepted at the inquiry of the Japanese Radio Technical Consulting Committee, Ministry of Posts and Telecommunications, in 1952.

2 IGNITION RADIO NOISE FROM AUTOMOBILES IN JAPAN

Radio-frequency noise interference from automobile cars in Japan was studied by the author in 1950, and the results of a survey on city noise were used to estimate the service area at the beginning of Japanese commercial radio broadcasting in 1950. The results of another survey on noise from automobile ignition, and its distribution with time and location, were used at the start of Japanese TV broadcasting in 1952 (3) (4). From the elaborate field surveys of VHF city noise, the author determined the ignition noise that had most effect on VHF broadcasting and land mobile communications.

An equivalent circuit was tested with noise measurements of the ignition system, together with sine wave signals inserted into the noise source terminal. Sharp pulses from spark plugs and distributor gaps were also inserted. By this system, and with measurements of circuit impedance and circuit constants, automobile RF noise characteristics were easily simulated and the effects of many methods of suppression were tested. Details of these methods will not be given here as it is intended to present a summary of the results of automobile RF noise measurements and suppression effects (4).

2.1 Measured results for automobile RF noise field strength of automobiles in the range 30–200 MHz

From 1950 to 1957, radio-frequency noise measurements for automobiles were carried out for typical production cars, and studies were made on the effectiveness of suppression techniques using, for example, a 5–15 kΩ resistor or resistor plug (5). In 1961 a resistance cord was developed, and 1964 saw the development of a resistance wire, or a resistance wire with a ferrite core cable. Examples of the average values of many results are shown in Fig.

The MS. of this paper was received at the Institution on 23rd March 1972 and accepted for publication on 26th June 1972. 22
* Society of Automotive Engineers of Japan Inc., 16–15 Takanawa 1 chome, Minato-ku, Tokyo, Japan.
† References are given in Appendix 114.1.

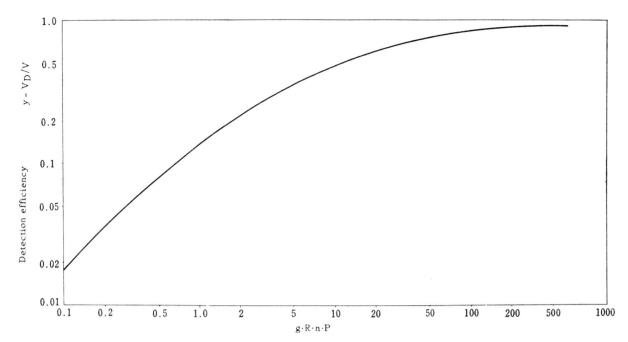

Fig. 114.1. Response of the quasi-peak detector with an input of periodic pulses

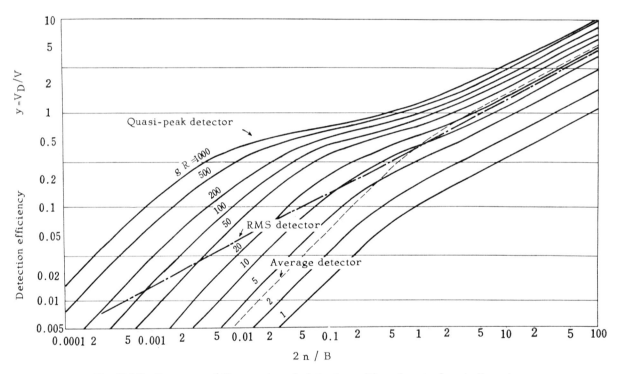

Fig. 114.2. Response of the quasi-peak detector with an input of periodic pulses

114.4, where suffix 1 indicates the 1958 results, 2 the 1962 results, 3 the 1964 results and 4 the 1966 results (6) (7). No suppression was used for group A curves, while group B curves were obtained after the application of several suppression methods; these curves show average values for many samples of production cars. Curve C1 is an upper limit and curve C2 a lower limit of the results obtained using some suppression methods for typical production cars in 1968. Fig. 114.5 shows some results of the suppression effect using a common suppression resistor, resistance cord and resistance wire with ferrite core cable. Group A curves show the results of the resistance wire with ferrite

core cable: A3 for 1964 and A4 for 1966. Group B curves are for the resistance cord: B2 for 1962, B3 for 1964 and B4 for 1966. Group C curves are for the resistance wire cable: C3 for 1964 and C4 for 1966. Group D curves are for the suppression resistor: D1 for 1958, D2 for 1962, D3 for 1964 and D4 for 1966. At the higher frequencies the suppression effectiveness is clearly shown in the case of a resistance wire with ferrite core cable and secondary resistance cord, and equally clearly the ineffectiveness of the common suppression resistor. This tendency increases at the higher frequencies of 1000 MHz although some resonance effects exist.

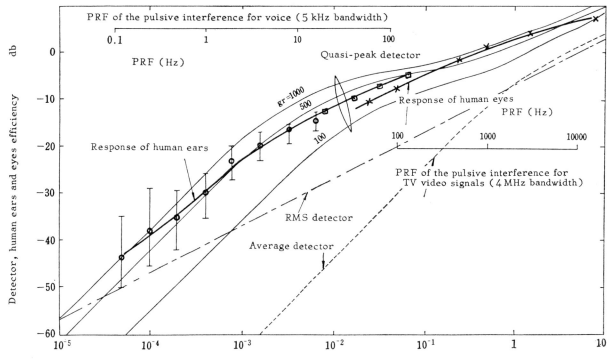

Fig. 114.3. Response characteristics of various detectors, human ears and eyes

2.2 Measured results in the range 200–1000 MHz

In 1969, at the start of the utilization of UHF for TV broadcasting in larger cities, the Radio Consulting Committee of the Ministry of Posts and Telecommunications sought a permissible level of RF noise for automobiles.

During the last three years, the committee of which I was the chairman has been surveying the RF noise field intensity and suppression effect for various automobiles (7). Fig. 114.6 shows the results of 37 types of common production cars with engines of 360–2600 cm³—sedans,

wagons, trucks and minis—and the results of motorcycles with engines of 90–750 cm³, using as the suppressor a resistance cord or a resistance wire with ferrite core cable. In addition, a shielded resistor is used at the head of an ignition plug to increase the suppression effect.

Fig. 114.6a–e shows results obtained with and without suppression and for horizontal and vertical polarizations of the CISPR type RF noise field meter. Curves present the recommended permissible limits of CISPR, the median values of measured samples, and levels for a sigma or twice sigma estimated probability. These results show that the recommended limits of CISPR are satisfied, i.e. 85·3 per cent by the resistance cord, 90·8 per cent by the resistance wire ferrite core cable, 92·5 per cent by the resistance cord plus shielded resistance at the plug head and 94·0 per cent by the resistance wire with a ferrite core cable plus shielded resistance at the plug head. Further studies show that the limits of CISPR are easily satisfied by proper bonding of the engine bonnet and body.

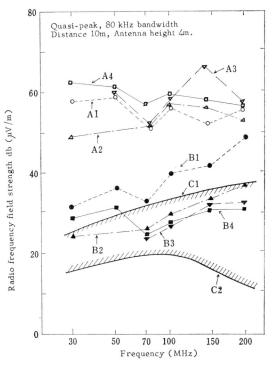

Fig. 114.4. Radio-frequency noise field strength measured results for various automobiles

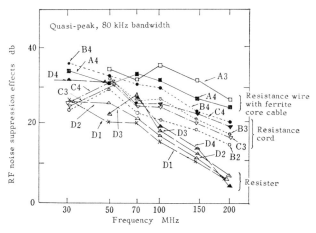

Fig. 114.5. Radio-frequency noise suppression effects for various automobiles

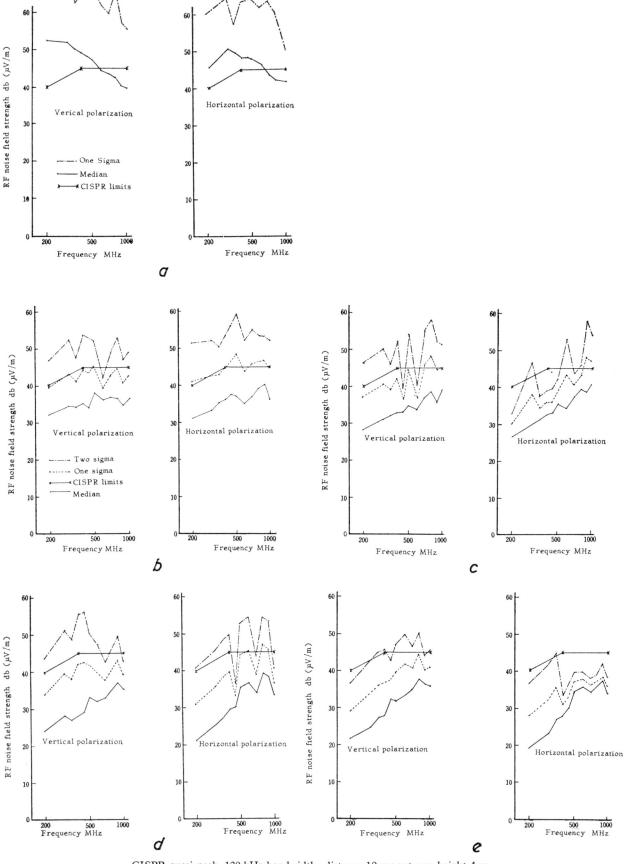

CISPR quasi-peak, 120 kHz bandwidth; distance 10 m; antenna height 4 m.

a Without suppression.   b Resistance cord.   c Resistance wire with ferrite core cable.
d Resistance cord plus shield resistor.   e Resistance wire with ferrite core cable plus shield resistor.

Fig. 114.6. RF noise field strength for 37 various common production automobiles

2.3 Measured results in the range 30 to 1000 MHz using automatic frequency sweeping with electronic tuning and switching

In 1969 the author was commissioned to design an automatic frequency sweep type RF noise intensity meter; after overcoming budget difficulties it was completed in 1971 (8). Fig. 114.7 shows measured results in X–Y plotter displays for some typical cars with simple noise suppres-

sion (9), but since this equipment is designed for computer displays after A–D conversion, the frequency response characteristics do not permit the use of strict calibration levels. The speed of the automatic frequency sweep is 1·5 s in cathode ray display, 15 s in the X–Y plotter display and 150 s in computer display, and even at the slowest speed strong carrier interferences can be eliminated from the noise data.

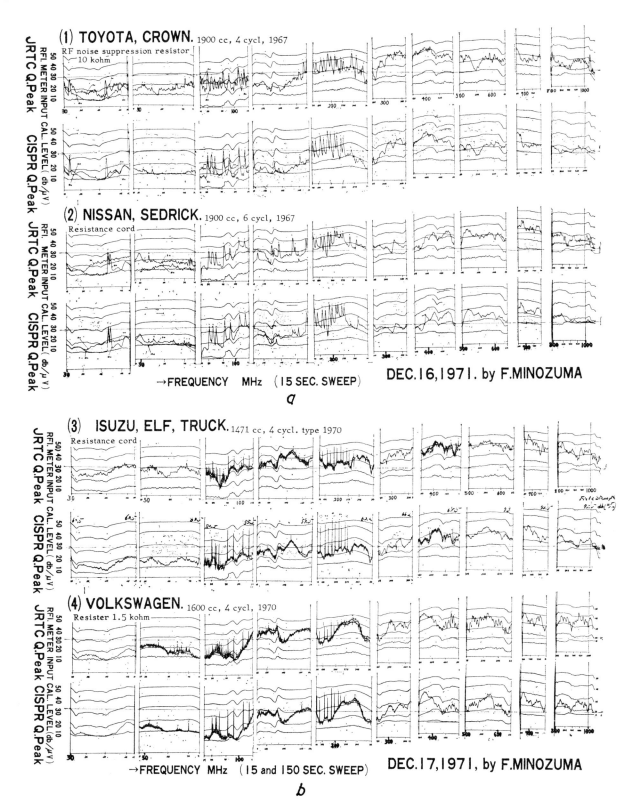

Fig. 114.7. Radio-frequency noise field strength of automobiles

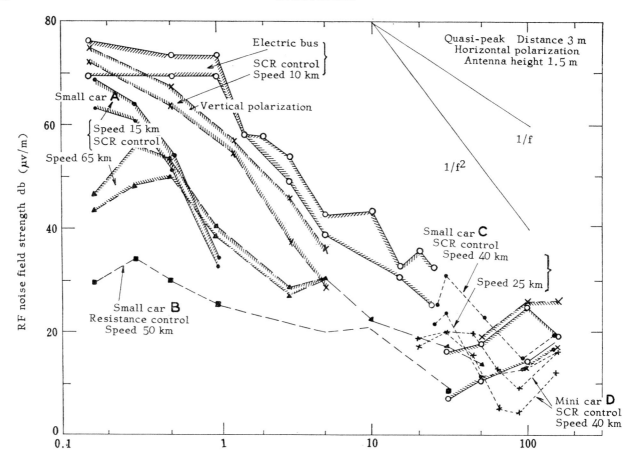

Fig. 114.8. Radio-frequency noise field strengths for electric bus and small cars

This interference protecting effect for RF noise measurement characteristics is a very predominant feature which does not require a specially shielded room for measurement.

The range between 30 and 1000 MHz was divided into 10 bands, using bands 1 and 2 (30–75 MHz) for wide band dipole and bands 3–10 (75–1000 MHz) for wide band log periodic antenna. These bandwidths are selected easily and conveniently by a choice of vari-cap diode and required circuit Q or sensitivity, but it should be possible to reduce the bands by half in the near future.

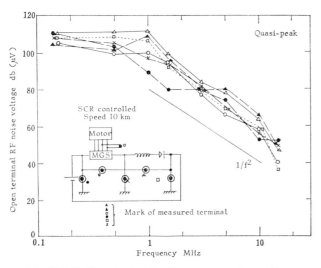

Fig. 114.9. Terminal radio-frequency noise voltage for electric bus

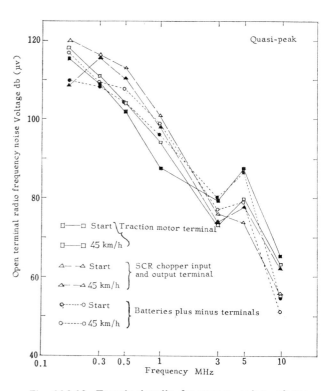

Fig. 114.10. Terminal radio-frequency noise voltage for SCR controlled small car

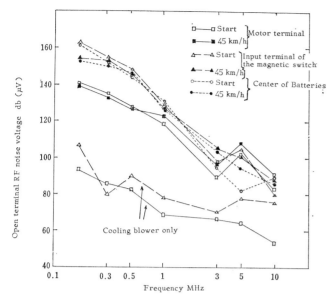

Fig. 114.11. Radio-frequency noise voltage at the pick-up small loop coil for SCR controlled small car

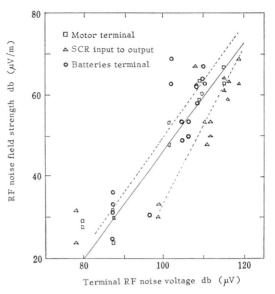

Fig. 114.13. Correlation between radio-frequency noise field strength and terminal voltage for SCR controlled small car

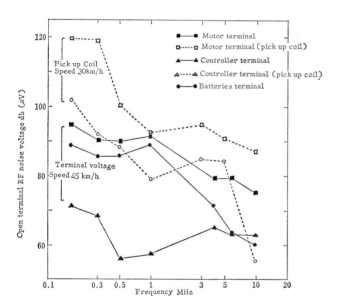

Fig. 114.12. Terminal radio-frequency noise voltage for resistance controlled small car

A. General Circuit

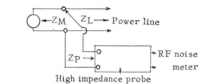

B. Insertion of the LC in power line

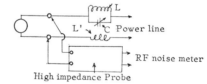

C. Equivalent circuit of a Motor

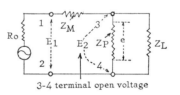

3-4 terminal open voltage

Fig. 114.14. Measuring circuit for corrected open terminal voltage

3 RF NOISE, MEASURED RESULTS FOR ELECTRIC VEHICLES

The first electric vehicle in Japan was developed about 30 years ago, and about 4000 cars were used for several years after the Second World War. Since 1965 we have been concerned with a new type of electric vehicle. An investigating committee was established in 1968 and about 70 cars were used at Osaka EXPO 1970; several hundred are now in use.

The electric vehicle generates severe radio noise interference for the unit's radio receiver, and interference is especially severe at the lower frequencies. The author has been surveying the radio noise characteristics of the two types of electric vehicle, resistance and SCR chopper controlled car.

Fig. 114.8 shows the measured results on experimental cars of radio noise field strength between 150 kHz and 150 MHz, and the field strength dB (μV/m) is roughly proportional to the inverse square of frequency, but some resonant frequencies exist. Interference is not severe above 10 MHz but is very strong below 1 MHz. From a comparison of the SCR chopper and the resistance controlled d.c. series motor types, the SCR chopper type gives much more severe interference than the resistance type, where the noise source is the d.c. traction and cooling blower motors.

Fig. 114.9 shows the open terminal (measuring equipment) radio noise voltage of an electric bus. The six curves show different measured points in the control box, but there is no significant difference between these curves because the circuits are close together at the terminals of the box. Terminal voltage dB (μV) is measured by the RF noise meter using a low input impedance probe of

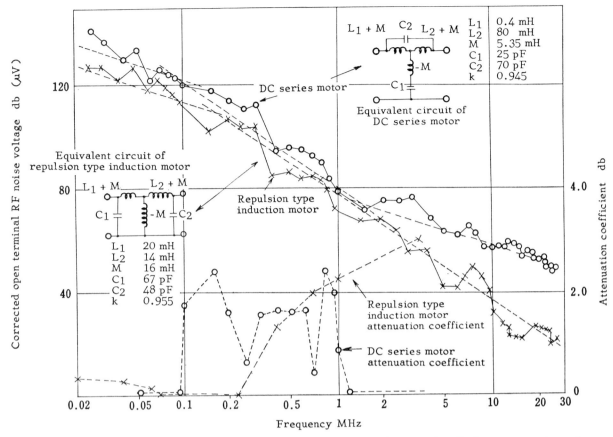

Fig. 114.15. Corrected open terminal radio-frequency noise voltage. Corrected radio-frequency noise voltage

known value, corrected to the open terminal voltage condition.

Fig. 114.10 shows the RF noise voltage at the open terminal of a traction d.c. motor, at the input and output of the SCR chopper and at battery positive and negative terminals. Batteries are installed in three divided portions, back and both sides under the floor. The SCR chopper with a blower motor and magnetic switch is sited left of centre and the traction motor is at front centre, coupled to a transmission box. The wirings between them are routed in the open air and no attempt has been made to shield or bond them. The RF noise voltage is measured at starting torque and at a speed of 45 km/h. Fig. 114.11 is the result of the RF noise voltage measured by a 15 cm diameter shielded pick-up coil at a distance of 2 cm from the wiring; the measured voltage is corrected to the open terminal RF noise level. The two lower curves show results for the cooling blower motor of the SCR control unit only, and while values are not very significant they cannot be neglected. During these measurements, d.c. loading current was between 30 and 150 amperes.

Fig. 114.12 shows similar results for a resistance controlled car. Fig. 114.13 is one example of a correlation between the RF noise field strength and the terminal voltage, but these cannot be measured at the same time. RF noise induced currents on the body are measured at about 20 points, but are not shown here. The distribution of such induced currents, measured in two-dimensional co-ordinates perpendicular to the surface, is very important information for the improvement of noise interference and for checking the effectiveness of shielding or bonding.

The above examples were measured and discussed by

the research committee consulted by the author, and this committee is one of the sub-committees of the national project on electric vehicles. The author has been studying the equivalent circuit analysis method and the characteristic simulation method of RF noise, i.e. inserting sine wave signals into the RF noise source, separating the transmission network from the noise generating source. The important characteristics of RF noise analysis of d.c. series and repulsion type induction motors were reported 18 years ago, but the report was written only in Japanese (4) (10). As this method might be seriously considered for electric vehicles at the present time, it will be described briefly.

The measuring principle is shown in Fig. 114.14. Fig. 114.14a shows the general measuring circuit, a high impedance probing the RF noise terminal voltage—Z_M is the internal transmission impedance of the motor, Z_L is the power line impedance, and Z_P is the probe impedance of the RF noise meter at the measuring terminal. The author intended to isolate the power line as ideally as possible and it has stabilized impedance at each measuring frequency. In order to decrease the effect of the power line high impedance, he inserted LC and tuned the circuit at each frequency to compensate for the imaginary part of Z_L, as shown in Fig. 114.14b.

In addition, to measure the RF noise terminal voltage of an electric motor (or equipment) without including any effects of the external circuit, it is necessary to keep Z_L and Z_P at much higher values than Z_M, but this is rather difficult in practice. For this reason he used an equivalent circuit, as Fig. 114.14c, and the noise voltage at terminal 1–2 (E_1) was corrected and obtained for the measured noise voltage at terminal 3–4 (*e*) and the measured impedances Z_M, Z_L and Z_P at each frequency, respectively.

The voltages of this corrected open terminal and line free terminal voltage should be calculated by the following formula:

$$E_1 = e.Z_M + \frac{Z_L.Z_P}{Z_L+Z_P} \cdot \frac{Z_L.Z_P}{Z_L+Z_P}$$

The impedances Z_M, Z_P and Z_L are measured with a general impedance bridge at each frequency, with the Zs estimated as absolute values. These measured impedances and the originally measured terminal voltage of RF noise at each frequency are not shown as these measurements are time-consuming and require much laborious work. Finally, the results of RF noise voltage E_2 at the line free open terminal 3–4 are shown in Fig. 114.15, assuming that the internal transmission function of the motor is given as Z_M. The tendency of these curves shows an important phenomenon, i.e. that the transmission coefficient (loss) between terminals 1–2 and 3–4 is proportional to the square of the frequency.

In addition, he calculated the equivalent LC values from the measured Z_M and the measured mutual impedance M at 50 cS, by the voltage–current method, and also compared these values with the measured leakage inductance at 50 and 500 cS. The equivalent circuits and the measured or calculated values are shown in Fig. 114.15.

He finalized the design of equivalent circuits of a band attenuation type filter and a band pass type filter as shown in Fig. 114.15, and the characteristics of an approximate attenuation are also given. We can easily choose a suppression method from these results: a simple C type suppressor is quite effective for d.c. series motors (e.g. a drill motor) above 2 MHz and is not very effective for repulsion type induction motors above 0·2 MHz, which

indicates that a more complex rejection filter type is needed.

APPENDIX 114.1

REFERENCES

(1) MINOZUMA, F. 'Fundamental characteristics for radio noise measurements', *Dempa Jiho* (Radio Review), Ministry of Posts and Telecommunications, 1951 **6** (No. 1), 24–32.

(2) MINOZUMA, F. 'Review of study on radio noise measuring equipment', *J. Inst. elect. Engrs Japan* 1954 **74** (No. 787), 479–493.

(3) MINOZUMA, F. 'Calculation of required radio field intensity for the sufficient service at the starting of TV broadcasting', *J. TV Engrs Japan* 1952 **6** (No. 5), 1–64.

(4) MINOZUMA, F. *Communication and radio noise*, Communication Engng Series 12-B, 1956 (Kyoritsu Pub. Co.).

(5) MINOZUMA, F. 'Report of Committee—Radio noise interference suppression for automotive vehicles', *J. Auto. Engrs Japan* 1959 **13** (No. 7), 264–267, 272; 1959 **13** (No. 8), 306–309, 315.

(6) MINOZUMA, F. 'Report of Committee—Radio noise of automobiles', *J. Auto. Engrs Japan* 1967 **21** (No. 8), 852–856.

(7) MINOZUMA, F. 'Suppression methods and characteristics of radio noise for automotive vehicles', *J. Inst. Elect. Engrs Japan* 1969 **89** (No. 970), 62–73.

(8) MINOZUMA, F. 'Panoramatic automatic frequency sweep type RF noise meter, using XY plotter and computer display', Japanese Automotive Research Inst., Tech. Rept (in the press).

(9) MINOZUMA, F. 'Report of radio noise limit for automobiles and measuring results, amendment of measuring procedure', Report of the inquiry of Japanese Radio Tech. Consulting Committee, Ministry of Posts and Telecommunications, 1972 (in the press).

(10) MINOZUMA, F. 'The new consideration for the measurement and suppression techniques of RF noise from electric motors', *Denki* (J. of Elect. Engng), Japanese Elect. Engng Industry Ass., 1954 (No. 75, September), 1–6.

C115/72   AUTOMOTIVE SWITCHES AND SWITCHGEAR

L. J. NEVETT*

This paper sets out to deal with the full range of automotive switches from the simple manual two position ON–OFF type to the complex multifunction steering column mounted assemblies. Aspects of styling and ergonomics are considered in addition to basic design criteria. Some reference is also made to electromagnetic and other switching devices which are not directly within the driver's control.

1 INTRODUCTION

A SWITCH HAS BEEN DEFINED AS 'a mechanical device for making and breaking the load current in an electrical circuit'. Less seriously it has often been described as twisting two pieces of wire together. Indeed, it is the apparent simplicity of the function of circuit control that often leads to insufficient attention being paid to correct specification. The examination of automotive switch warranty returns over a period of some years provides considerable evidence that incorrect specification bears as great a responsibility for failure and malfunction as does unsatisfactory design. Basically a switch can be divided into two sections; the contacts which perform the electrical make and break and the actuator or mechanical device which moves the contacts together and apart. Since there are a variety of applications for switchgear in the motor vehicle, there must necessarily be a multiplicity of contact, actuator and operational mode forms. The choice of combination of the three factors must be influenced equally by electrical load requirements, environmental conditions and human factors considerations. In a highly competitive market, cost aspects must also play a large part and value engineering is therefore an important factor.

2 CONTACTS AND CONTACT ARRANGEMENTS

2.1 Materials

Contact materials used in automotive applications as in any other field of switchgear design should ideally combine certain characteristics. They are:

(1) freedom from surface films;
(2) high electrical and thermal conductivity;
(3) resistance to electrical and mechanical wear;
(4) low cost.

In such a highly competitive market the latter factor of low cost dictates the use of base metals wherever possible and completely precludes the use of any metal more exotic than silver and certain silver alloys.

The MS. of this paper was received at the Institution on 28th June 1972 and accepted for publication on 4th July 1972. 23
* Joseph Lucas (Electrical) Ltd, Northbridge Works, Elm Street, Burnley, Lancs.

Copper, brass, phosphor bronze and beryllium copper are widely specified in many shapes and forms to suit a wide variety of applications. Bimetal contacts in strip or rivet form are often used to obtain optimum conditions at minimum cost. Even when cost considerations are not taken into account no one single material is ideal. Those that are least subject to surface corrosion may have a high wear factor and, conversely, materials which are resistant to wear tend to form oxide films. The presence of oxide film on the contact surface can cause high or variable contact resistance. This is particularly troublesome on light duty switches where contact pressures are low. Heavy duty switches usually have a much higher pressure and this tends to break through any surface contamination.

The thermal conductivity of a material is particularly important in the design of heavy duty contacts, and will determine the current-carrying capacity for a given size of contact. High conductivity ensures that heat generated at the point of contact is rapidly dissipated and minimizes arc erosion.

Rate of mechanical wear of contact materials is usually related to their hardness and can therefore be predicted with some accuracy. Electrical wear, however, is a somewhat more complex phenomenon and is due to material transfer during arcing. Taking a given voltage, there is for every material a value of current below which a stable arc cannot be maintained. This is known as the limiting current. When switching direct current loads some metal transfer may take place at levels below the limiting current and this will determine the life of the contacts. Harder and denser materials usually have a higher melting point and are therefore most resistant to transfer. In heavy current applications the rate of erosion is controlled by two main factors—the current flowing during arcing and the duration of arcing. Despite the considerable amount of research that has been carried out on contact arc erosion, it remains the largest single problem in the design of switchgear. The designer can minimize its effects by his choice of material, by ensuring that the bulk of contact material provides adequate thermal dissipation, by providing adequate contact gap and by keeping the duration of arcing to a minimum by correct contact movement control.

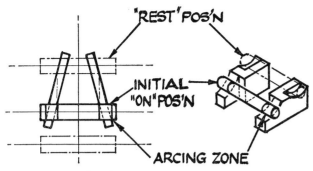

Fig. 115.1. Contact zoning

When wiping contacts are employed measures can also be taken to prolong contact life by zoning. This means that the area in which contacts touch during the make and break period of movements is removed from the area of contact when the moving component has reached the end of its travel. Fig. 115.1 illustrates this theory which is equally effective when the roller type of moving contact is used.

Wherever possible contact break should take place in air. Transferring the moving contact in a wiping action, from the live fixed contact on to some insulating materials, will produce burning and subsequent tracking breakdown. Plastics based on phenolic resins are particularly prone to this and should be avoided if an air break cannot be allowed for. Melamine and alkyds have excellent anti-tracking properties in the low-voltage non-burning sense. Many thermoplastics are also good but are liable to melting in the arcing area. Plastics which maintain combustion should be avoided at all costs in the contact area.

2.2 Contact lubrication

The difficulty of keeping contact surfaces clean is a constant thorn in the flesh of the designer. Surface films and arcing both create contamination which will reduce the life and efficiency of the switching device. To combat this problem two alternatives are available—contact cleansers and contact lubricants. A cleanser will remove most types of contamination but it leaves the surfaces in a dry unprotected state and often actually promotes the further formation of tarnish film.

Contact lubricants are acknowledged as the most efficient method of protecting electrical contacts. Modern contact lubricants not only possess useful mechanical lubrication properties which greatly facilitate a reduction in contact wear due to friction, but also the resulting surface films play an important part in the operation of the contacts. The film of lubricant provides a greater area of contact, thus decreasing current density. This, together with normal heat conductance, produces a subsequent drop in overall contact surface temperature and therefore greatly reduces any tendency to form welds.

Manufacturers of contact lubricants make a particular point of the arc inhibiting properties of their products as a means of prolonging contact life.

2.3 Contact control

From various points made in the section on materials it can be seen that the mechanics of contact movement control rate equally with the choice of materials in the design of efficient switching devices.

When deciding the method of contact control there are a number of criteria which must be considered. The following points should be borne in mind during the preliminary selection of a contact system:

(a) In general terms, the current which can be safely interrupted by a pair of contacts varies inversely as the product of the frequency of operation and the impressed voltage.

(b) In inductive d.c. circuits the contact gap and the speed of contact separation should be great enough to interpose an air gap sufficient to prevent excessive arcing before high peak voltages are induced across the contacts. As has been stated, the choice of contact material for such conditions should be capable of minimizing arc erosion.

(c) When controlling tungsten filament loads the rate of contact closure is the important factor for similar reasons.

(d) In order to ensure minimum contact resistance and temperature rise the highest possible contact pressure, compatible with mechanical contact wear, should be used.

(e) Increase in contact pressure leads to decrease in voltage drop or contact resistance between the contact surfaces. This is particularly true when materials are used which tend to form surface films.

(f) Contact life can be considerably increased by using a design which will mechanically eliminate contact bounce at make and chatter at break.

(g) Contact alignment is important. In general, a domed contact form used in conjunction with a flat faced contact is most satisfactory. The radius of the domed face should be approximately two to four times the head diameter.

(h) Material transfer is a directional phenomenon in d.c. circuits. It is frequently possible to decrease transfer by using dissimilar materials for the positive and negative contacts.

2.4 Contact support springs

In any switch design contacts have to be urged together by some form of spring. When the spring itself is a separate component from the contact and does not have to carry current, steel is most often used in coil or leaf form with suitable treatment against environmental conditions likely to be met in service.

When the contact support spring is part of the current-carrying system then a non-ferrous material of high electrical conductivity and suitable mechanical properties must be specified. This applies particularly to springs in leaf form.

Phosphor bronze is perhaps the most frequently used non-ferrous spring material, but for electrical purposes it suffers from the disadvantage of having an electrical conductivity which is less than 20 per cent that of copper. The only material which is superior to both in respect of conductivity and spring properties is beryllium copper, which has a conductivity of 25–30 per cent in the heat treated state and, as an added advantage, spring properties almost equal to steel. Its optimum characteristics can be utilized whatever the shape of spring. Hard rolled brass is a material which is often used where cost considerations are of prime importance. This material has a conductivity

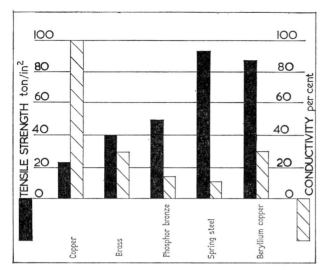

Fig. 115.2. Comparative electrical conductivities and tensile strengths

equal to beryllium copper but has an inferior fatigue strength. In practice, therefore, extra backing is required to prevent early fatigue failure. As an electrical material beryllium copper is superior from the fatigue strength point of view, particularly in a corrosive salt spray environment. All three materials are suitable for silver tip contact attachment by the Schlatter process of resistance welding and forming. (See Fig. 115.2.)

3 ACTUATOR MECHANISMS—MANUAL

The number of ways of linking man's action to the ultimate result of closing a pair of contacts is probably as multitudinous as the number of contact forms and variations themselves. The factors of current level, type of load, environmental and life requirements must be considered in equal depth as when choosing the contact material.

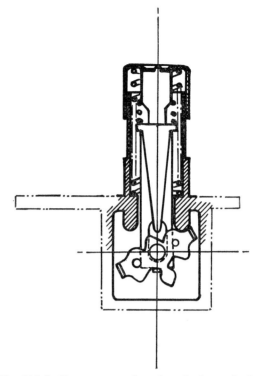

Fig. 115.4. Foot operated push switch employing progressive quick make and break action

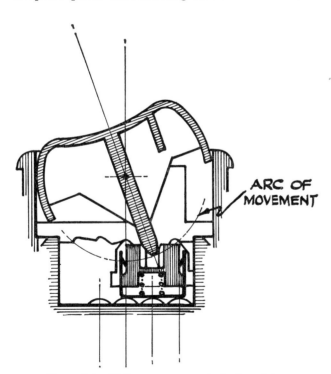

Fig. 115.3. Sliding contact switch; 3 position

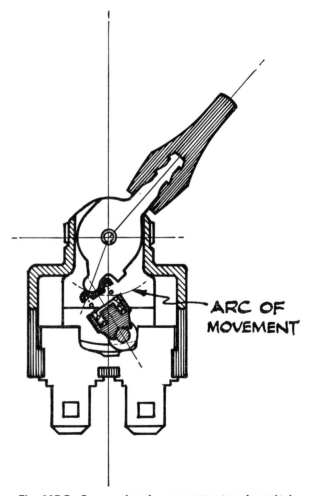

Fig. 115.5. Conventional over-centre toggle switch mechanism; 2 position

In the design of manually operated switchgear for automotive applications, sliding contact—whether linear or rotary—and quick make and break mechanisms are both employed with equal popularity.

Sliding contacts have the advantage of being self-cleaning, but since more often than not the contact carrier is directly mechanically connected to the operating lever or knob, make and break is partially controlled by the speed of hand movement, the only other influence involved being any positional location action designed into the device (Fig. 115.3). There is a tendency therefore to a reduced life due to contact arc erosion. This also applies to some extent to the type of switch which incorporates spring blade contacts operated by a cam.

The most satisfactory mechanism is that in which energy is built up via the operating lever or knob to a critical point past which it is suddenly released, moving the contact at high speed. This type of actuation can be achieved by either a latch-release device or by an over-centre mechanism. Fig. 115.4 is a good example of the former used in a foot dip-switch design. Spring pressure is built up under the operating cap to a point where the catch releases the contact carrier and the mechanism flies over to the alternative position.

There are several ways of creating a quick make and break movement with an over-centre device. Fig. 115.5

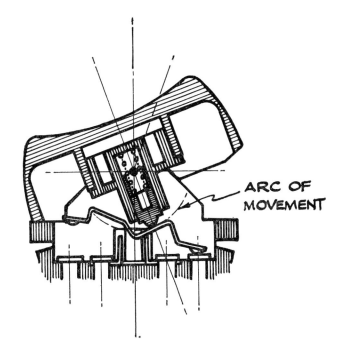

Fig. 115.6. Rocking blade over-centre switch mechanism, forward pivot; 3 position

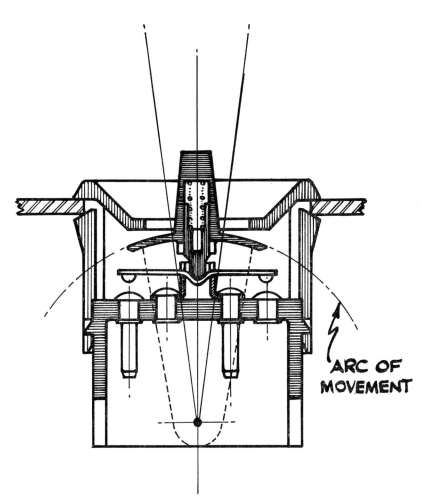

Fig. 115.7. Rocking blade over-centre switch mechanism, rear pivot; 3 position

shows the conventional 'toggle' spring loaded roller type. Figs 115.6 and 115.7 show the rocking blade variation in two forms. In both those shown in Figs 115.5 and 115.6 there is some disadvantage in that contact pressure is reduced immediately prior to break. The fact that this problem is avoided in the form shown in Fig. 115.7 renders it particularly suitable for controlling inductive loads.

Both the rocking blade mechanisms are often chosen by designers for the light and pleasant action feel in addition to the electrical properties. Figs 115.8 and 115.9 show diagrammatically a two-stage over-centre switch of rather unique design. One half of the switch remains stationary when the other half is being operated, providing a high level of circuit versatility. Contact wipe takes place before break and after make, thus ensuring that the contact rest point is removed from any arcing area.

Popularity of the panel mounted push button switch has increased of late, particularly on the Continent. A typical catch-release mechanism is shown in Fig. 115.10.

4 ACTUATOR MECHANISMS—REMOTE OR AUTOMATIC

4.1 Mechanical

The modern automobile requires a number of remote or automatic switches. Mechanical types include gearbox mounted units to automatically operate reverse lights when

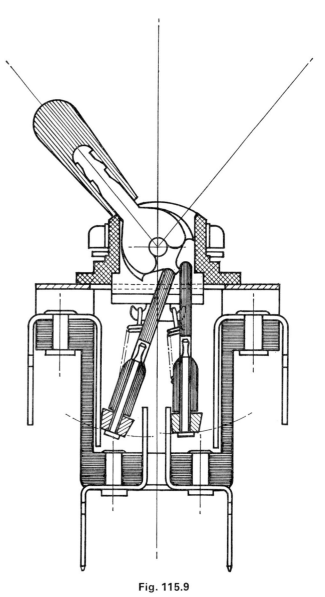

Fig. 115.9

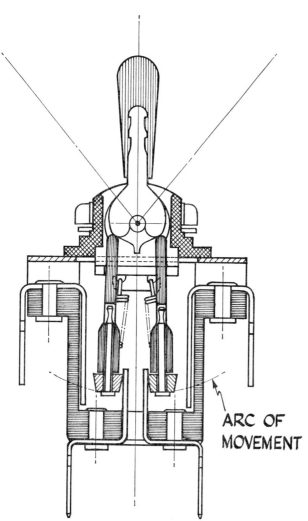

Fig. 115.8. Two-stage, three-position over-centre switch mechanism

ARC OF MOVEMENT

that gear is engaged, and inhibiting switches which prevent starting in other than neutral gear.

Both of these are fairly conventional in form, being plunger operated via the gearbox selector rods. Beyond mentioning the obvious necessity to provide adequate protection from external water ingress and preventing gearbox oil from entering via the plunger bore by efficient sealing, they merit no special attention. Combination switches which incorporate both functions for use on automatic gearboxes are very similar, but since there is sometimes a temperature problem designs have been recently developed for external mounting with operational control via a shaft through the gearbox casting.

4.2 Pressure switches

Pressure switches are used on road vehicles for mainly low oil pressure warning and operating stop lights from the hydraulic brake system. Problems encountered in the design of both are basically non-electrical and concern diaphragm sealing and life rather than contact durability. Hysteresis due to friction and lost motion in the switch mechanism can be predictable and, therefore, allowed for in the design.

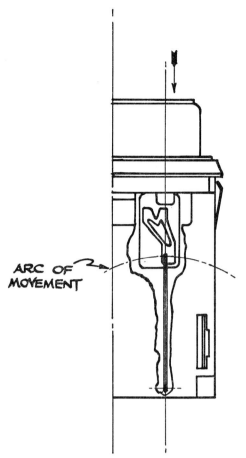

ARC OF MOVEMENT

Fig. 115.10. Push–push latch/release actuator

4.3 Electromagnetic devices

Solenoids

The most important use for the solenoid in automotive applications is starter operation. In its simplest form, used with the inertia starter, it is an electromagnetic switch. In its more complex form with a pre-engaged starter it performs the mechanical function of engaging the pinion before energizing the starter.

In either case it must be capable of switching from the normal level of running current to the upper levels encountered during stall for any given starter application. On the private car this can be from about 250 amps to approaching 1000 amps.

The contacts are designed with sufficient bulk of material to allow rapid dissipation of heat. To ensure that contact welding does not take place without impractically large contact areas and high pressures, a feature known as inertia break is incorporated in all heavy duty solenoid designs. After initial contact is made when the solenoid is energized, the plunger is allowed to travel further before the magnetic gap is totally closed. A contact follow-through spring takes up this extra travel and applies pressure to the moving contact in so doing. When the solenoid is de-energized the follow-through spring pulls the shouldered plunger rapidly back causing it to impact against the moving contact, so breaking any welding that may have taken place (Fig. 115.11).

Since starter solenoids are usually mounted in very exposed positions they must be proof against water, oil and dust ingress and be adequately protected against salt corrosion.

Solenoids are also used in differing forms and sizes to actuate overdrive systems, electrical door locking, in emission control systems, and for engine manifold venting to prevent run-on, etc.

In some applications continuous operation rating is required where space and cost is at a premium. In these cases two windings are employed. The first a short-rated one designed with adequate pull/stroke characteristics to perform the specified function. This winding is automatically switched out when the plunger travel is completed and a smaller continuously rated hold-on winding takes over.

Relays

The relay as used in the motor vehicle is principally a load shedding device. As a remote switch it can be used to control relatively heavy current functions from a lightly rated switching source. It can be intermittent or continuously rated with single or multiple contact arrangements in normally open, closed or change-over forms. The relay is a good example of a butting contact device where the choice of contact materials greatly affects its durability and performance. With light load where metal transfer is minimal, silver is specified, but for heavier current applications dissimilar metals are used with advantage. A combination of a nickel–silver alloy moving contact against a copper fixed contact is commonly employed for fairly heavy tungsten filament lamp loads—polarity being observed. There are occasions where system current resistance is high and voltage drop is therefore at an unacceptable level. A relay can, with advantage, be employed to switch the function locally. Where interlocking is required and circuit complexity renders normal switching impractical, multipole relays are used. Dual level signalling, which will be required by U.K. laws in 1973, is an example of such an application in which the relay is energized from the vehicle lighting control and switches series resistors into the flasher and stop lamp circuits to lower the night-time light intensity levels. A ballast resistor is also switched into the flasher circuit to maintain the flashing rate at a lower current level.

5 OPERATIONAL MODES

5.1 Human factors

The sophistication and complexity of every type of electrically powered or electrically controlled machine has increased beyond measure since the early days. The road vehicle is no exception. When the motor car reached the advanced stage of being equipped with electric lamps, self-starting and coil ignition, it only required three switches: one for lighting, one for ignition and one for starter operation. The advent of the electric windscreen wiper added the requirement for one more. All of these manually operated controls of the simplest lever, rotary or push–pull type of actuation were mounted in any conveniently clear space on the fascia panel. The same modes of operation are still in use but rarely in the original simple form. New technologies, new materials and value engineering have all had their effect on both contacts, actuation mechanisms and modes of operation, but it is only in recent years that human factor considerations, which have been almost instinctively applied to driving controls since the first motor car coughed its way out of the workshop, played any significant role in switchgear design.

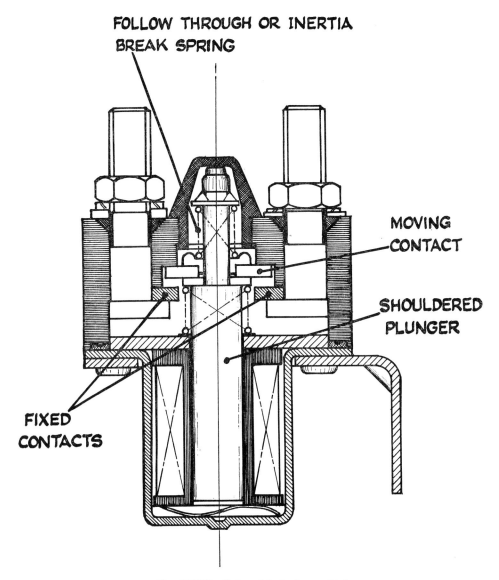

FOLLOW THROUGH OR INERTIA
BREAK SPRING

MOVING
CONTACT

SHOULDERED
PLUNGER

FIXED
CONTACTS

Fig. 115.11. Solenoid starter switch

It can be said that in no other field of design is the application of human factors or, to use the popular term, ergonomics, of greater importance than in automotive electrical controls.

In an emergency or under stress a machine operator will react with natural or stereotyped movement to maintain control of a situation. The success of his response depends to a very large degree on how well the controls are designed to match the natural and instinctive movements. Similar conclusions are reached when the vehicle driver environment is critically examined.

5.2 Types of control

The choice of control should be governed by compatibility considerations, but special situations may affect the appropriateness of the ideal and justify variation from accepted practice based on research or experience. Below are shown the types of control in common use, examining modes of operation and applications in relation to environment.

Rotary selector switch

The rotary selector switch provides discrete positions indexed by detents with a spring-loaded action mechanism. It is usually designed with three to five positions with a minimum angular movement between positions of 20° to a maximum of 30°. Knob styling depends on application, but bold shapes such as square or heavily fluted circular are most suitable. Pointer styles may be used where index markings are required.

Compatibility depends on application and location. If a rotary switch is used, it should not be lower than elbow level so that it can be gripped with the fingertips with the wrist in line with the forearm.

Toggle switch

Toggle is often the term used for the type of panel-mounted switch operated by a short lever. This mode of operation has long been preferred for its compatibility to most locations and applications. In a three-position form, the desired positional setting is easily located and errors are minimal. Despite ergonomic advantages, the toggle switch has lost favour in recent years due to passenger protection requirements. The most suitable knob shape for ease of operation is unfortunately potentially hazardous under impact conditions, and panel styling that provides adequate masking of the projecting knob tends to detract to some extent from the advantages.

Manual push button

The spring-return push-button control is an activation device applied to intermittent functions such as windscreen washing.

A push-button mode of operation can also be used for progressive and discrete position selective devices. In the progressive form the number of positions will depend on mechanical design. The disadvantages of difficult selection of the desired position inherent in cyclic operation increase with the number of positions.

Discrete position devices of the push-button type use latch-release mechanisms. Only two positions are possible with single units, but interlocked pairs of switches will perform normal three-position functions. Light finger pressure to latch the button in the inner (ON) position, and further light pressure to release, renders a control device of this mode eminently compatible in any operational plane.

Direct finger-end push operation as a continuation of forward arm motion or downward pressure with the ball of the finger are both recommended for speed and accuracy. In piano key form, controls can be styled into

energy-absorbent crash pad areas satisfying aesthetic and functional safety requirements.

Foot push switch

In the field of automotive electrics, foot-operated push-button controls have been used predominantly for high/low beam selection. In the U.K. and on the Continent, location of this function has been largely moved to the steering column area. This will be dealt with in Section 6.

Rocker knob

The rocking knob is a mode of operation for panel switch controls that has been popular on the Continent for some years. The adoption of this style in the U.K. was largely influenced by the early Federal safety standards requirements on fascia panel protrusions.

As a two-position switch, the rocker is reasonably acceptable—providing the location is carefully chosen. As a three-position control, spring-loaded to a centre off position, the rocker is again acceptable under good locational conditions, but as a three-position switch with the off position at one end of the knob travel, it is most unsatisfactory.

A well-defined centre position to prevent accidental override demands a heavy action feel unless an expensive gating mechanism is used. If a light action is embodied in the design, location is limited to definite areas if reasonable manual control and accurate positional selection are to be maintained.

Fig. 115.12. Long lever arrangement giving complete primary function control with added rotary lighting switch

Long-lever controls

Long-lever controls are designed mainly for steering column mounting—the turn signal switch unit being the best example of intrinsic compatibility. The extension of application of this mode and location to other functions will be discussed in Section 6 (see Fig. 115.12).

5.3 Classification of controls

Classification of importance of electrical controls within an ergonomic study is based on whether or not they are used when the vehicle is in motion and on the frequency of use.

All signalling controls—turn signal, main/low beam changeover, main beam flash, and horn push—can be classified as primary controls since they are used with high frequency under all conditions. Similarly, the windscreen-cleaning controls, wiper, and wash come under the primary classification. The lighting switch may be classed as a secondary control except in countries where it is not obligatory to use headlights when the vehicle is in motion; here it may be moved to the primary class.

Controls for auxiliary lights that are only used under poor driving conditions would be given secondary classification in the countries where they are allowed.

Other controls that are operated before the vehicle moves off or when it has come to rest are third class. This latter class is not dealt with specifically and would only need the basic rules of compatibility to be applied to avoid irritation.

5.4 Location

The introduction of seat belt restraints has tended to narrow the field of compatible location of controls.

Accepting the statement that both of the driver's hands ideally should remain on the steering wheel while the vehicle is in motion, it follows that the fascia panel is not now a satisfactory area for the location of primary controls unless vehicle construction brings it close to the wheel in the form of a binnacle.

If the fascia area must be used, then the most compatible types of control are those whose plane of operation is a continuation of the hand's motion. Change of direction between motion and operation introduces time delay and chance of error. This rule applies to a greater or lesser degree, depending on how drastic is the change of direction. For instance, a forward motion to operate a rotary control has a lower compatibility factor than a forward motion to operate a toggle switch in a vertical plane.

The steering column is an ideal location for primary controls since motion time is minimized and operation is possible without visual distraction.

For class two and class three controls, the fascia panel, centre console and door panel are all acceptable areas.

The steering wheel bar is not an ideal location for controls other than horn operation or devices that will be used solely when the wheel is in the straight-ahead position—such as cruise-control switches that are mainly used during freeway or turnpike driving.

Fig. 115.13. Panel arrangement of rocker switches showing good grouping but poor angle of mounting for easy operation

6 GROUPING AND COMBINATION OF CONTROLS

Once the problems of compatibility have been resolved, control grouping must next be considered. In terms of human sensory perception, where sight or touch is employed, rapid resolution is limited to selection from three groupings.

If controls have to be grouped on the fascia panel or centre console, maximum groups of three should be utilized to avoid confusion. Since, in forward motion of the hand, horizontal discrimination is the more efficient, horizontal separation is preferred in these particular areas. Figs 115.13 and 115.14 show panel groupings.

From every point of view, the steering column is the most desirable area for mounting primary controls, since, for almost all of the time that the vehicle is in motion, the driver's hands are or should be holding the wheel. It is logical, therefore, that to obtain the highest degree of driver efficiency, the hand should not need to stray far in order to operate any other primary control. From experience it appears that one hand ideally should be used for all signalling functions and the other for windscreen cleaning—thus providing a complete group of primary controls operated by two levers (Fig. 115.12).

To effect this, some combination is required, which, if compatibility requirements are properly observed, can be acceptable to all drivers. Here national preferences based on custom and practice tend to influence what is acceptable in the choice of combination and the left- or right-hand positions.

It is customary in most countries to mount the turn signal switch on the outboard side of the steering column, which means that cars for left-hand drive countries are obviously opposite to right-hand drive countries. There is a marked reluctance in the U.S.A. to acceptance of the specification of multifunction column-mounted assemblies, which have been used in one form or another in most European countries for the past 10 years or so.

It may be, therefore, that ergonomicists from different cultural areas may hold different opinions on choice of combination, but the evidence of consumer research shows that a pattern of preference is emerging in the U.K.

The signalling unit combines turn signal, high/low beam selection, high beam flash (if allowed) and horn control. The turn signal control obviously has a radial movement and should preferably combine a lane-change feature. The high/low beam selector should, if possible, observe intrinsic situation compatibility in having the high beam position uppermost and move axially away from the driver to low beam. This does create design problems when a main beam flash feature is included.

Having a spring-loaded knob at the end of the lever allows the addition of horn control. This, in terms of compatibility, is better than a wheel-centre horn pad but marginally less satisfactory than a full-width horn bar or ring. Economics will often dictate the choice.

The windscreen-cleaning switch unit is operated radially for two-speed wiper control with a spring-loaded knob for washer operation. A further feature that has become known as 'flick-wipe' can be added. This is a

Fig. 115.14. Complex panel grouping improved by masking of centre lighting controls

Fig. 115.15. Static pad ergonomic control layout

spring-loaded position in the opposite radial direction to normal providing a single sweep of the wiper blade or sustained wiping while the lever is held—a low-cost alternative to complex, intermittent wipe systems.

Two alternative column-mounted arrangements to the long-lever concept have been studied and found to be equally acceptable ergonomically but less attractive economically. Both are designed so that the total primary function switch requirement for a motor vehicle can be contained in one preassembled unit.

In the first case, the switch housing is in the form of a moulded box with energy-absorbent material on the upper surface statically mounted in the centre of the steering wheel but actually rigidly mounted on the column outer tube. The drive between the wheel and the live shaft is achieved by a gear train. By using an arrangement of gears in epicyclic form, it is possible to bring out the cable connections to the switch box between the main drive gear on the steering wheel hub and the final live shaft drive. All the light action switches are mounted close to the wheel rim so that the operating knobs are accessible to the driver's thumbs with minimum hand movement.

Half-ring horn operation and a high-beam flash, large-area pressure pad are provided, with the turn signal function being operable by either hand (Fig. 115.15). In the second scheme, a similar box form mounted below the wheel and projecting outward to the wheel rim is used to house similar light-action press-button switches, as in the

first scheme, but they are arranged at the outer extremities within easy reach of the fingertips. Both schemes provide excellent ergonomic switch layouts which avoid controversial multifunction single units.

6.1 Standardization of location and layout

Compatibility has been dealt with as a subject basic to ergonomic control arrangements. If a scheme with optimum compatibility from every point of view could be agreed upon nationally and internationally, and used as a basis for a standardized layout and grouping of controls, then a major success in safety improvement would be achieved with certainty.

6.2 Identification and illumination

When the basic rules of compatibility can be observed, control identification in whatever form should only be required for initial instruction or occasional reference by the experienced driver operating a new vehicle. Adoption of a standardized ergonomic layout would remove the necessity for this, except for student drivers who would learn the positions of electrical controls in much the same way as they learn the location of the accelerator and brake pedals.

Since we have not reached this happy state, some identification is necessary for daytime use. Should this be visual, or tactual, or both? If they are visual, literal markings present language problems, and many symbols have nationalistic traditions that make them difficult to understand outside the cultural zone of origin. This is another area where international agreement is required. Tactual identification in isolation is very difficult to absorb and retain. Within the scope of styling acceptance, shapes of control knobs that can be related to familiar objects in the same way that the symbols can are almost impossible to design. Shape coding in simple form—for example, square for lighting controls and triangular for wiper—is acceptable if it is combined with symbol marking and a standard coding is used.

Illumination

Emphasis cannot be laid on the desirability of identification without considering the problems related to the hours of darkness. In areas other than the steering column, illumination to provide positional location is an unquestionable need.

This not only applies to electrical controls but to air conditioning, heaters, cigarette lighters and any other device that is likely to be used by the driver when the vehicle is moving at night. Methods and styles of illumination are many. Low-level switch-knob or knob-surround illumination is highly effective if the controls are arranged within normal compatibility relationships. Individual lamps or fibre light guides providing many outputs from one light source may be employed. Development work has been carried out on switch illumination with colour change to provide position and condition identification. During demonstrations, marked preference has been shown by designers and stylists for this method over single-colour illumination. The general opinion is that the contrasting colour change can be easily seen without any decrease in forward vigilance.

7 RELIABILITY

A great deal is heard in the automotive industry on the subject of reliability. Nowadays vehicle manufacturers are tending to produce their own product specification on standards by which a supplier of components must gain acceptance. This is not a bad thing providing there is agreement on all sides and that sensible standards are set. It does not seem logical that an item of electrical equipment should be designed to such a reliability level that by the time it is reached in service, the rest of the vehicle will have crumbled into a heap of rust. Adequate safety factors should be built into any product and this can be

Table 115.1. Numbers of switch operations taken from instrumented proving laboratory cars

Product	Operations per 1000 miles	No. of operations based on 50 000 miles	Durability test life target
Starter . . .	492	25 000	50 000
Ignition switch .	419	21 000	50 000
Brake lights .	4317	220 000	250 000
Trafficator switch .	1380	69 000	100 000
Headlamp switch .	140	7 000	50 000
Dip switch . .	440	22 000	50 000
Wiper switch . .	99	5 000	50 000
Screenjet switch .	48	2 500	10 000
Horns . . .	456	23 000	50 000

achieved without cost penalty by good design backed by full proving experience.

Table 115.1 shows operational life levels of switched functions measured on instrumented cars over a period of some years. Service experience of this type enables the designer to set his durability targets at sensible levels and helps equally to prevent costly overdesign or irritating early life failure.

8 SUMMARY

As in other fields of electrical engineering the complexity of the electrical system in the motor vehicle increases year by year. The necessity of providing for heavier loads and more severe environmental conditions imposes greater demands on the ingenuity of the switchgear designer. He must not only keep abreast of advancing materials technology and be capable of designing for modern manufacturing techniques, but must also be aware of styling and ergonomic factors involved in the equipping of the modern motor vehicle with controls which are inherently reliable and compatible with any and every type of driver.

APPENDIX 115.1

BIBLIOGRAPHY

Electrical Engineering Data Publication No. 1300 (Johnson & Matthew & Co. Ltd).

TURNER, H. W. and TURNER, C. 'Choosing contact materials', *Electronics and Power* 1968 (November).

'Electric controls' in *Design engineering handbook* 1968 (Product Journals Ltd).

NEVETT, L. J. 'Human engineering applied to the design and grouping of electrical controls in the motor vehicle', S.A.E. Paper 720233, 1972

'Properties of beryllium copper', *Design Engineering* 1966 (February).

Discussion on papers C89/72, C106/72, C61/72 and C65/72

G. J. Bell Dunstable
If we are to develop a 50 000 mile spark plug, which seems to be the current requirement, the whole ignition system must be capable of firing such a plug for this length of time without the emissions becoming prohibitive.

Paper C89/72 states, and it is known to many of us, that the major forms of spark plug failure giving rise to higher emissions are gap growth, carbon foul and lead foul with leaded fuels. If long burn times are required to reduce hydrocarbon emissions for lean air/fuel ratios to an acceptable level, how do the authors see the compromise of achieving fast rise times to combat fouling and long burn times to inhibit emissions being achieved?

The authors' studies here show burn times of only up to 1000 μs. Recognizing that there must be an upper limit to how far we can go with burn times, what effect on emissions do longer burn times have?

What work has been carried out, do they or any other members know of, with regard to series gaps in plugs to try to obtain the conditions required for a long life, maintenance-free spark plug with low emissions?

C. Bowden Member
I have no personal knowledge of the effect of spark plug design on exhaust emissions. I only know what I have been told. But there are a number of points I would like to raise with regard to Paper C89/72 and, more particularly, the discussion. I can offer some tentative explanations and some personal experiences.

I must query Fig. 89.5, in which the spark duration times are shown. I do not know whether this is a plot of voltage against a resistive load, but it is certainly not a plot of a spark discharge. 'A rose is a rose is a rose', as Gertrude Stein said, and there seems to be a tendency to say that 'A spark is a spark is a spark'. There are probably as many different kinds of sparks as roses, and the characteristics of the spark discharge vary very widely from system to system and spark plug to spark plug and from source to source. The actual nature and theory of the spark discharge itself is both complicated and complex in a mathematical sense. Clerk Maxwell and Hertz first discovered that a spark was a radio transmitter and could generate frequencies way up into the multi-megahertz range. This behaviour has considerable bearing on the way a spark ignites a fuel mixture, and it is demonstrable that successful ignition depends far more upon the nature of the discharge as determined by the source parameters, than upon the mechanical design of the plug, so that given a really efficient source and a correct knowledge of spark technology a 'universal' spark plug suitable for any engine becomes possible, and the large amount of empirical

investigation described in the paper, although commendable, is really wasted effort and a sad reflection on the inadequacies of the two voltage generating systems used in the experiments.

Another point not raised concerns the effect of a suppressor resistor. In this country it is illegal to run a car without suppression resistors because it makes white spots on television sets. But the suppressor resistor is also an essential part of the ignition system. The heat content of a spark and the ignitability quotient of a spark are very largely dependent on the nature and size of the suppressor resistor. It must be non-inductive and have an impedance between 10 000 and 50 000 Ω and should preferably be incorporated in the spark plug together with a series gap of not less than 4 mm assuming an adequate H.T. voltage source. The use of resistive leads is technically inexcusable on a number of counts, which time does not permit me to discuss.

We have heard a lot about the desirability of high rise rates and the effect of series gaps but no one has really explained why these are often effective in clearing or preventing plug fouling. The commonly offered explanation is that with a high rise rate the current does not have time to leak away down parallel paths. This is to a large extent nonsense. When I went to technical school Ohm's Law was not time dependent and I am not aware that it has since been altered. Further, extra parallel paths apart from fouling are likely to be mainly capacitive and give greater attenuation with rapidly rising voltages.

As a result of a great deal of thought and experiment I have concluded that the known effects can be directly attributed to a hitherto neglected factor, namely the negative temperature resistance coefficient of carbon and metallic oxides which are the most likely contents of conducting fouling deposits. With such materials, which are generally 'poor conductors', the resistance decreases with increasing temperature, and they are also usually what is known as 'pressure sensitive'—sewing machine controls and carbon pile regulators, carbon microphones and carbon pile variable resistors are well known. This pressure sensitivity has previously not been satisfactorily explained, and I can now state that it is related to the temperature coefficient. Consider Fig. D1a, which represents a block of conducting material with contacts on opposite faces; current will flow (on application of a voltage) along path A and also along a multiplicity of paths such as B with values inversely proportional to the length of path. In Fig. D1b, the block is of metal with a positive temperature coefficient, so that the resistance of the shortest path (with the greatest current) will rise at a greater rate than the parallel paths, tending to reach equilibrium when the current is widely

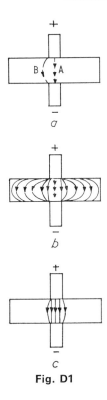

Fig. D1

distributed through the whole block, so that extra contacts will have little effect.

In Fig. D1c, the material has a high negative temperature coefficient and the reverse effect takes place, so that the current is confined to a narrow channel between the contacts, the whole process being cumulative.

It will be seen that this effect is also time dependent, the greater the rise rate the greater the 'channelling' effect. In the case of a spark plug with fouling, a slowly rising current will allow heat to be dissipated over the whole surface of the insulator reducing the channelling effect, while a rapidly rising current will intensify the effect, directing the discharge into a very narrow path with high current density, and consequent high local temperatures, possibly sufficient to evaporate or explode the deposit along that path, forming a plasma type arc to ignite fuel if present. This phenomenon can be very effectively and repeatedly demonstrated and I have no doubt that it provides a convincing explanation of previously puzzling effects.

With regard to Paper C106/72 and the comments on the standard type capacitor discharge system, the patented Bowstock system has all the advantages of a capacitor discharge system and none of the disadvantages.

This is a transistorized power amplifier giving up to one kilowatt output, not just a T.A.C. system, transformer coupled to the input for low contact or 'trigger' currents and voltages and low voltage switching of the transistors, and transformer coupled at the output to give correct impedance matching to a standard type of ignition coil, eliminating the 'time constant' problem and allowing full H.T. output up to 1200 sparks per second. The output across 1 $M\Omega$ and 50 pF is one complete cycle of a 2·5 kHz wave form with a strong second harmonic, starting off with not less than 10 kV positive then peaking to not less than 20 kV negative, giving rise to rates of up to 2×10^8 V/s. This type of discharge has been proved over ten years and 20 million miles to be extremely effective both

for starting and running conditions and can be positively stated to overcome all the electrical deficiencies of the conventional system apart from external insulation. As the system does not depend upon integration during 'points closed' it is independent of dwell time—during which the amplifier is completely quiescent taking virtually no current, which gives low current consumption so that a standard car may be run at 2000 rev/min on two flashlight batteries.

Even with this, we are still left with the crudities of the mechanically operated points and centrifugal timing system and for the past few years we have been testing many different kinds of triggering and timing systems and gadgets, one of which was intended to get rid of the 'lost motion' of a centrifugal system (slide). This worked quite well but still displayed considerable hysteresis. As a result of this we discovered that hysteresis is an inevitable companion of any centrifugal system, as the expression for the radius of gyration occurs on both sides of the equilibrium equation giving an infinity of solutions, which solution is accepted depends upon whether the system is accelerating or decelerating and at what rate.

We now have produced the PIRFECT (Position Indicating Radio Frequency Electronically Controlled Timing) system. In this patented system a radio frequency oscillator of a special type is amplitude modulated by a rotating plate or drum with a printed pattern to give the optimum or desirable timing curve. After demodulation and smoothing the output is a d.c. saw tooth type of waveform which contains all the information necessary for automatic or manual (remote electrical) ignition timing control *versus* engine speed or other parameters. The sharp edge of the saw tooth gives any required reference angle, e.g. bottom dead centre, the height of the sloping face the instantaneous position of the crankshaft, and the pitch of the teeth against a time basis gives engine speed. Apart from the simple rotating member there are no moving parts, all control being achieved electronically, automatic adjustment taking place after each individual cylinder firing without hysteresis, and as there is no dependence upon centrifugal action, auto advance can be effective from cranking speeds.

Fig. D2. A modified distributor fitted to a four cylinder car

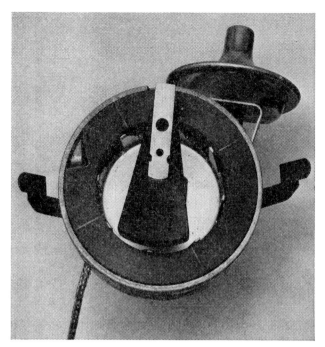

Fig. D3. An experimental conversion of a distributor including a vacuum advance transducer for an eight cylinder 'detoxed' luxury car for the American market

Fig. D2 shows a modified distributor fitted to a four cylinder car and Fig. D3 an experimental conversion of a distributor including a vacuum advance transducer for an eight cylinder 'detoxed' luxury car for the American market.

With reference to Paper C61/72, the use of the contact breakers seems to me to be a very retrograde step. Have alternative methods been considered?

The damp blade flow measuring device is a comparatively crude mechanical one which could be liable to errors due to sticking and wearing of the bearings. Has the use of other devices such as the hot wire anemometer, with no moving parts, been considered?

E. H. Ford London

With reference to Paper C89/72 spark duration in terms of time might be the wrong parameter; perhaps spark duration in terms of crank angle might be a better thing to look at. This would explain the fact that ignition requirements appear to be easier at higher speeds, and since a given spark duration lasts for a greater crank angle at higher speeds, and therefore until the pressure rise in the combustion chamber is actually established, I think we might find an explanation here of this phenomenon.

One of the authors has explained the fact that a relatively short spark duration system can equal some of the longer duration systems by the use of a wider spark plug gap. I would like to put the thought for debate that this might be due to the fact that with the wider gap we are releasing more energy in the same time to the charge, therefore spark energy released in the charge might be another very interesting parameter to look at, rather than some of the standardized parameters we now use.

As a supplementary question may I ask whether the authors have any evidence that spark gap erosion might be reduced by limiting spark duration to the point where the combustion is actually established? If we continue the spark discharge across the spark gap in the presence of combustion, will not this give the fastest rate of electrode erosion for their 50 000 mile system? I would prefer to relate the spark duration to the ignition advance angle.

With reference to Paper C106/72 dirt is the obvious enemy of opto-electronics and there are two ways of dealing with it. The simple way is to keep it out. The second is to design around it.

Dealing with the second way, since the first is obvious, we have operated very large numbers of opto-electronic ignition systems for more than the 50 000 mile period mentioned without maintenance and with success. The problems due to dirt in the ignition system can be dealt with by dividing them into two phases. One is the pure obstruction of the beam which might cause the system to fail to function. Clearly, if a flat-lensed detector having a chip of small size is used, 0·020 or 0·030 in square, a particle of this size on the lens will obstruct the beam, but with a relatively large diameter lens, focusing the beam to a crossing point and chopping it there, the whole of the lens surface would have to be obstructed before dirt is effective. We have designed a trigger so that 95 per cent of the light could be lost and it would still function. In practice it is very easy to make this work for the lifetime of the vehicle.

What happens to the timing as the dirt accumulates? Bearing in mind that we are focusing this beam to a crossing point, we come down to how small we can make the beam at the crossing point without high cost. The beam width can be limited to a diameter of roughly 0·025 in, including the fringing and spherical aberration one gets. If we make the chopper diameter such that 0·025 in represents less than the permitted timing shift we will allow (say 1°), then we make the chopping diameter such that we must always switch, no matter how much the dirt accumulates, within that 1°. We have been laughed at by some of our friends in the industry because of our obsession with dirt. They say, 'We can design around that and keep it out. Spend a penny on a seal and it is done'. However, we knew this would come up and have designed against it.

I would point to the advantages of opto-electronic triggering other than those I have mentioned. We get our square wave output from very few devices. We amplify it in such a way that we have inverse switching with only two additional transistors, and have a current level which is relatively high, clean switching with a very high repetition rate up to 10 kHz or more. This makes it possible to use one trigger to determine every one degree of crank rotation, and to that we can apply all our known digital frequency dividing techniques. To get this very-high-speed square-wave output, clean and free of noise influences, is the right answer, we submit, and this should be adopted in tomorrow's ignition systems and perhaps in some other systems in automotive use.

J. G. G. Hempson Member

One unequivocal point that seems to have come out of the presentation of Paper C89/72 is the desirability of maximum gap length and this is limited by the voltage capability of the ignition system and also by external breakdown.

Often a system which is capable in dry weather of dealing with a wide gap gives trouble in higher humidity, therefore anything which reduces the voltage requirement for the larger gap is of advantage. Some earlier work showed the very big gain, especially after prolonged service life, of fine-wire electrode plugs. We did some single cylinder test work showing that if we set a given voltage demand capability and the plug gap is set to give the equivalent voltage requirement, we can recover much of the short duration ignition system's loss in regard to running on weak mixtures. The change over the life of the plug shown by an earlier Champion presentation is nearly 2 to 1 of the final voltage requirements after long service. Does anybody think that, in the end, the gold–palladium or some other fine wire plug might come into use? Even where a fine-wire plug with the standard gap is used there is a small improvement in weak mixture ignition probability due to less thermal quenching effect.

Paper C106/72 is a clear exposition of the options open to the ignition system designer but the author has not, perhaps wisely, prophesied which type will prevail.

I was particularly interested in the system combining fast rise and long duration of discharge and would like to know if this has been realized in practice.

From the discussion on Paper C89/72, it is now evident that spark duration is an important characteristic. I remember in the pre-pollution days saying that discharge time was of little importance, and, as long as only near chemically correct mixtures are involved, this remains true but the coming of weak and diluted mixture operation has changed our criteria.

I would endorse the remark in section 3.4 regarding doubts on the suitability of photo-electric triggering systems. While these are very convenient for laboratory rigs, fouling of the optical elements eventually occurs, causing malfunctioning. On balance it would seem that a simple electromagnetic system has the best prospects of reasonable cost and long life. However, I admit this is open to controversy.

M. W. Weeks Member

Paper C61/72 is one of the first papers I have encountered in which all the advantages of fuel injection are drawn into one paragraph (section 3.6). There the advocacy of the use of the electronic fuel injection system as a means to an end in relation to pollution regulations is summarized in concise detail.

With regard to the modification in this system whereby the airflow measuring principle is utilized, some two years ago my company tried to use this sort of method as a means of giving us a signal of direct airflow. We used an offset butterfly blade which in turn was connected to our control cam. One of the problems with this blade was that the law deteriorated (in other words, the rotational angle to air flow) as the blade tended to seal, especially where we were using idle bypass. In a normal carburettor system the blades would be washed clean by the fuel itself, whereas with fuel injection there is no fuel to wash the dirt away, causing silting of the blade and consequently a deterioration in the law. Could the author give us details of any disadvantages found in this connection?

With regard to Fig. 61.11 (fuel pump), it would appear that the fuel enters through an inlet (a), travels down into the pump chamber, out of the pump chamber and into the armature section, and through the outlet (d). What effect has this in regard to induced vapour within the fuel itself, and what is the effect of motor heat on the fuel in transport through the motor?

I noted that on the previous system a capacitive resistive network was in series with the injectors. This it would appear was used:

(1) to provide a current bypass via the capacitor to open the nozzles faster,
(2) to reduce voltage across the nozzles by way of the resistor being in series with the nozzles, thus reducing closure time.

It would appear that this network is partly missing from the 'L-Jetronic' system, and I would like the author's thoughts on this point, since it would appear to play an important part in nozzle operating time.

J. Reed Member

With reference to Paper C61/72, why have potentiometers been chosen to measure the air movement? The life of these is very suspect indeed, particularly that of the logarithmic potentiometer. I would have thought that something more on the lines of what was discussed previously—the transducer type—would be much more sensible here. The use of a primitive method of sensing will restrict the life of the gauge.

Many cars spend most of their lives running cold, simply doing the few miles from home to work. The method of temperature sensing possibly is subject to considerable delays, according to the illustrations shown. The time lag is likely to be sufficient to cause cold running on the injection when the engine is actually hot.

M. Ford-Dunn (Student)

To achieve the 1976 U.S. Federal exhaust emission limits catalytic reactors and extremely close control of mixture strength, probably ± 1 per cent, will be required. Will the system described in Paper C61/72 give this accuracy or will we require additional controls such as oxygen sensors?

C. S. Rayner Solihull

I understood from Paper C61/72 that acceleration inputs are now not required in the 'L-Jetronic' system and yet there is still a throttle switch used (see Fig. 61.2). Does not this produce an acceleration input?

M. S. Windisch London

Paper C65/72 appears to have omitted one of the methods of improving diesel engine starting—excess fuel. The author has mentioned that engine oil viscosity varies considerably when a vehicle has been in service for some time.

Has much work been done to check how much it varies? Is there an attempt to simulate the effects of this variation in the cold room facility? It appears that the cold room is a rather expensive and difficult thing to keep up. Has any thought been given to simulating what happens to an engine under cold conditions? In other words has it been considered whether it is possible to produce a test rig which is capable of being fully controlled to avoid the down time occasioned by preparation of the cold room?

M. W. Shepherd Member

I would enquire of the author of Paper C65/72, in view of the many variables which he has discussed, how good a correlation is obtained between field tests and cold chamber starts.

Also I would enquire whether any allowance is made when determining the battery and starter combination for service deterioration of the ignition system along with maladjustment to the engine settings and particularly of the ignition timing.

Recent surveys carried out by my company both in the United Kingdom and North America show that the majority of cars on our roads suffer from some maladjustment to the ignition system. Perhaps I could quote some figures to illustrate this.

The North American survey was carried out over a five-year period during which some 50 000 cars were inspected. This particular survey was aimed specifically at establishing the incidence of and reasons for poor starting, during both summer and winter months. It established that 25 per cent of all car owners have either a singular or recurring starting problem. Of this 25 per cent, the problem could be traced in 44 per cent of cases to deterioration of the ignition system, and approximately another 10 per cent to the battery condition. Of the 75 per cent who did not experience any problem, 34 per cent of these were still in need of attention to the ignition system.

Additionally it was found that 70 per cent of the cars surveyed had incorrect ignition timing, 33 per cent being over-advanced and 37 per cent retarded.

It is also of interest to note that the fan belt condition of 10 per cent of the samples was poor. As this item almost invariably drives the generator the battery could also be in a poor state of charge leading to low primary voltage which, as the author details, has a detrimental effect on available high-tension voltages.

The United Kingdom survey on 1200 cars showed that 65 per cent required some engine setting adjustments. A massive 77 per cent needing servicing of the contact breakers, while 62 per cent had incorrect ignition timing with 42 per cent being over-advanced and 20 per cent retarded. These latter figures, while in opposition to those recorded in the North American survey where the greater percentage had retarded ignition timing, nevertheless illustrate that this engine setting is too often incorrect. Furthermore 13 per cent of the cars required servicing of the sparking plugs and 20 per cent had over-rich carburetion which could give rise to fouling of the sparking plugs and poor air/fuel ratios for starting purposes. Here again the fan belt required attention in 19 per cent of the vehicles checked.

The Chairman

Presumably the ignition timing is different from vehicle to vehicle as between manufacturers so maybe the difference in the statistics is due to the fact that some people specify $\pm 1°$ and others $-2°$.

M. W. Shepherd

Correct ignition timing was taken as being within the manufacturers' tolerance.

T. E. Cadmus (Author)

In reply to G. J. Bell, how do we reach a compromise between the fast rise time we feel may be necessary to overcome fouling for long life of spark plugs and yet keep the long duration which seems to be necessary for lower emission levels? Unfortunately, we would like to have both very fast times and very long durations, and as we are not involved in ignition system design, all we can possibly do is present the effects of both of these factors on engine performance and emissions and hope that maybe we could encourage the use of faster rise times associated with longer durations in ignition systems in the future. Longer durations and higher discharge energies do tend to cause higher electrode erosion rates, which also could cause adverse effects on longer life for spark plugs.

As to the compromise, this is something that each engine manufacturer is going to have to study for his application and decide just what duration he feels is the minimum necessary for acceptable emission levels, and get the fastest rise time he can with that necessary discharge time.

With regard to the second question, concerning the effect of discharge times longer than 1000 μs, this depends on the application. As we mentioned in the paper, there is a minimum level for duration above which we do not see any additional advantage. In other words, if we can ensure consistent ignition with a duration of 1000 μs, I do not think an additional 500 μs would show any advantage, and the longer spark duration does cause higher erosion rates for electrodes.

With regard to E. H. Ford's first point of spark duration as opposed to crank angle, this is probably well taken; in fact, we should have mentioned this as one of the reasons why at higher speeds the shorter duration system seems to be less critical.

With regard to the second point, as to spark energy as opposed to spark duration or gap size, this is also well taken. Unfortunately, spark energy is much more complex as far as measurement to determine what it is, which is probably why we tend to use spark duration and gap size rather than spark energy measurements.

We do not have any specific data to confirm the last point of E. H. Ford but I suspect that this is probably true.

L. R. Lentz (Author)

I think G. J. Bell's questions should really be directed to the people concerned with ignition systems.

With regard to series gaps in spark plugs, they are an effective tool for overcoming fouling, and particularly carbon fouling. Their benefit is in relation to the voltage requirement of that series gap. A narrow series gap of perhaps 1 mm would have a very slight effect in overcoming fouling, but a wide series gap of 2 to 4 mm would have a very pronounced effect in overcoming carbon fouling. The problem is that with these series gaps, the overall voltage requirement of the spark plug is increased. The increase is not the sum of the voltage of the series gap plus the voltage of the spark gap. But there is a substantial increase in the voltage requirement as the series gap is increased to 4 mm, and this problem always must be considered in connection with the voltage available from the ignition system. Most of the American systems have a voltage output higher than most of the U.K. and

European systems, and in many cases, the American system has been able to tolerate a series gap of $1\frac{1}{4}$ to $1\frac{1}{2}$ mm.

With regard to the question raised by E. H. Ford on the pictures of the spark duration (Fig. 89.5), admittedly those were rather stylized versions of spark discharge. In the case of the first long duration spark, there were undoubtedly many refirings of that 1000 μs duration. However, this is the typical inductive breaker point system used on American cars. There were resistor cables used on this car but not resistor spark plugs. The suppression of the spark plug does effectively reduce the number of refirings and effectively reduces the length of the spark duration.

We would confirm every point made by J. G. G. Hempson. With a fine-wire electrode, there are two benefits gained. One is a lower voltage requirement. The other is that the gap is more open to the combustion gases. Platinum would be an ideal material but it is not usually available, and with the advent of catalysts, it will probably be even less available and more expensive. We have developed a less expensive substitute material, a gold–palladium alloy, and it has had quite good success in specialized applications. We are not advocating it for everything. We do not think it is necessary. But J. G. G. Hempson pointed out two very important advantages of it.

H. Scholl (Author)

Replying on behalf of N. Rittmansberger: J. G. G. Hempson asked whether we have any experience with the dual system, the combination of a capacitive discharge and the normal coil system. We have made a great number of samples and done experiments in our engine test field in combination with exhaust emission systems and also given prototypes to some of our customers. We know that the system really works. The cost of the actual design is high, but this might be reduced by further work.

With regard to the Hall effect, the special system shown by the author uses not a normal Hall sensor but a sensor which is designed by Siemens, Germany. The sensor is a special semiconductor. The resistance of this device changes as a function of magnetic flux. Together with an appropriate electrical circuit the output voltage is much higher than that of a Hall generator.

With regard to E. H. Ford's contribution, it is agreed that this system is advantageous in principle, and we are happy that people are working hard to overcome the difficulties which we actually see.

With regard to C. Bowden's remarks concerning the ignition timing, this is to a great extent related to the exhaust emission systems which will be used in the future. We have certain indications that for the model year 1973–74 the requirements of the motor industry with respect to the accuracy of the ignition timing will be very high, because people are trying to overcome the difficulties presently experienced by ensuring very precise timing. There is a certain tendency to solve this problem with a digital timing system which allows such high accuracies as are required for the 1973–74 systems. On the other hand, for the additional requirements of 1975–76 in the United States it is obvious that it will be necessary to use thermal and catalytic reactors which change the requirements on the ignition timing, because then the emission level is not so much dependent on the accuracy. Lifetime and low maintenance will be very important factors for the

1975–76 standards. So there might be a tendency for analogue timing systems to be introduced, with an accuracy comparable to the actual mechanical system when it is new and this accuracy will be maintained over the useful life.

With reference to the discussion on my own paper, M. W. Weeks' first question referred to the deterioration of the air flow meter. We have found that there has been a very small effect on the accuracy, because we use a logarithmic function between the blade angle and the air flow. The range of air quantity per unit time is 1 to 30 and it is very important to have sufficient accuracy at idle, where the air quantity is very low. The accuracy is ensured by the special design which I showed (Fig. 61.5).

With regard to the vapour locks in the pump, this is a very complex problem and we don't believe we really have the answer completely.

We did a lot of experimental work on this. Vapour lock is affected by influences of the design of the fuel chamber inlet of the roller type pump; but it seems that more important factors are that the fuel temperature is not increased too much by the exhaust system, and that the distance between tank and pump is as short as possible.

M. W. Weeks' last question is related to the capacitor-resistor network for the injectors. The reason we used a resistor in series is to reduce the time constant. This way we dissipate more energy in order to improve the response. The capacitor is used to reduce the transient voltage. For the L-Jetronic system we have basically the same circuit but we made some changes concerning voltage versus capacitor size.

C. Bowden asked whether we have made experiments with alternative methods to solve the air measuring problem. We are looking at several methods. Some we have eliminated already in the stage of paper work. We are doing some experiments with heated wire, but, as I have already mentioned, the range of the air flow between idle and wide open throttle at maximum speed is 1 to 30. We don't believe that with a heated wire it is possible to obtain the accuracy over the whole range which is necessary for a system like this. The air flow meter must have an accuracy in the range of ± 1–1.5 per cent over the whole range.

Why do we use a potentiometer? We use inductance to measure the manifold pressure but it changes only by a factor of 1 to 4 between idle and wide open throttle. There is no problem of measuring a parameter in the range of 1 to 4 with an inductive sensor. We did not find a solution with inductance at the ratio of 1 to 30 for the accuracy which I have already mentioned.

With respect to the time lag of the temperature sensor, this device is mounted normally in the cylinder head reaching the cooling water. The housing of the temperature sensor is directly in contact with the cylinder head but the NTC tablet is very small, and it is insulated thermally from the temperature sensor housing. The response time of the sensor is very low, and it follows with practically no delay the temperature of the coolant water. The time constant is approximately 5 seconds.

There was a very interesting question concerning the accuracy of the system in relation to emission control systems. There are several possibilities for solving the emission standards for 1975–76. All three emission components must be very low. The normal solution at nearly all automotive companies is to have two catalysts and an air injection pump. The accuracy requirements on the fuel system in this solution are not much higher than in the present fuel systems. We are working on an emission system with one catalyst only. We are using a reducing type catalyst and no air injection. In this case, if we use a one-bed catalyst to reduct all three components, it is necessary to achieve an accuracy of air/fuel ratio in the range of 1 to 2 per cent. This can only be obtained by a closed loop system with an oxygen sensor.

The question from C. S. Rayner was related to the acceleration enrichment. The contacts in the throttle switch of the L-system are not the same as in the D-system. We still use the throttle position switch but only to have a signal for wide open throttle enrichment, and to correct the air/fuel ratio at idle. The switch has only two contacts, one at idle and one at wide open throttle.

A. J. Barber (Author)

The checking of oil viscosity after the vehicle has been in service is difficult. Some testing has been done using the CCS, by I believe Perkins, and they had problems in actual wear of the apparatus. Using the engine as a viscometer is possibly the best way to do this but to my knowledge an exercise of this nature has not been carried out.

To create a facility which would simulate cold cranking is, I suppose, possible. One has to simulate the resistance of the engine, de-rate the battery and increase the performance of the starter motor by an amount corresponding to the test temperature.

One way of increasing engine resistance is to use oil of higher viscosity, but it would take a lot of work to correlate such results with actual cold room work.

M. W. Shepherd's question concerned correlation between testing in the cold room and in field tests. My experience is that once a system has been specified for the vehicle in the cold room there is something like a 5 K advantage in the field. A system which would start down to, say, $-30°C$ in a cold room would start down to $-35°C$ in practice. This is probably due to the fact that air temperature can increase quite rapidly during the early morning and this gives a slight starting advantage as opposed to the cold room where the environment is strictly controlled.

We do not take any account of deterioration in engine or ignition systems. The only possible concession we make is that we do de-rate the battery to 70 or 80 per cent state of charge for cranking tests which allows for the sort of nominal battery state on most cars. All engines tested are timed correctly, normally with new plugs, and the carburetion is set correctly. If settings were altered to simulate deterioration or poor maintenance it would create two problems, first that of maintaining consistency between tests, and second there are sufficient difficulties encountered in starting engines at very low temperatures with the system correctly set and testing with conditions other than this would inevitably lead to over-design of the starting system.

Perhaps setting the ignition to the limits of tolerance could be done and this would seem sensible, but how we would cater for the individual who neglects his car and has a slack fan belt and ignition 22° advanced I do not know. I do not think it is our job to cater for these conditions.

The following corrections to the paper should be noted:
Page 21. Right column, third line. For 'crank-performance' read 'cranking performance'.
Page 24. Fig. 65.5. For 'resistive curves' read 'resistive torque curves'.
Page 29. Fig. 65.12. For 'TIME ($\frac{1}{10}$ s)' read 'TIME (1 s)'.

Discussion on papers C63/72, C72/72, C115/72 and C111/72

M. M. Bertioli Solihull

The authors of Paper C63/72 have mentioned the necessity to limit the turbine temperature to a safe working value during the start-up. Is this not taken care of by the normal temperature loop which performs this function as part of the main engine control? Or is it a special function of the start-up routine?

They have given a figure in the paper of a no-load speed of 22 000 rev/min for the motor. What special constructional features are necessary to permit this high speed?

With regard to Fig. 63.12 my interpretation is that we must work between extremely narrow margins, between the 27·5 kN/m² atomizing pressure line and the weak ignition limit. This is an extremely narrow band. Is this correct?

Lastly, what changes would the authors expect to see in the system to make it compatible with automotive pricing if we see the introduction of automotive gas turbines?

J. D. Heath Newcastle under Lyme

Paper C72/72 has given a very clear picture of the way in which the present-day auto harness evolved and has outlined the environmental conditions which the harness must withstand.

Although the basic requirements are similar, there must clearly be differing parameters controlling the physical design of wiring systems between the public service vehicle, the agricultural tractor and the family saloon car but, apart from these, there are tremendous physical differences in the harness design for each of the major vehicle manufacturers. Overseas requirements concerning the volt drop in various circuits, lighting regulations, etc. and, of course, the left- and right-hand drive, all serve to increase the harness designs and can result in a multiplicity of designs for even one model of a manufacturer's range. It is this wide range of harness designs which presents probably the biggest problem to the harness manufacturer today and the way in which this is resolved can affect the economics of production.

Can the authors give any facts on the sort of improvement which can be gained by using modular harness designs? Do they think this is the answer for the future? Harness fitments—terminals, mouldings, grommets, cable clips, etc.—are continuously being developed to meet the demands of the industry. Terminal designs are changing to enable automated harness manufacturing processes to be used. However, at times, an apparently minor feature of a harness design can prevent the use of automatic cut-length, insulation strip, terminate and insulate techniques being used, resulting in increased manufacturing costs.

For the immediate future, I would add to the authors' list investigations into cables and fitments which will be required to meet the high reliability standards of the sophisticated electronic equipment which is being transferred from the air-conditioned computer room to the automobile environment.

D. R. Crockett Stanmore

From the discussions and papers we have seen that the electronics revolution in other industries has now come to the automotive industry. It is starting to pose questions that hitherto the electrical engineer in the industry has never had to consider. Already we have had references to some very sophisticated electronic techniques, and these will bring in their wake very many attendant problems, these being in the important area of how to integrate a series of electrical and electronic black boxes. It will necessitate a definite upgrading of the basic standards of the connection and wiring system to an integrity level that today is only associated with the computer industry.

In Paper C72/72 the authors mention the trend towards the use of new wiring media and cite particularly printed circuitry both in the rigid and flexible form. It is clear from the very nature of the phrase 'flexible circuitry' that it is more adaptable than rigid circuitry and therefore could become a very practical innovation for the automotive industry. May I have their opinion as to what time scale they see involved before flexible circuitry could be considered a majority application for future wiring media?

K. L. Leech Member

In Section 9 of Paper C72/72, reference is made to the problem of temperatures. It is stated that under-bonnet temperatures are going to increase because of the inclusion of exhaust emission control equipment, but the authors have not put any value on what these new higher temperatures are going to be. I have seen a figure of 205°C quoted. Is this a realistic prediction for the future? If this is so it will cause considerable problems not only with harnesses but with other items of under-bonnet equipment, particularly those including semiconductor devices.

The figure of 400°F (205°C) came from an American source and related to passenger vehicles of V8 engine configuration and it was a predicted level for 1975. In present-day European vehicles, temperatures of 100°C under-bonnet are quite normal and hot spots of 120°C and 130°C have been measured. What the predictions are for the next four or five years on European vehicles is more difficult to answer, but I think this question should be directed to the vehicle manufacturers.

R. W. Mellor (Chairman)

As one of the few engine designers here may I state that the problem with under-bonnet temperature is that it depends how we clear or cool the air under the bonnet. This may not be the critical factor; it may be a matter of the heat sources present, the routing of the wiring and its thermal behaviour may have just as much effect on the performance of the loom as the actual measured under-bonnet temperature under a certain set of conditions.

G. H. Leonard London

Paper C72/72, albeit indirectly, highlights the conflicting interests of the vehicle designer and the auxiliary equipment designer. Mention is made of standards for voltages at various lamps and the possibility of the use of electronic circuitry in a pulsed switching arrangement is referred to. The use of such circuits would involve a volt drop in the switching semiconductors.

Similar considerations arise in the case of monitoring and diagnostic equipment, the sensing of current presupposing some volt drop. In the case of the direction indicator 'flasher', the equipment designer wishes to introduce an appreciable voltage drop in order to facilitate the reliable indication of lamp failure with an economic design, but the vehicle designer, who wishes to minimize his requirement for copper in the wiring harness (on economic grounds) wishes to lose a minimum of volts in the equipment.

Future regulations should be formulated in such a manner that the auxiliary equipment designer is allowed sufficient volt drop to give scope for economic design, and vehicle designers should not restrict this scope by employing wiring which drops an excessive voltage.

E. H. Ford London

Can anyone give me any estimate of the family car, or even the higher performance cars, under-bonnet temperature as it is likely to be in the next five or six years?

The Chairman

I see people using motors with extra fans on to cool their batteries.

E. S. Tye Enfield

Regarding Paper C72/72, we harness manufacturers are all capable of supplying wiring assemblies, incorporating sophisticated terminations, plugs, sockets and cable, manufactured to stringent specifications, so that, provided the design parameters are correct and the loom is installed with due care, it should give the minimum of trouble in service. We indeed know this to be fact.

As with any type of product, problems do arise with changing conditions.

Currently we have the need to develop our cables, insofar as the insulation is concerned, to withstand the much higher temperatures recorded under-bonnet with the advent of the so-called 'hot' engines, together with equipment required to meet legislation on emission. This same problem also affects the side-engined single-deck buses, as much of the wiring passes through the engine compartment and fires have occurred due to the effect of the high temperatures encountered on the p.v.c. insulation of the cables, causing short-circuits.

There are other problems, but we believe that a satisfactory answer has always been forthcoming and that development is a continuing process to enable us to meet our various customers' requirements.

Printed circuitry and flat-strip wiring have been discussed, and we feel that there is definitely a place for both of these applications. The former is ideal for dashboards where complete grouping of instruments and switches is contained in a fairly small area, but becomes less attractive where 'consoles' are used.

Flat-strip wiring shows promise, yet has not gained favour in the U.S.A., although it was manufactured there in various forms in 1965. As it is, however, in its very early stages of development, perhaps it is not politic to dwell too much on this subject.

C. Surridge Basingstoke

With reference to Paper C72/72, when are the motor car manufacturers going to consider the vehicle's future owner? There are a list of commonly fitted extras, fog light, reversing light, rear fog light, radio, etc., which, if not supplied by the manufacturer as original equipment, will almost certainly be fitted by the owner or his garage at a later date.

It is our experience that unless tampered with, modern wire insulation will last the life of the car. Shoddy workmanship on the part of the professional or the owner's lack of knowledge can and does cause damage to other wiring. Badly insulated clamping devices which cut through insulation are often used to make connections. Wires are strewn along the vehicle, under the carpets and even on one occasion along and wrapped around the petrol pipe.

Why don't the car manufacturers make provision for the commonly fitted extras by having the necessary wiring available in the loom?

Why do the car manufacturers include ignition resistance wire in the loom? We have had reported and have seen instances where they have over-heated and damaged the insulation of other wiring.

When are the car manufacturers going to adequately protect the wiring with fuses? At least one car in current production made by a major manufacturer has no fuses at all.

F. C. Ayres Hoddesden

The subject of Paper C115/72 is not given enough consideration in the motor industry but often takes the blame for the electrical problems encountered.

With regard to the switch in Fig. 115.6, it is stated that there is a low contact pressure immediately before break. This problem is eliminated in Fig. 115.7. I do not see this personally, because this type of design must be such that the pressure of the contacts at break is zero.

In modern switches the styling by the motor manufacturers is creating a lot of problems for the switch designer. While I accept that the styling of the car body has a great influence on the selling potential of the car, I consider that the styling of the switches used within the car has very little influence on the selling of the car. This being so, we are finding that, due to styling of switches and switch knobs, the switches themselves are more expensive than they should be. They are reducing the quality and the efficiency and creating masses of problems for the designer, making it more difficult and therefore far more expensive in the design stage. I would like to see the situation in regard to switches where the considerations are economics, reliability, safety, and ergonomics, rather than styling.

I endorse the author's remarks in Section 6.1 with regard to standardization of switch controls and the positioning of switch controls, taking into account ergonomics. This is one of the most important things in switch design today. It is even more important for those who drive different cars on different days. If I am not driving my own car I have a job to find how to start it, let alone drive it, so I think this is a very important factor and will help to make motoring safer.

Standardization is very important. It will reduce cost. More manufacturers will be able to use the same products, therefore bigger volumes can be manufactured. If we can take the fingers of the styling people away from our switches, the models that we design can go on for many model changes, and with the continued production of these switches and the improvements made over long production runs this will increase the reliability of the product, at the same time bringing down cost. I think this is a very important factor.

We are moving forward to a very interesting era in which electronics will be taking over quite a lot of the things we have been doing with twisted wire—once the manufacturers of electronic components reduce their prices!

J. C. Coyle Crewe

With reference to Paper C115/72, I have listened with interest to the author's remarks regarding the feel of switches, the positions that they have to be made to work in, and to what he said about the possibility of electronics taking over. I would like to ask him about proximity switches or touch switches and how far away he thinks they may be.

J. G. G. Hempson Member

Have reed switches had any consideration in this context?

R. S. Emerson Buckingham

Paper C111/72 is an excellent résumé of some of the techniques available to us for testing the various components of vehicles. But I would like to make some comments of a more fundamental nature.

Firstly, from the technical standpoint, what are the purposes of test equipment? Test equipment is absolutely necessary to set the adjustments of a number of components, such as ignition timing, contact breaker gap, etc. These operations may be required for a number of reasons such as (a) routine servicing as part of the procedure or after the exchange of parts on the vehicle (since as the author says, they are not always directly interchangeable), or (b) an adjustment may be directly requested by the customer—we have all done this, I am sure. This is a specific type of equipment needed in the back shop. It may be classed as a tool.

Next, there is the necessity to diagnose faults. Again, this operation may become part of the routine service, or, a customer may report an unknown malfunction which

may well be fictitious. He may say, 'It doesn't seem to pull very well'.

This second type of equipment is entirely different from the first. Essentially it is front-shop equipment. The prime requirement here is speed of operation coupled with technical integrity of the readings displayed. The aim might well be for the receptionist to make the initial test while the customer waits. In this way the customer reaches agreement immediately as to the work to be done —thereby reducing turn round time and parking space.

The same type of equipment also has the opposite requirement—to establish vehicle health. The customer is going on holiday and wants a quick check.

Thirdly, we have the equipment necessary to establish that a vehicle conforms to the law. The requirements here differ in that the tests are concerned more with the safety aspects of vehicle integrity than the performance aspects. The whole schedule is differently orientated.

Vehicles are rapidly increasing in complexity and it is becoming more and more difficult to make tests at all without specially tailored—and probably automatic—test equipment for such things as electronic petrol injection, etc.

Finally, we have the requirement to overcheck work done by the mechanic. This type of equipment should provide the proof to the customer that he is getting what he pays for. And I think this would be something of a luxury. Nearly every time my vehicle is serviced it has to go back for something—probably more than once—to say nothing of the items which are completely omitted.

Such equipment will need to operate automatically in order to be sufficiently fast in operation. It will require an input peripheral containing all the necessary information pertaining to each type of vehicle. Here I am not so worried about the updating of this information; I do not anticipate any difficulty. However, perhaps I am wrong. It must, of course, produce a printed-out result for presentation to the customer. To do this effectively some instrumentation of the vehicle is desirable but it must nevertheless operate with the vast majority of non-instrumented vehicles already on the road. It must do both jobs equally effectively.

On the question of transducers, in my opinion there is no necessity to fit a multiplicity of special transducers to a vehicle in order to test it thoroughly and quickly. Certain simple sensors are certainly desirable—for instance, to locate t.d.c. and perhaps minimum permissible brake lining thickness—but most of the other measurements can be made using existing connections, preferably hard wired to a plug socket.

One motor manufacturer (who shall be nameless) put a price of 100p on the complete instrumentation assembly including sensors, wiring and plug socket. The project was dropped because the total cost with labour amounted to 150p.

Again, as J. Bushnell has said, the correct place for instrumentation is on the floor-mounted off-vehicle peripherals in the garage which do not require any connection to the vehicle at all.

My second point is this. Apart from the technical standpoint, what other aspects are of importance to test equipment? (1) Test equipment obtains and retains customers. (2) It may have to conform to a franchise policy. (3) It can save money in a number of ways: firstly, by saving time;

secondly, it can help to overcome labour shortage—I believe that at the present time there are 60 cars per mechanic and in the 1980s the estimate, I believe is 72; thirdly, it can permit the use of a lower grade of labour; and fourthly, there should be a very great saving on re-work.

Test equipment, used properly, goes a long way in combating the growing customer disenchantment with the service he gets.

There is no problem in the testing procedure itself. Equipment is available and components are available to do any sort of test. The real problem lies in establishing a viable proposition which benefits the garage, the motor manufacturer and the customer. And it seems to me that it comes down to these three types of equipment: one for making adjustments in the back shop, one for examining the vehicle in the reception area to give the customer a report of what needs doing and for overchecking what has been done, and one for mandatory safety checks.

The customer already pays for the right to proper testing. But the equipment itself can only materialize out of (a) the will of motor car franchisers to give good service, (b) their close co-operation with equipment manufacturers and, above all, (c) education of garages and service stations in using—to their own advantage as well as their customers'—modern, purpose designed, test equipment.

E. Wharton (Author)

In reply to the first question concerning engine temperature limitations, unless there is a satisfactory rate of acceleration during start-up, turbine blade temperatures can reach a critical limit at which failure occurs as a result of creep. If we examine Fig. 63.1 it will be observed that the first portion of the engine restriction curve, if continued without light-up occurring, would have the form of a typical fan characteristic, increasing in torque in relationship to increasing speed. If light-up occurs, however, there is a positive power developed by the engine. From that point, both the starter motor and the engine provide accelerating torque. Theoretically, when the engine characteristic crosses the zero torque axis, the engine can be left to its own devices. If this were the case, however, prolonged acceleration would result in turbine blade overheating. The starter motor is therefore designed to assist the engine until the engine is capable of accelerating itself at a satisfactory rate. The point at which the starter motor is no longer required is known as the self-sustaining speed. The performance of the engine beyond this condition is an aspect outside the topic of the paper.

The second question refers to the high speeds associated with gas turbine starter motors. Starter motor speeds as high as 22 000 rev/min are mentioned. In Paper C65/72 typical starter motor speeds associated with internal combustion engines are in the order of 2 000 rev/min. The difference then is in the gear ratio between the starter motor and the engine. The internal combustion engine requires a starter motor with high torque and low speed whereas the gas turbine starter motor has a relatively high speed and low torque. Consequently, the higher speed of the gas turbine starter motor results in a smaller size. It should be emphasized, however, that not all starter motors for gas turbines attain speeds as high as 22 000 rev/min.

Higher powered machines of the order of 4 hp or more would tend to run at lower speeds. Such speeds do not present a particularly arduous problem of design but it is important that proper consideration is given to such aspects as commutator construction.

There was a question as to the changes that could be foreseen which might make the system more compatible with automotive practice.

I have made reference to various types of ignition unit and these comments were, of necessity, generalized. There are likely to be two distinct philosophies emerging according to the application. For example, gas turbines for trucks rated at 400 hp or so and gas turbines for motor cars rated at 70 hp or thereabouts would demand different consideration in relation to cost, life and reliability.

Because of the difference in speed range by comparison with the internal combustion engine, the starter generator concept may be quite a suitable proposition for passenger car applications, considering the limited brush-life. Trucks on the other hand, demanding longer life between overhauls and greater reliability, may not be so suited to the application of starter generators.

In the choice of ignition systems, there will be a question of cost which influences choice. Transistorized versions are likely to give greater reliability but on the other hand a simple contact breaker type may be cheaper but this requires the provision of a drive shaft independent of engine speed.

E. Carr (Author)

With regard to the question on Fig. 63.1 it is necessary to operate the engine within the narrow stability limits shown. The results given are for a very small combustion chamber with a combustion annulus of only approximately 1 in depth and this small size is the main cause of the narrow combustion limits. The development work required on the small annular chamber is therefore usually greater than that necessary on the automotive engine pipe chamber where the problems are reduced by the inherently wider stability limits.

C. H. Hartop (Author)

J. D. Heath mentioned passenger service vehicles, tractors and passenger cars as items which we had not specifically talked about. On the PSV side, we build the chassis but do not put on the body, therefore we are not really involved. I would hardly have thought there was much difference in the techniques necessary to wire a passenger service vehicle and, say, a heavy truck. I admit that tractors are somewhat different, but there are techniques which could be used to handle that side fairly well. One could use a metallic conduit without a great deal of difficulty but it would be frowned on if we tried to use metallic conduit down the frame of the truck.

With regard to passenger cars, generally speaking these suffer from having every single penny taken out of them, and a lot of the problems that we suffer come from just this philosophy. If we were allowed to spend a little more money, probably only pennies, we could improve the quality of wiring harnesses out of all recognition. We are talking perhaps in terms of not more than 50p. That is the sort of figure I would have in mind.

J. D. Heath also mentioned volt drop—something I omitted to mention. A couple of years ago the Federal Government of West Germany issued a draft regulation for the control of voltages on the lamps of a vehicle at the time of type approval. This proposal was unanimously condemned not only in this country but in every country in Europe, as far as I know. The draft regulation required that certain specified voltage drops were permitted in circuits to all external lamps. When you are starting from a variable and working to a fixed volt drop then you are in difficulty. As a result the SMMT, through the Electrical Equipment Committee, set up a Working Party that produced a counter-proposal in which there was willing and full co-operation from all motor manufacturers. A large number of vehicles were measured to provide the base line data because, as we understood, the idea was not to make the vehicle more efficient but to put on a control, so that good engineering practice was carried out by all the vehicle manufacturers. I do not think anybody would disagree with this. Our counter-proposal defined minimum voltages at the various lamps throughout the vehicle under a prescribed set of test conditions. We had to do this because there are so many variables involved. This draft counter-proposal was submitted to GTB in February of this year at Rome where it was discussed, but not in any depth because the delegates were not fully briefed. The Italians and French were very much on our side, and since then I understand, both support the British proposal very strongly. I know of nothing from Germany at the moment and as I am now out of that side of the business, I probably will not hear. I think we may end up by having legislation which will require us to build vehicles for type approval in which minimum voltages will have to be available at all the signal, driving and positioning lamps. This may not be a bad thing, but it does mean that connectors will have to be very good because we will not be able to tolerate any more volt drop than we have at present.

We have taken measurements on the vehicles that we build, using the modular system, and find we should not be in any serious trouble, although we might have to make some fairly minor alterations. But some companies that have used single piece harnesses have shown up some fairly substantial volt drops.

I thought I would mention the question of the possibility of legislation controlling the voltages on the vehicles as this could be very important in the future. I do not know how long it will be before we are faced with this situation.

I agree with D. R. Crockett that the problems of integrating electronic black boxes with the existing type of harness in current use will be considerable. I do not think anybody knows the answers; in fact, I do not think that we have any electronic black boxes to integrate at the moment. If we are talking about the ring mains and pulse switching then we are probably talking in the time-scale of five years at the minimum; probably five to ten years.

D. R. Crockett also mentioned flexible printed circuits and the time scale for introduction. I personally do not see a big increase in the use of printed circuits. They are fragile, have handling problems and are easily subject to damage. Some forms of strip wiring have been used in the United States and all suffer from some shortcomings. For example, if there is a screw or other sharp object resting on

top and you step on it, there is an almost certain dead short-circuit. This is unlikely to occur with an ordinary harness. I always have reservations about the value of using flat strip wiring, ribbon wiring or printed circuits. Printed circuits in general do not have the carrying capacities required for motor vehicles.

K. J. Leech mentioned the high temperatures of engine compartments. I do not know the answer. I know that the problem exists and that certain firms have been very concerned about this, particularly on rear-engined buses. I do not know the figures but have talked to various people who have mentioned very high temperatures and this has prompted me to mention the possibility that they may have to use ceramic bead insulation. There is, first of all, an enclosed engine at the rear end of a vehicle and sound problems which, because the engines are encased in insulation to keep down the noise, are raising the temperature. None of these things are really compatible. I am sorry I do not have an answer to this problem.

With regard to C. E. Surridge's plea for the 'do it yourself' people, that is difficult to answer. This a personal opinion so do not hold it against me, but the motor industry seems to go through phases. We have been through periods where there has been a cost consciousness to such an extent that we have gone beyond the point where we can build a really sensible vehicle. I think now the present-day atmosphere is towards reliability, therefore with the increased reliability that we are all striving for I think most of us have probably been allowed to do things that would not have been possible a few years ago, so I think we shall be using many more fuses. Ford, on some of their vehicles, are using as many as 12 or 14 fuses. Certainly there is an increase in the number of fuses. I can remember trucks being built with one fuse not so many years ago. I think about 12 fuses are required for sensible protection. The next generation of vehicles will have fuses covering almost all the circuits except the main feeds. From a 'do it yourself' angle, the colour coding which is universal in this country must be a great asset, because a brown feed on a Ford or Vauxhall is the same circuit, I believe, or it was the last time I talked to them. They are all the same, green, red or brown, and I do not think any other country can make this claim. This is the great thing for all concerned. The speaker talked about clamping terminals. I think I know the one he means. I do not like it either. That is all I can say. It works, but for how long I do not know.

Regarding C. E. Surridge's second point, on the passenger vehicles that we build there are facilities and the owner's handbook gives a diagram listing all accessories available and the tapping points. Those points exist on the vehicle, therefore there should be no necessity to use any of those fancy devices, except for some peculiar thing you might want to fit, like a time clock or something of that nature.

L. J. Nevett (Author)

I expected there would be comments on the two particular rocking blade designs. If we study their configuration we see that the front or rear pivot is the whole point of this argument. With the rear pivot design, because of the arc of movement of the knob, one is tending to build up a contact pressure. On all the switches a zero point is reached, whatever one does, even on the toggle switch, when the thing flies over, but if the switch is operated normally a pressure is built up before the blade lifts. With the front pivot design there is tendency to lessen the contact pressure before going over. One is sliding down towards the centre. This is based on these two configurations only. The other point is that with the rear pivot there is a much more acceptable positional feel. It has a much lighter action giving equivalent contact pressures. It has obvious advantages in this way.

Styling is always a problem. I hardly know where to start. It is a very difficult problem to satisfy the stylists but we have to try. That is all. F. C. Ayres started off with economics and ended up with ergonomics. It was sad to think that he put ergonomics last, although later he said it was important.

On the subject of standardization, this reduces costs, of course. I have found personally that standardization is a battle lost before it has started. There is a new design on the drawing board and almost before the draughtsman has lifted his pencil there are a dozen different variations. We produce 160 different models and we have 2000 variations of those 160 different basic types of switch. There is standardization for you!

I did not mention touch switches, although I vaguely referred to them when mentioning electronics. This idea is good provided we can get the costs down; in fact, there are some exercises going on at the moment in this area. But touch switching is the ultimate when one does not make any movement of the switch operating pad. You are all quite familiar with the American elevator type of switch, where one touches the square and it lights up red. That is a similar type of thing but it works differently in their system. Nevertheless the final operation is the same. It is an excellent system if we can get the cost down. With the constant reduction of solid-state components I am sure it will come in time, perhaps in combination with other solid-state functions.

With regard to reed switches, we have only tried using them in failure monitoring devices, otherwise they have no significance that I am aware of in the automotive field.

J. Bushnell (Author)

With regard to updating of information, the average service station has the greatest difficulty in keeping its own records straight as a financial body, and finds it difficult keeping up with the plethora of information which comes out from the vehicle manufacturers every day, as well as bringing its own details up to date. Human nature being what it is, the tendency is to keep the paper on the service manager's desk until it is really wanted, and by that time it is too late. Doing it with punch cards or computer information would make the same difficulties. The problem is capable of solution, I agree, but it will be difficult.

The basic operation of Volkswagen is an 88-test routine of which 74 are mechanical inspections of which the results are the opinion of the mechanic. He punches YES or NO to whether the head lamps work, the side lamps, the screen washers, wipers, etc. They are dual opinions and he has two buttons, YES or NO. There are 14 other tests. One test is the automatic measurement of toe-in and camber, which is done very rapidly and very excellently, in 15 seconds. This is stored in the machine and printed out instantaneously. There are four other checks taken, one for the electrolyte level of the battery, and three voltage checks. The next range of automatic tests are done by inserting a temperature sensor to get the oil temperature, etc. Any other tests, such as timing adjustment or dwell angle, are done independently of the device at this stage; they may be added later but they are not part of it at the moment. The plug is a 28-pin plug which is standardized on the back of the chassis and has a limited number of connections to it at the moment, with the capability of adding more. So basically a lot of the tests are still done by mechanical inspection.

Discussion on papers C90/72, C75/72, C113/72 and C79/72

W. W. Bischoff Fellow

With regard to Paper C90/72, the advantage of solid-state displays is their compactness; these displays are very shallow.

This feature does not only contribute to greater safety by providing the desired space into which the steering column may collapse, or adapts itself to the ever diminishing space available for instruments as windscreen angles become more acute, but it also releases space for airbag paraphernalia. I believe that one American car manufacturer is proposing to put the pressure cylinder and diffuser into the space normally taken up by the instrumentation. Such an approach demands a shallow instrument display.

Another advantage of the solid-state display is to eliminate the flexible drive to the speedometer. The flexible drive is a nuisance where right-hand drive and left-hand drive versions of a vehicle are required, or even where there is a change in the speedometer position between the de luxe model and the standard model. This is because, for such a variety of requirements, it often becomes impractical for the vehicle manufacturer to provide ideal flexible-drive routing conditions in every case, and therefore concessions are made resulting in inferior installations with corresponding sacrifice of life

and stability of indication and drive noise. However, today this problem can be overcome using conventional electronic instruments which present the speed information in much the same manner as the mechanical instrument, but without the need for a flexible drive. Electronic speedometers are currently fitted on commercial vehicles, and we would expect to see them on private cars within the next two years. This is becoming possible because realistic assessments of the total cost implications of speedometer installations are now being made. For instance, the cost of the flexible drive, its installation on a vehicle, the speedometer drive components required in the gearbox transmission, and their assembly will probably equate with that of the latest type of electronic speedometer plus signal transducer. This means that adverse cost differentials for the remotely triggered speedometer will shortly disappear.

The major attraction of a solid-state display is that it provides the opportunity for concentrating into a relatively small space all the information provided by existing types of instrumentation.

Fig. D4 is an artist's impression of such a solid-state display. Behind the steering wheel is a small screen. If we make it as flexible as a television screen it will be possible to portray almost anything we want. I do not believe this

Fig. D4. Artist's impression of a solid-state display

Fig. D5. A head-up display

is entirely original thinking. The screen would have to be based on a close-pitched dot matrix system. If we had such a screen we could continuously indicate speed on it or we could project speed onto the windscreen as a head-up display and use the small screen in the fascia to provide information only by exception. For instance, if anything goes wrong, such as the fuel being almost used up, or if oil pressure has disappeared, or the coolant has leaked away, this information would appear on the little screen automatically, and the driver's attention would be drawn to it by audible means or by a combination of audible and visual means.

In normal circumstances the driver could also use this small screen to interrogate any of the services on a vehicle connected to it, possibly by the type of touch button briefly referred to in Paper C115/72. He could also call up time from the clock, or pressure or fuel when he is ready to do so, when it suits him and when he has no other distractions. The information would stay on the screen for a short time and then disappear again. Certainly in that context, solid-state displays will offer us something we have not already got.

Current instrumentation has been developed to a high degree of visual appeal. Whatever we replace it with must therefore not solely be new, but must be capable of competing successfully as a styling feature of the vehicle interior.

Solid-state displays are not the only new display techniques. Fig. D5 shows a head-up display. A speed image is projected onto the windscreen where the driver can always see it. The image is produced by a mechanical speedometer carrying a skeleton printed disc in place of the pointer. The disc moves in front of a light source, and the image is transmitted by a simple optical system to the windscreen. The image is focused near infinity so that the driver can see his speed while still observing the traffic scene ahead. In this way continuous attention on the road

is maintained. This type of speed display is particularly useful when a knowledge of vehicle speed combined with undivided attention on the road are required, for instance in fog or generally poor visibility and when driving fast. In addition to speed, a danger warning, showing when any critical vehicle services are at risk, is projected onto the windscreen. In Fig. D5 this takes the form of a red horizontal bar below the speed image. Finally, two vertical parallel lines projected onto the windscreen just above the speed image, provide a measure of safe following distances. The spacing of the lines is controlled by vehicle speed and wet or dry conditions, and the gap between the

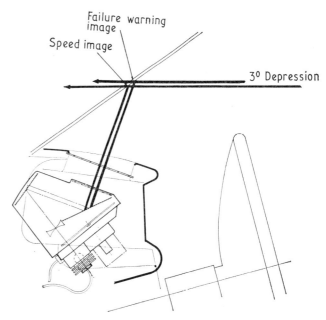

Fig. D6. Speed head-up display

lines should equate to the width of the vehicle in front for adequate reaction and braking time.

The mechanical head-up display installation is shown in Fig. D6. The unit needs to be designed into a new vehicle fascia. Solid-state displays will also play a part here in reducing the size to more convenient dimensions.

D. J. Neville Buckingham

With reference to Paper C90/72, it seems to me that all the important displays for the driver which are associated with his actual driving need to be analogue as the majority of us do not actually 'read', for example the speedometer. We know already the positional meaning of the pointer and just glance down to see its position. If it were a digital display we would have to do some reading and we can make a mistake over that. We would continue to want the main displays as analogue displays.

With regard to head-up displays, it would seem to me that these will be very distracting unless they are associated with the actual driving. The two pointers which show the width of the car in front are good. Other information could be distracting, especially if it was changing information not immediately helping the driver in his driving.

The idea of a panel on which the optional instruments can be called up allowing one to see a particular parameter if desired, seems to have a big disadvantage that one is not aware which instrument will show a fault condition. When I am driving, I often look down and quickly scan all the instruments, and I am immediately aware if there is one indicating an unusual situation. This is a problem when one is trying to select an instrument.

If it would automatically display anything which is at fault as the author says, this would obviously alleviate some of the problem but greatly increases the complexity and so the possibility of failure. I think it would also be difficult to obtain agreement as to what is an indication of pending failure.

C. Bowden London

Some 30 years ago I was closely associated with the design of a gyroscopic gun site fitted to Spitfires and producing a head-up display on the pilot's windscreen. It was a fairly simple sort of display device consisting of six small spots which moved inwards and outwards and also across the target. This display gave the pilot information about the range, size and gun settings for an accurate firing and was one of the factors in winning the Battle of Britain. I take no credit for that! What was done 30 years ago is just slowly beginning to filter into the automobile field.

With reference to D. J. Neville's remarks on Paper C90/72, I would comment that this did not seem to distract the single-seater pilot of a Spitfire, who also had to fly the plane while reading his head-up display.

With regard to analogue displays, can the author tell me whether he has had any experience of the reactions of the public to a 270° to 300° display on a speedometer or tachometer as against a 90° or 110° display, which can be done with a much less sophisticated instrument?

In this country I have found that there is a great objection to a 90° display, whereas in America and Japan it is accepted by the public quite readily.

With reference to Paper C113/72, may I draw attention to two rather unusual motor cycles which we had the problem of dealing with? The first of these, which I think contradicts some of the author's statements about contact breaker speed operation, was a projected Czech motor cycle, a four-stroke four-cylinder machine with an expected top speed of 14 000 rev/min. It was a 90° twin, with twinned big-ends on a two-throw crankshaft, which meant it had an asymmetrical firing distribution, so that between no. 1 and no. 4 cylinders the firing angle was only 45° instead of 90° (distributor), and over this interval it was running as an eight-cylinder engine. This demanded a contact breaker operation and spark production of something like 800 per second. Various systems were tried, all of which—as in any other system, apart from ours—demanded a current integration during the dwell period. None of these would produce satisfactory ignition at this speed, even with contact-less operation. We had a prototype of it here and successfully ran it but unfortunately political happenings brought an end to this project.

The other one is a side-car machine which carries a Saab two-stroke three-cylinder engine. This is running at 11 000 rev/min and this demands quite a high rate of operation. It is racing quite successfully and I believe it came second at Silverstone in early September.

I was once an enthusiastic motor cyclist myself. Unlike the saloon car, one is very largely exposed to the elements, and although some riders seem to think this is an advantage, the high tension distribution system certainly does not, and it is one of the failure spots of the motor cycle. Our system permits the use of a comparatively low tension commutator system, which is possible because there is no current taken except during the time when the spark passes, so that one can use small metal contacts with large insulation separations which do not burn when the brush leaves them and do not track to cause short-circuiting because of the large ratio of insulation to contacts. It is possible to use one ignition system, but it demands a coil for each cylinder. This is practically weather-proof, and apart from the actual insulator of the spark plug, if this is sufficiently insulated against wet, one can run the whole machine completely submerged in water except for the exhaust and air intake.

C. W. Spencer Cannock

It is obvious that we lighting engineers have a common technical objective, particularly so with respect to head-lamp aim. Having made the headlamps we feel they should be used efficiently.

With regard to sealed beams, I feel that the author of Paper C75/72 has been a little short of generous in regard to the sealed-beam principle. There have been quite significant changes, at least in the United Kingdom, since the introduction of the first sealed beam. We now have a higher wattage, higher efficiency, halogen units, rectangular units, and a European beam pattern. Further, the difficulties he mentions of manufacturing a single device to perform two functions apply equally to replaceable bulb units. With regard to replaceable bulb units, there is a contradiction between the advantage the author has stated in the precision possible in manufacturing two discrete components and the disadvantage quoted in regard to the large number of variables. Could he explain this?

With regard to headlamp alignment, this is a very important feature that is too often neglected or ignored. With the increasing traffic on the road and with the improvements in headlamp efficiency and the subsequent potential to inflict glare, etc., it is increasingly more critical that the beam should have aim control. I agree entirely that this control should be fully automatic and not left open for misuse or neglect, as with a manually operated system. The control must start with the initial aim of the lamps, this being mainly a matter of discipline and possibly enforced legislation. The technically more difficult control is the maintenance of the initial aim under all driving conditions. However, you have mentioned one means of doing this and there are others.

The work with which I have been associated has led us to believe that a mechanical system offers advantages over a hydraulic system from a cost point of view, which is an important factor. It offers simpler fitting, with probably less 'tailoring' and less maintenance, and it can be easily controlled to give the desired frequency response. This latter point is still under discussion and, as you have pointed out, it is a compromise between the headlamps responding quickly to change in attitude and at the same time ironing out the 'flutter' from the road surface. Being a convert to headlamp aim control, I feel it is a pity that road users are not demanding this on their vehicles. Possibly this is because a good system is not very obvious and the purchaser is not aware that he is getting anything for his money and perhaps because it benefits other drivers as much as the man who has bought the equipment.

With regard to direction control, I would suggest that this is of dubious value. Having driven with these devices I believe that they are gimmicks—maybe attractive but at the same time expensive. Increases in headlamp output allow main beam light to be given at angles of the order of 6° to 9° left and right of centre, which illuminates around fast bends while the vehicle is still travelling along the straight portion of road towards the bend. This is the important time when decisions are made with regard to the speed at which the vehicle is put into the bend. It is debatable whether meeting beams should move at all and I would be glad of the author's comments on this.

Finally, if you are the type of driver who drives 'on the door handles', as I believe the expression goes, or are just an unfortunate conventional driver on a slippery surface who has lost control, then the steering has to be turned to the opposite lock with the directional control lamps then pointing in completely the wrong direction.

A. M. Judson Leyland

With reference to Paper C75/72, the lighting regulations refer to changes of headlight angle in terms of arctangents. I wonder whether the introduction of headlights which also aim about a vertical axis may lead to confusion between percentages and degrees?

The retarder system discussed in Paper C79/72 only applies to commercial vehicles and I expect that only a limited number of people are directly concerned with such systems at the moment. I endorse the author's suggestion that this is an example of an electrical item which must be installed at the design stage.

Fig. 79.12 indicates that present retarders weigh approximately one per cent of gross vehicle weight and it is clear that the weight must be placed between the gearbox and the rear axle (on conventional vehicles). Chassis-mounted versions require increased stiffness in the chassis side members and rear axle mounted versions adversely affect the performance through an increase in unsprung weight. It may well be that the increased weight of the rotor on the axle pinion will create noise and accelerate wear problems.

The present German regulation requiring a sustained braking performance, if adopted by the E.E.C., will force a more thorough consideration of electric retarders and development by vehicle manufacturers will commence.

I feel that a column-mounted control for the system may encourage 'driver abuse'—a very serious problem, especially on public service vehicles. At present, many exhaust brakes are operated through a floor-mounted switch and I believe that progressive application of the retarder should be through a foot control, preferably in conjunction with the existing footbrake and will be less liable to abuse.

Present PSVs comprise an increasing quantity of electronic equipment which is very often adversely affected by r.f. (radio-frequency) interference and noise within the vehicle electrical system. I should like to ask whether investigations into the output from retarders have been made.

The problems associated with relative movement between two very close rotating members, such as those of salt and dust ingress, may be increased since ferromagnetic materials will also be liable to contaminate the system.

Perhaps the original equipment installation of retarders might also be encouraged by developments of the system such as preventing the engine over-revving, a fail-safe method of control and reductions in the unit weight.

V. A. Murari Birmingham

Regarding Paper C75/72, in India we had a problem of deciding which headlamp standard to adopt, the Anglo-American or the European, and finally it was decided to have both, so that over a period a preference would evolve for an Indian standard. Both beam patterns are being produced in that country. One fact that emerged was that the European beam pattern is very narrow and the Anglo-American is considerably wider while the illumination is the same. It is a question of whether there is something to be seen on the side of the road. Is this the reason why headlamp aiming has been found necessary?

J. E. Ridley Birmingham

Paper C113/72 shows how important the electrics on motor cycles have become. What concerns me is that the demand for electrical power is increasing all the time. In a recent check on a twin-cylinder motor cycle we found that for night time driving the continuous electrical power requirement was 160 W and the additional total intermittent power without electric starters was 111 W. These are electrical loads that are steadily increasing. There is now legislation in some areas of the United States which requires that, during the day regardless of weather conditions, the dipped headlamp be switched on, and therefore in urban areas, where there are speed restrictions, the alternator has a very difficult job of supplying sufficient power.

I would like to ask the author if it is possible for alternators to be produced that can meet these and future requirements and yet not be unduly heavy.

My second point concerns the mechanical contact breaker assembly. As engine speeds are now getting faster and faster, in the region of 10 000 to 12 000 rev/min, are we not now reaching the limit at which mechanical contact breakers can be successfully used? Shall we be forced very shortly to turn to contactless ignition systems and fit them as standard items?

J. G. G. Hempson Member

The author of Paper C113/72 has given an extremely good summary of a very complex story, and added further facts to the written paper.

It is surprising that, with the relatively unanimous nature of the solution in the four-wheeler field with the changeover from the d.c. generator to the alternator, there has been great complexity and rather peculiar solutions adopted in the motor cycle field, with much smaller production. The early motor cycle alternators, mentioned in the paper, without any form of charge rate control, seemed to be a retrograde step at the time and over-charging became much more prevalent than with the previous generation of d.c. machines, but this has been largely overcome.

The author mentioned the tendency to go to three-phase connection for the alternator, which, as far as I know, is universal in the car field. It seems rather odd that, with the very low cost of diodes, this has not been adopted earlier in the motor cycle field.

The explanation has been given with regard to breaker-less systems. It is there but so far people will not pay for it. I think it will have to come. I was interested in Fig. 113.6, showing what would appear to be a rather high cost solution involving three transistors of which one presumably has to be highly rated, compared with a much simpler thyristor solution, where a single thyristor can handle the power required. What was the motive behind the design shown in Fig. 113.6?

I was very interested in the figures at the bottom of section 1.7 of Paper C79/72, 'Power dissipation and cooling', in connection with the steady-state losses of these retarders. Engine designers are under very considerable pressure to make very small improvements in engine friction, such as re-designing water and oil pumps, and small changes of ring configuration on pistons to save the odd horsepower. In the case of the Bosch example, it is a matter of throwing away 6·7 kW in steady-state con-ditions. Admittedly the Telma is more reasonable at 2·5 kW but there is no mention of losses in connection with the Pye design.

E. H. Ford London

I would like to mention, in the absence of any reference to opto-electronic switching in the motor cycle application, some of the work we have been doing which at the moment appears to be quite promising. Could the author of Paper C113/72 give me the maximum temperature at the normal contact set mounting location in the motor cycle application? The maximum ambient temperature

there would be of help. We originally ran into a tem-perature problem at this point, but we now function in the range of 158° to 162°C, at which point we stop switching, without damage, I might add, to the system. Our work to date in applying Lumenition to the motor cycle application seems to indicate that the opto-electronic trigger could have certain advantages. Some magnetically-triggered systems are subject to the effects of wobble and false triggering as the magnetic path is altered or the reluctance of the air gap alters as the shaft wobbles. That is one factor. Perhaps contact sets in the motor cycle application are even more of a nuisance than they are in a motor car, requiring very frequent adjustment if accurate timing is to be maintained. By using the opto-electronic trigger, timing variations are completely removed. There are no contact points to adjust. Both the dwell function and the firing point accuracy are fixed. We do not have the high and low speed limits of operation. If we can operate the Jaguar V12 to 6000 rev/min we should be able to take care of the motor cycle. This is using one coil, and if we duplex the thing, we double these engine speeds. This is with very high energy levels in the spark at top speeds. So we would by no means rule out the opto-electronic trigger, the only true replacement for the contact set which both turns on and off the circuit, whereas the magnetic trigger only does half that job and requires mono-stable circuits with constant reversion times, when what one is looking for is constant crank angle reversion. Our work to date does not rule out opto-electronics provided we can limit the temperatures at the trigger to 150°C maximum.

C. M. Elsey Arborfield

With reference to Paper C79/72, the Army are users of heavy automotive equipment and there is little doubt that the use of electric retarders would be most advantageous. However, retarders must create considerable local mag-netic fields which could influence the performance of on-board electronic equipment. What does the author think the magnetic effect would be on a navigational aid that relies upon the earth's magnetic field for its operation?

E. Wharton Hemel Hempstead

I should like to offer a comment on Paper C79/72 with reference to the apparent problem of radiated magnetic fields from electrical equipment on vehicles. Although I am not familiar with retarders in particular, they are nevertheless electrical machines closely related to genera-tors. Although it is true that stray magnetic fields exist, they tend to be relatively small and more generally confined to the region of the machine. That these fields do not constitute a problem is evidenced by examples of genera-tors in aircraft where I know of one installation with almost a megawatt of installed capacity. In my opinion, I think it most unlikely that retarders fitted to vehicles would present insurmountable problems with respect to navigational aids.

T. P. Newcomb Fellow

The author of Paper C79/72 presents a very informative account of electric retarders and rightly emphasizes the importance of a subsidiary brake to reduce the load on the main brakes during hill descents.

Although the author mentions that future regulations will perhaps favour the increased use of retarders, mention must also be made that regulations are continually upgrading the cold braking performance of commercial vehicle brakes to try to ensure parity of brake performance with that obtained on cars. These higher brake performances can only be economically obtained by using a compact friction brake, and an electric retarder would provide little assistance in meeting this aspect of braking requirements.

For this reason it is unlikely that any changes to the design of current brake systems, such as reducing the brake size, would be made possible by fitting an electric retarder as suggested by the author. The stable brake performance now obtained from friction brakes could be seriously affected if a smaller brake incorporating more self-servo was used to obtain the required torque for the brake actuating forces now available, especially with greater vehicle weights coming into use.

On the subject of lining fade, although standard materials may show some loss of performance on hill descents, fade never falls below an acceptable limit, and all materials regain their original performances on cooling down. Fade tests are a standard part of any test to ensure acceptability of linings for vehicles, both for original equipment and as suitable replacement materials, and permanent loss of lining performance would be exceptional for any reputable make of lining. As linings are tested not only by the friction material manufacturer but also by the brake manufacturer and vehicle manufacturer, and probably in the future by official bodies, there should be little chance of any material fading beyond prescribed levels.

With retarder fade, one can appreciate the increase in air gap owing to expansion of the drum in the Pye type of retarder but not in the Telma retarder, where the expansion of the disc should be towards the poles. Therefore, a comparison of the fade behaviour of the two types of retarder should indicate how much of the fade comes from the change in air gap. Has the author any figures comparing the two types of retarder?

One of the biggest problems with electric retarders is the difficulty of installing them on articulated vehicles, which have had the greatest growth rate in commercial vehicle production in recent years. If electric retarders are used they should be used on the trailer as well as on the tractor. Generally, tractors are made as short as possible to permit the greatest length of trailer. There is therefore little ready space for installing a retarder on the tractor, but there is plenty of room available for fitting one on the trailer. This creates the need for using a live axle on the trailer or another method of driving the retarder, and although the cost of a retarder is only a small percentage of the overall vehicle cost, it is expensive in relation to the cost of a trailer unit itself if a live axle is included. Quite often two axles are fitted and it would be necessary to use two retarders plus live axles. These difficulties make the use of a retarder a far less attractive commercial proposition on articulated vehicles, and the author's comments on these matters would be most welcome.

B. Shepherd Witney, Oxon.

I would be grateful if the author of Paper C79/72 would enlarge on the use of this retarder in anti-lock braking systems. It seems to overcome some of the problems associated with such systems—for example, the fact that the braking effect drops to zero as the wheel speed drops.

With regard to the need for heavy cables, one would have thought that with new types of electronics one could control the heavy current at the wheel and only send signals up and down vehicles. It would then only be necessary to have switching means inside the loops to the various retarders. What effect would this have? There is only one paragraph in the paper on anti-lock braking systems.

P. Ledger Reading

I would like to ask the author of Paper C79/72 the following questions:

(a) Does provision exist at present for coupling up Pye or other makes of retarder directly into the main braking circuit of the vehicle? In this way retarder braking would take place when the footbrake is applied and would remove the need for the driver to operate a separate control. This could be of considerable use with fire-fighting vehicles travelling at speed to fire calls.

(b) Are there any problems envisaged when installing retarders in fire-fighting vehicles, bearing in mind the close proximity of the main pump drive (Hardy-Spicer drive shaft type almost invariably) to the propshaft between gearbox and back axle?

(c) An increasing number of applications of electronic equipment are being encountered in fire-fighting vehicles. In the Berkshire and Reading Brigade, one current example is the investigation of various systems of control equipment for changing traffic lights in favour of a fire appliance proceeding to a fire call. In addition, all operational fire appliances are fitted with short wave radio. Could the author advise on the possibility of interference from the magnetic field of the retarder?

T. J. L. Dobedoe (Author)

In reply to W. W. Bischoff, the point is taken about air-bags. This is obviously one of the benefits we gain. Hopefully we do not gain airbags!

With regard to the electronic speedometer, this is a question of time scale. The sort of displays I have been discussing are a long way off compared with the normal electronic instruments, which I am sure will come in a few years.

I specifically did not talk about head-up displays because I have not been acting in this field myself. It does seem to me, however, that one of the reasons we are talking about putting the instruments into the panel is to avoid reflections in the windscreen. There is a lot of human factors work to be done in assessing head-up displays. Should they be found to be desirable I am sure one can do this either electro-mechanically, as now, or by using a projected electro-optic system as discussed earlier.

I did say early on that one really considered only a minimum number of instruments, and I think that the philosophy of calling up information is a very good one. It means that one clutters the driver's vision field by the minimum amount possible, also minimizing, in cost terms, the amount of display area needed to be available.

If we ever go to something like the type of television projection—I too suffer from artists' impressions—then the complexity of the matrix used is likely to be quite severe. Otherwise I would agree with 95 per cent of what has been said.

On D. J. Neville's comments regarding analogue displays against digital, this is a very interesting question. People do have different viewpoints on this. I tend personally to believe that for certain display situations, the analogue information is the ideal way to proceed, but this may be a function of the environment in which we live, which is basically tuned to things like analogue clocks. We are getting used to digital clocks and used to times coming up on the corner of the television screen during the Olympics. This may change with time.

With regard to the disadvantage of call-up instruments, this again is a question of exception. One lets the driver know when he has problems.

With regard to exceptions, can we ask C. Bowden about the difference in quality between drivers and pilots? There is a difference in the training situation and in the aptitudes. I think that the question of the desirability of head-up displays in the driving situation needs investigation as that and not perhaps with reference to semi-analogous situations.

With regard to angles of display, regretfully I cannot answer that. Display angles tend to change quite a lot. It is not my field; it is the field of the human factors and design people.

P. Cibié (Author)

I do not think this is the place at which to enter into a discussion of the advantages or otherwise of the sealed beam. Everybody will have been interested, I am sure, in C. W. Spencer's remarks.

A. M. Judson asked why we speak in percentage terms instead of in degrees. I agree that it is wrong but it is used by the GTB Committee which prepares the texts for Geneva, and I will continue to use it. In practice, it is a very convenient way of measuring in the laboratory, because the angles we have to consider are very small. That is the only reason, but he is right and I think in the future it would be better to speak of degrees.

With regard to the accuracy of measurement, there are three methods that we use. The first is to put a gyroscope on the car and to try to record the levelling of the body according to the plane defined by the gyroscope. The second is to measure the position of the wheels relative to the body. One has to take into account the independent movement of the wheels, but experiments show that this is not a problem as the wheels only move at a frequency of about 10 Hz and with very low amplitude, so one can just as easily use the recording of the position of the body relative to the wheels. The third method consists of putting a camera on the car and recording the shadow at a great distance; this is a very convenient method. Afterwards we put an accelerometer in the car.

Looking at Fig. 75.10, we have a recording of the accelerometer. The position of the body is shown by a dark line and above that we have the position of the headlamp relative to the position of the body. Here there is a difference between the two and that is the position of the headlamp relative to the road. There is less than 0·5 per cent of movement not corrected by the apparatus and I think all these methods are very easy to use. It is interesting

that many laboratories are doing experiments with these problems.

C. W. Spencer spoke about mechanical advantages and he compared it with the hydraulic ones on self-levelling systems; I think the two systems can work very well and we have them in production for the Citroën car—the mechanical one on the DS21 and the hydraulic one on the SM. On this car the hydraulic one is better but that does not mean that the mechanical one could not do the job. The problem is to define what is best and to avoid the fluttering movement of the beam, as the research laboratory calls it. It is necessary to avoid this fluttering (or butterfly) movement but to have a response so fast that there is no risk of dazzle. The main thing is to have a response fast enough for speedy driving. That is the reason why we propose to limit the time of this response. Fluttering is a problem of comfort and so it is a commercial problem. The public, being the users, will choose the system which is more agreeable. This is not really a problem of safety. The main thing is to fix the speed of response.

C. W. Spencer spoke also of the system of directional control of headlamps. I am sure that is an expensive solution and it is very agreeable to have it in certain cases, such as in mountains, but I do not know whether the advantage warrants the price. I am sure it is very useful on a winding road and especially in the mountains, and on fast roads it is very pleasing to see the curve and what is going to happen in 100 or 150 m. One cannot often use the main beam but we can say that it is like the fire extinguisher. It is not used very often but when we need it we prefer that it works well!

With regard to the main beam, it is exactly the same, and we are always surprised that drivers make observations about the main beam more often than about the passing beam. I think the public especially in France can sometimes drive with the main beam!

In reply to V. A. Murari, for the main beam the width is not sufficient to avoid the turning system. It is not obligatory to have this turning system. It is a luxury on the car. It is not easy to see a curve at 100 m. For overtaking, the European beam is not so wide as the sealed beam unit. We intend to put more light on the road where the obstacles are and we do not think it is so important to have the light on the side, where there is nothing interesting to see from the point of view of safety. We think it is necessary to put more light on the centre part of the road.

D. W. Norton (Author)

In reply to J. E. Ridley, I agree entirely that the output of the current range of generators has been severely taxed. We have effected an improvement which has come into production for the 1973 motor cycles by using a higher energy magnet in the rotor of the present alternator. This has pushed up the output from approximately 7·25 A at 2000 rev/min to 8 A at 2000 rev/min.

I would question slightly his wattage figures; I feel that they err a little on the high side. It is my opinion that the output of the alternator we have just introduced is *just* capable—I will admit this—of supplying loads of the order that we have on the machine at the present time. Tests carried out by his own development department, where a motor cycle was equipped with the earlier alternator and subjected to a continuous operation round a circuit chosen partly in an urban district and partly in a city centre, proved that the battery became flat in 3 to 3½ days. The same test carried out with the higher output alternator was abandoned after a fortnight's running.

I agree that we must produce higher output generators. I would suggest that we are barely keeping pace with demand, and for the future we must try to introduce a generator of a different type with markedly increased output. I would say that the absolute minimum would be an output of 10 A at 2000 rev/min and a maximum of approximately 16 to 17 A.

Taking J. E. Ridley's second point on contact breakers, he mentioned a maximum engine speed of 10 000 rev/min. You must remember that the contact breaker is driven off the camshaft and therefore only runs at half engine speed, 5000 rev/min, which is well within the capability of the present contact breaker to supply satisfactory ignition.

With regard to change-over to contactless ignition systems, at the moment it is quite true to say that this is only held back by virtue of increased cost. If we could produce a system at the same price as the contact-breaker system I am sure there would be a 100 per cent changeover.

In reply to E. H. Ford, the ambient temperature for the contact breaker housing is 150°C. With regard to the adjustment of contact breakers, it is rather a laborious job. We tend to use a separate contact breaker and coil for each cylinder and we make each contact breaker assembly adjustable independently of its neighbour. The ignition timing of the engine is set, incidentally, by moving the one contact breaker in respect of the other, so that once it has been set it is merely a matter of keeping the contact gap adjusted to give satisfactory timing.

J. Reed (Author)

In reply to A. M. Judson, with regard to the weight of retarders, I agree that on commercial vehicles it is a penalty. However, the ratio of costs to savings is not overcome; it is just reduced. A certain amount of revenue per ton mile is lost but this does not overcome completely the savings made on the retarder, especially on the large commercial vehicles where a set of brakes will cost up to £100. On coaches it matters not at all because the unladen weight and gross vehicle weight usually do not bear any comparison to the actual load carried. I have never heard of a coach company, user or manufacturer complain of the weight of the retarder.

I agree with you on driver abuse; in fact, from experience, I would say it will not damage the retarder; it will damage the transmission. I have known a case where a driver was going down a long hill with a retarder on and was not going fast enough and so put his foot on the accelerator.

Foot control has been tried—not very successfully. I really think it is a matter of driver education. Once they get used to it they usually do not misuse it too badly, and the manual actuator is the cheapest system; anything else will cost more.

I have not come across this problem of electrical noise before. I would think that the noise generated is of very low frequency and, as such, is not likely to disturb anything else.

There are eight poles on the rotor and the speed is up to about 4000 rev/min at full speed. This is a frequency of only 270 Hz.

With regard to engine over-revving, one can certainly fit a control system, but this is a question of driver education again. They have got used to going downhill by changing down and revving the engine to the limit. Once they have been told how to use this gadget they usually do it the right way.

With regard to corrosion resistance, it is a problem. They usually have a guard to keep pebbles out. On the test bed we deliberately got one red-hot and then threw a bucket of water at it. It just went straight through or over it—no problem at all. The main problem is salt on the electrical connections. It is under consideration to provide some form of encapsulation to prevent this problem. Apart from that we have not had very much corrosion trouble.

C. M. Elsey is quite right. There is a considerable magnetic field in relation to the earth's field. If alternators are fitted they also have a considerable magnetic field, and the chassis is bound to set up its own field around it, so that there is something of a problem. Shielding does help. The whole field can be biased usually to give correct results but I appreciate that it is a problem. You have a rather special circumstance there.

The reason we have no figures for air flow is that we have not measured it. The Bosch and Telma figures were taken from a report by a German organization which did some comparative testing.

This correction to the paper should be noted. Page 47, final paragraph: 300 rev/min should read 3000 rev/min. 6·7 kW is a lot, it is nearly 10 hp! We are, however, talking about a retarder suitable for a vehicle of up to 25 tons. In that context, where the engine is delivering in the order of 200 hp, the problem is not perhaps as significant as it sounds. It is a problem, though. There is always some loss in the transmission due to the fan effect. I will endeavour to measure ours as soon as possible.

In reply to E. Wharton, this is true, but we are relating this to the earth's magnetic field and stray fields stretch out a long way from the machine. They are immeasurable. But compared to the earth's magnetic field they are considerable distances.

Attenuation of the stray magnetic field we find is approximately 50 per cent per centimetre.

Taking another point, it is quite true that not only do we need the controls to be carried through to the trailer; we need some very heavy current cables or another battery, and, if so, we need charging means for it. This is very complicated.

I agree with T. P. Newcomb that ideally on an articulated vehicle it should go on the trailer. He has pointed out the problems and I cannot see a trailer being fitted, except for a very special reason, with a retarder. This can be a very nasty problem.

There are different mountings for retarders which make it easier to fit them on various portions of vehicles.

Telma started off with a transmission-mounted retarder. I showed it in Fig. 79.5. They found that on certain vehicles, particularly rear-engined vehicles, it could not be used properly. For instance, in the case of one rear-engined bus to which they tried to mount it, they had to put a four-point differential on and drive it from the fourth point, which is a very expensive method, so that they have designed a version which will mount on a differential casing or gearbox. The same applies to all the makes. It becomes a lot shorter when used on the articulated prime mover. I think the main field is that of coaches and passenger carrying vehicles. I do not think the commercial field is yet ready for them.

With regard to the wheel brakes, he is right in stating that there are advances and improvements, but the very fact that there is an accepted standard of fade on them does mean that there are problems. The point is that if one has the retarder one does not use the wheel brakes. One can stop with the retarder under normal traffic conditions and use the wheel brakes to bring one to rest over the last three or four mile/h.

I do not necessarily agree with him about the size of brakes but he is the expert so I will not argue!

The Telma fade that he knows about is virtually common to all retarders. There is a slight degree of variation in the initial slope of fade between the ones I know but they finish up at near enough the same level. This tends to make one think that the Curie effect on the magnetic circuit is much higher than the effect on the air gap.

The regulations on friction brakes are made without consideration of other braking systems. If the friction brake is the sole method of retardation, then the cold performance must be uprated to conform with increased speeds, weights and safety standards. I would respectfully suggest that the uprating of cold performance is partly to bring hot performance to an acceptable standard. I was speaking some months ago to a driver who regularly drove 30 ton loads down the M1. He said that, after one application of the brakes, it took nearly half a mile to stop the vehicle from motorway cruising speed. Granted that there may have been some exaggeration, it still highlights the problem of fade. I do not dispute any of T. P. Newcomb's statements on brake performance, but when he mentions 'stable performance' he is, perhaps, overlooking the fact that 'cold performance' is the criterion when a retarder is used. When I say used, I mean fully used as an integral vehicle control, not as an afterthought. Again, I am suggesting merely that advantages could be gained and should be investigated. I doubt if anybody at this time could accurately predict the braking performance of a large vehicle with a retarder designed in, since this has never been done.

If friction brakes are used to the point of serious fade, surely this will cause wear which, itself, will reduce subsequent performance.

The fade behaviour of the Pye Electric Retarder is within 5 per cent of the Telma Retarder. This is partly due to the more effective air cooling of the Pye Electric type, but does indicate quite clearly that Curie effect has a much greater effect than mechanical expansion.

The matter of fitting retarders on the trailers of articulated vehicles was fairly thoroughly discussed at the Symposium. It is an area where a high-speed brake is not particularly suitable. However, a differential-mounted retarder on the tractor will take up only a very few centimetres of drive shaft and will do nearly everything that a trailer-mounted retarder can achieve. It should be said at this point that the major area of use is, in the foreseeable future, the p.s.v. market, including coaches.

With regard to the anti-locking braking question put by B. Shepherd, I had a long section on that and a beautiful set of diagrams. I based this on a talk with a man at MIRA who described to me how the jack-knifing is due to taking the load off the drive wheels because the front wheels of the articulated prime mover are the ones that do the main braking. It lifts up the back and everything goes. I had it in the paper and was shot at from all quarters and promptly removed it! All that is left is the fact that it cannot lock the wheels. B. Shepherd is quite right. Although there may be a speed difference between the wheels and the road it is not necessarily anti-skidding completely, although it is a great deal better than wheel brakes. On the other hand, this sort of condition usually only occurs with emergency braking, and I would never claim that a retarder can provide the degree of retardation required in an emergency.

With regard to the question about power on the trailer, yes, this can be done. It is now possible to obtain alternators which will give sufficient power to provide the necessary excitation for the retarder on their own without any backing up from the batteries. One could do it this way but it is expensive again and it is necessary to fit another alternator to the vehicle.

In reply to P. Ledger, it is not normal to operate electric retarders from a foot pedal. The main reason is, I suspect, that this involves altering the existing mechanics of the vehicle. Since the retarder is regarded almost exclusively as 'add-on' equipment, the general practice is to treat the control gear in the same way. A further problem exists in the difference between normal foot brake operation (which is progressive) and the sequence-switch operation of the retarder. Rapid and repeated changes of switch position could cause transmission shock loading and induce relay contact deterioration.

The operation of a hand switch is no more difficult than a pre-selector gearbox. It has been found to give a straightforward control, readily understood by the driver. If a foot pedal control is required, coupled to the braking system, any retarder manufacturer will be able to supply such a control, but probably at extra cost.

To fit a retarder in a transmission line where due allowance has not been made at the design stage can be difficult. Ancillaries can be moved readily, but a pump drive shaft will be a problem. The best solution is to obtain a retarder which is coupled direct to gearbox or differential, where there is only one shaft and a reasonable amount of space.

The frequency of alternation of a retarder magnetic field is generally low enough to prevent interference. For instance, an 8-pole device revolving at 3000 rev/min has a frequency of 200 Hz. Switching will cause only a fraction of the interference produced by the ignition system and is comparable to headlamp switching, trafficators, etc.

Discussion on papers C108/72, C114/72, C88/72 and C107/72

A. H. Ball Birmingham

If I understand his work correctly the author of Paper C114/72 shows in Fig. 114.3 that a quasi-peak detector produces results closely corresponding to the response of the human eyes and ears. This confirms in a scientific manner what we have believed in the U.K. for about the last 25 years when it was established by subjective tests by, if I remember rightly, the Electrical Research Association, the B.B.C. and others. It confirms the basis on which all the C.I.S.P.R. ignition interference limits have been established. It is also gratifying to see that the author has shown in Fig. 114.4, quite independently, that the well known forms of resistive ignition suppression on production cars effectively produce compliance with C.I.S.P.R. and E.C.E. limits. This is again in accordance with European work.

The author of Paper C108/72 indicates that suppression methods have been based on measuring equipment. I would rather say that measuring equipment and techniques of measurement have always lagged behind the practical know-how. In this connection it might surprise the author of Paper C114/72, who mentions 1961 as the date for the introduction of resistive cable, that I was working on this with my own company in 1937 and it was used extensively on military vehicles during the last war.

This leads me to emphasize that we must not lose sight of our objective which is not to measure interference but to get rid of it. Do not let measuring techniques become an end in themselves.

Ignition interference is the only automobile source which significantly exceeds the E.C.E. limits. Effective suppression methods have long been known and applied in almost all industrialized countries for many years. In Japan and the U.S.A. where no mandatory requirements exist this is also the case. It has been effectively demonstrated as shown by the results in D. W. Morris's Table 108.3, and confirmed by independent reports of the E.R.A., that application of the methods shown in Table 108.5 and Fig. 108.6 will effectively meet the E.C.E./C.I.S.P.R. Standards. In practice this means that conventional metal-bodied vehicles will fulfil all requirements when fitted with resistive h.t. cables. I would suggest, therefore, that mandatory controls should be based on suppression by approved devices already shown to be satisfactory on a world-wide basis rather than by extending the laborious and unnecessarily expensive system of control by measurement which seems to be the present trend. Measurement would, of course, be necessary to specified limits as the ultimate criterion in the event of disputes or for abnormal vehicles or equipment. In operating a system of suppression by approved devices, as an alternative to measurement, which has already been practised for years in many countries, for example, Germany, Belgium, Holland, U.K., U.S.A., Sweden, etc., it is desirable to control the performance of the devices themselves. This can very simply be done by a radio-frequency attenuation bench test which is, of course, very much simpler and less costly than measurements on a complete vehicle. Such a method has already been devised and documented by C.I.S.P.R. Perhaps the authors would comment on these views.

One aspect of ignition suppression which has not been mentioned is the effect on engine performance. Although I would be the first to take the view that with current engines and suppression methods there is no significant adverse effect I am not so sure that this will continue to be the case in future. I have in mind the increasing demands of exhaust pollution control which are causing engine designers to investigate the transient conditions of engine operation which are the most difficult periods for ignition and which are most likely to be affected by ignition spark characteristics which, in turn, are dependent on the suppression fitted. Abnormally weak mixtures are also under investigation for emission purposes with air/fuel ratios of 18 or 20 to 1. Such conditions may necessitate increased spark energies which may conflict with suppression techniques.

I wonder if the sophisticated interference measuring equipment now available might better be employed looking at such future problems rather than largely wasted in formalizing a long established satisfactory situation on existing vehicles?

E. H. Ford London

With reference to Paper C114/72, ignition systems may be classified according to the amount of radio interference they generate, the worst being the very fast secondary voltage rise time systems and those which have oscillatory characteristics of the secondary current spark discharge. In our system we have done a number of things to reduce radio interference at its source. The first one I would like to mention is the slowing of the rate at which the primary current is turned off by the power device. This can be slowed to 25–30 μs without the loss of secondary voltage output. All we lose are the fast, rather large spikes of induced primary voltage which are a source of radio interference. The second thing we do is to throw out the primary condenser, which is not necessary when solid-state means of switching are employed at a controlled rate. We do not want to play football with the energy by taking it into a condenser and having it ring back into the primary, so we eliminate the condenser. This also eliminates some of the harmonics in the secondary because changes in the primary current, which are fast, are reflected in the secondary. Thirdly, we separate the primary winding entirely from the secondary, so that the very fast, very large, initial capacitive strike as the gap ionizes is removed entirely from the primary low-tension circuit of the car.

Those are the main changes which we make in order to produce clean uni-directional discharge and a minimum amount of interference.

T. J. L. Dobedoe Basildon

There are one or two questions arising out of the technical side of Paper C88/72 which I should like to ask. The first is that of discrimination of the unit in terms of the people and devices it is liable to meet on motorways. In motorway driving the discrimination problem will not, I hope, be so severe, but presumably there are limits to the discrimination, which one would be interested in hearing.

Secondly, it would appear that the bandwidth of such a system is liable to be rather large. What is the attitude of the Post Office to such a large number of motor cars radiating around 30 GHz up and down the country? Have the authors discussed this with them?

Coming away from the technicalities, we are on rather more difficult ground. If we take the model chosen, the two-car following situation, this is not a normal motorway situation. It would be very interesting to know whether the later work you may have done has indicated the stability at the back of the queue, not just in the acceleration mode, which is, I feel, the simpler mode, but in a motorway situation where one is likely to have a system such that the speed of the convoy is the same as the speed of the leader and inevitably there will be overtaking. What would be the response of the system to a step function when an overtaking vehicle comes in front of the queue?

I would also welcome comments on road utilization if we all drive at 10 ft per 10 mile/h. I have heard it said that we are bound to use more road therefore we shall not have such good road utilization. On the other hand, it has been suggested that because of the more uniform motion it is less likely that we shall have traffic congestion and problems.

Finally, I would be interested to know what conclusions Lucas have reached on the effects of this sort of system on driver concentration and fail-safe. One has the fear, perhaps, that a driver will become accustomed to such a system on a motorway and not on a minor road and that he would tend to rely on a system that no longer exists in a vehicle.

B. Shepherd London

With reference to Paper C88/72, I would question the point of the rather large bandwidth. I am somewhat worried when I imagine a large number of vehicles equipped with a system of this sort, with 30 GHz split into channels. There would be interference and drifting through as one vehicle overtook another. I know that the Americans are very worried about this with regard to the use of radar detectors for triggering airbags. What happens when every American car is fitted with a radar transmitter when a random coincidence can trigger an airbag?

C. Surridge Basingstoke

For the system described in Paper C88/72 to work, it will need to have a very directional aerial system and a high discrimination level, to enable it to 'see' only the 'target' ahead, at the vehicle spacing distances necessary and not roadside furniture, etc.

With such a narrow beam pattern, will slight changes in vehicle direction cause it to lose or gain a target and possibly reverse the desirable control?

J. F. Miles Mitcham

With reference to Paper C107/72, the basic anti-lock system, in which a wheel deceleration measurement, combined with an approximation to a measurement of wheel slip, is used to determine the correct time to release the brakes, is now fairly well established. The difference between the systems I have seen concerns the way in which we determine when to put the brakes back on and this is what controls the quality of the system. A simple system can be designed which, fitted to almost any vehicle, will give some improvement in braking performance. If we want to optimize a system, as mentioned in the authors' introduction, we have to take into account the parameters of the particular vehicle to which we are fitting it, and specific adjustments are required. Then we are in trouble because it does not work on the next model of car. The owner changes from cross-ply to radials or his shock absorbers wear out and it needs further adjustment. I would be very interested to hear whether the system that Bendix are producing is designed as a universal system or whether it has to be adapted to each vehicle.

A more detailed point of design that came out of the very interesting system in the paper is the response time. This is extremely critical. If the pressure in the brake line is relieved too late we have two factors. Not only is the wheel decelerated further in towards lock than we want but also we have pumped too much oil; this has to be pumped out again before the wheel stops decelerating and it will go even further into lock; therefore a long time constant, a long delay in releasing the brakes, severely degrades the performance.

The paper refers to a 30 ms dive from 40 km/h. This is equivalent to the wheel decelerating at $30g$, and I have seen oscillogram traces of up to $40g$ on some road surfaces with small wheels, so the time constant we are talking about is small compared with 30 ms. The type of pick-off illustrated is a fairly crude system which the automotive industry insists on because it is fairly robust. This is the toothed wheel, with a limited number of teeth, and therefore small number of pulses on each revolution. I was surprised to see a reference to a counter in order to turn this into a measurement of frequency. That suggests you are counting teeth in a period, which means you cannot get your informaton in less than a multiple of the tooth period, and I would suggest that this is a little slow. The magnetic pick-off is rather prone to shock. If the car hits a bump and the shock absorbers go into resonance, signals are generated which are not related to car speed, and this can interfere with the antilock system. Do the authors consider that their system is viable on a four-wheel system? This effect is probably of little significance on a rear-wheel system. Perhaps American cars are more rigid on the front end than most British cars.

I would question the choice of the radio as the starting point when they talk about reliability. Perhaps that is the ultimate example of an electronic product designed down to a price. Reliability can be built in if one is prepared to pay for it.

F. Minozuma (Author)

At present, our electronics engineers are attempting to revolutionize the application of electronics to automobiles. I have organized an Automotive Electronics Committee in the Society of Automobile Engineers of Japan. This Committee comprises of three groups. The first deals with electronic devices, concerned principally with the requirements of a thermal and atmospheric environment, as well as with the requirements of vibration. This group is also concerned with electromagnetic susceptibility, for, in future, we may be using a great deal of electronic equipment in a automobile, so that electromagnetic susceptibility will be a very important requirement. There are also questions of reliability, accuracy and cost; these we are discussing now. Also very important is our sensor for the future system. We know that the automotive mechanical engineer is very conservative when designing a car. The second group deals with communication from car to car and from car to land. This will be used for car or traffic controlling, and for the automotive telephone or data communication system. The third group is related to control systems, such as car following, speed control, etc. I am concentrating on the spin-off of space technology as related to the automobile industry because my past experience is in space technology and development.

There are one or two ideas that we have in mind relevant to the ignition system. Why is electromagnetic energy (i.e. electromagnetic power transmission system or oxygen molecule resonance at mm wavelength) used as the igniter? What about an ultra-violet (i.e. oxygen atomic excitation at around 2000 Å) laser? When we succeed with such a powerful igniter instead of the present match-like point flame we may decrease the air/fuel ratio and the compression ratio considerably and we can also expect a low exhaust air pollution. Of course, these things may require several years of development before they can be put into practice.

The following corrections to the paper should be noted. Page 116, Fig. 114.2. For 'periodic pulses' read 'white noise'.

Page 123. Left-hand column. The formula should read:

$$E_1 = e \cdot \left(Z_M + \frac{Z_L \cdot Z_P}{Z_L + Z_P} \right) \left(\frac{Z_L \cdot Z_P}{Z_L + Z_P} \right)^{-1}$$

A. P. Ives (Author)

T. J. L. Dobedoe has highlighted a number of interesting points.

With regard to discrimination, obviously the smaller the target the more difficult it is to see, and this is why we have mentioned that a system like this is only likely to emerge on motorways or where pedestrians are restricted and small vehicles are restricted. Some work has been done on measuring the sort of target areas that vehicles present to radar frequencies but this is not at all extensive. It does indicate that in X-band one can get several tens of dBs difference between lorries and Volkswagens. It is not only the size of the vehicle but the attitude that is involved. One

particular difficulty is with the rather large flat-backed truck which, whilst looking large at the moment that it is square on to one, diminishes, as soon as it makes a small angle, to a very small target; so there are vast problems, and at the moment I cannot say whether we can solve them or not.

With regard to bandwidth, this is an interesting matter; we have talked to the Post Office and are operating under a development licence. Their attitude is, 'it is wide but we are not sure'. They are asking us to keep them informed of the work we are doing so that they can take it into account —a reasonable attitude. Clearly, though, the smaller the bandwidth the more advantage there is to the Post Office and the more chance of its coming into use. This is very true.

On the braking side, we have recently done some tests and are making a small film. In it we show what we call a 'three car trick', with two cars following and a third coming along and driving in between them. The effect of this is not what one might expect. We found that there was still relative velocity, i.e. positive relative velocity, between the car coming in and the trailing car. The system relies on a certain amount of derivative control and that relative velocity does not cause what one would expect to be a very sharp braking effect. The trailing vehicle drops back nicely and settles down at the controlled distance behind the car now in the middle. In our film we drive the car out again and the controlled vehicle takes up its station behind the leading car and accelerates up to its correct distance. It is the rate of change of velocity which is so important and gives one the clue to the emergency braking. It is no good looking at distance alone and expecting to get vast changes of distance in a short time. The reaction time of the system is fast if we look at the velocity term, and we get $0 \cdot 4g$ under certain conditions. That is not nearly good enough and a lot of work has to be done here.

With regard to road utilization, 10 ft per 10 mile/h— $0 \cdot 7$ s is roughly what we have at the present time, and the human driver is said to have that reaction. If we can get the system to be tighter and have a faster reaction, there is no reason why this cannot be closed up, but there is a certain psychological effect and one finds oneself driving very close to something which feels uncomfortable. If we are looking at future road systems with large numbers of vehicles, we may have to stick with the sort of spacing we have now because this is what we are used to.

With a breakdown in the system, the human being has to be in a position to take over and if he is stuck hard up against the back of the car in front he will not like that either.

This brings us to the matter of fail-safe. I have nothing to say on fail-safe and nothing to say on driver concentration. It is a very difficult problem and it is too early to make any comment.

With regard to B. Shepherd's question on interference, and the large number of cars operating with the microwave equipment on them, the output frequency we have been looking at is the result of a transit time in the order of nano-seconds, and the output is in the audio range of a few kHz. This means that, as far as the system is concerned, it does not need to recognize high frequencies, and one can put in a filter which cuts out everything beyond a few kHz. The probability of another vehicle coming towards one and modulating at exactly the same rate and time as oneself, giving an output frequency which will be in that audio band, is very slim. The probability is there, but it is slim. So I think the answer is that we have got some sort of restriction in what the controller sees.

Biological effects, as far as I know, only start to be felt when the power levels become high. We are talking at the moment of 3 mW and not more than 5 or 10 mW in the future, and by the time this power gets to the aerial, the power density is very low.

With regard to C. E. Surridge's point about safety, and the presence of 'roadside furniture', at present we are talking about someone steering this car. Maybe in many years' time that will not be true either. I do not know. But there is somebody behind the wheel and he is the direction controller. If the system responds to something from the front and the brakes are applied and the car takes some change of direction, first of all we have got the feedback in the human being driving the vehicle in the direction he wants to go, which will counteract that effect. It may be a valid point and experimental evidence might show that up eventually. We have not got that far.

D. R. Elliott (Author)

The first question put by J. F. Miles dealt with the pressure reduction turn-off point and its importance in the proper control of braked wheel speed. This control depends really on more that just the turn-off point. I would not acknowledge that by itself the turn-off point is that sensitive. It can be, depending on the type of logic and pressure schedules that are used.

I agree with J. F. Miles regarding shock absorbers wearing out and the suspension becoming loose. I should have brought this out in the paper and welcome the opportunity to do so now. Recognizing that a system had to be compatible with those changes that were expected in the life of the vehicle—not just the normal life but a more adverse life—we elected to design our system as an 'adaptive braking system', and the degree to which it is adaptable can be demonstrated by the fact that we met certain goals. The first goal is that there is no mating of any of the major top assemblies. Any modulator will go with any electronic control unit. The second is that in the four-wheel system, which is used on a fairly heavy, luxurious American car, the control logic settings are identical to the rear axle control logic settings of the two-wheel system. The two-wheel system is used on a utility vehicle which is often used for off-road work as well as on highways. (Probably the closest companion to this utility vehicle would be the Land Rover, though the Land Rover is a lot more an off-road vehicle than the one I am thinking of.) Lastly, we do not make any provisions for the production system to be adjusted in the field. For service applications, all adjustment is done at the factory, on the individual assemblies.

With regard to the second question concerning adequate time response to avoid 'deep slip' cycles. We would agree with that, we typically require of our modulator assembly response times of about 10 ms, and this means that the solenoid valves ideally would be somewhat faster than that. I think he is well aware that the slowest thing in the entire control loop is typically the brake. Introducing any significant further delays by something we are adding does not enhance the situation at all.

With regard to the speed sensing function, I used the term 'counter' which may be a jargon developed in Indiana. Let me explain that we do not wait for the time period of several teeth. We simply generate pulses for each tooth that goes by, a very well defined pulse in amplitude and width, and we arrive at a d.c. voltage which is proportional to pulse frequency.

I agree with what he said about a magnetic pick-up. Any magnetic circuit with an electrical output involving changes in flux linkages which produce the voltages is subject to any form of mechanical motion that is not indicative of wheel speed. Our solution has simply been to encapsulate the coil itself and hold it in a fairly rigid bracket, and the toothed wheel that we are utilizing is also fairly substantial. I am not acquainted with the natural frequency but we deliberately made it well above control frequencies for this very reason.

The last point dealt with the radio as a reference. I agree to this extent—that we are trying to achieve aerospace performance and reliability at low cost. The reason for selecting the radio is that it is the largest volume automotive electronic device produced, and I thought it might work as a nominal reference of automotive electronic equipment to begin with. It certainly is not a safety-related item, though, and we should have brought that out more forcefully.

List of Delegates

ABBOTT, A. J. M. — Joseph Lucas Ltd, Birmingham
ALCOCK, B. J. — Ministry of Defence, Chertsey, Surrey
ATKINSON, T. R. — Chrysler U.K. Ltd, Coventry
AYRES, F. C. — D. H. Bonnella and Son Ltd, Hoddesdon, Herts.
BALL, A. H. — Joseph Lucas Ltd, Birmingham
BARBER, A. J. — Joseph Lucas Ltd, Birmingham
BAREHAM, E. G. — British Leyland Motor Corp., Birmingham
BARNES, L. D. G. — Champion Sparking Plug Co., Feltham, Middx.
BARROW, J. H. H. — Vauxhall Motors Ltd, Luton, Beds.
BEARTON, F. — A.C. Delco Division of General Motors, Dunstable, Beds.
BELL, G. J. — A.C. Delco Division of General Motors, Dunstable, Beds.
BENNETT, R. S. — The B.S.A. Group Research Centre, Birmingham
BERTIOLI, M. M. — Joseph Lucas Group Research Centre, Solihull
BISCHOFF, W. W. — Smiths Industries Ltd, London
BOUCHER, G. D. — Ministry of Defence, Chertsey, Surrey
BOWCOTT, J. T. — Joseph Lucas Ltd, Birmingham
BOWDEN, C. — Bowstock Engineering, London
BREWER, C. D. — Consultant, Cold Weston, Shropshire
BROOKS, P. J. — Texas Instruments Ltd, Bedford
BUDEK, J. A. — Texas Instruments Ltd, Bedford
BUSHNELL, J. — Crypton-Triangle Ltd, Bridgwater, Somerset
CADMUS, T. E. — Champion Spark Plug Company, Toledo, Ohio, U.S.A.
CAPSTICK, D. L. — British Insulated Callender's Cables Ltd, Helsby, Cheshire
CARR, E. — Lucas Aerospace Ltd, Burnley, Lancs.
CIBIÉ, P. — Projecteurs Cibié, Paris, France
COLLINI, D. N. — Ministry of Defence, Chertsey, Surrey
COOPER, R. H. — Smiths Industries Ltd, London
COYLE, J. C. — Rolls-Royce Motors, Crewe, Cheshire
CROCKETT, D. R. — A.M.P. Inc., Stanmore, Middx.
DAVIES, E. — Ministry of Defence, Chertsey, Surrey
DAVIES, G. — Autocar Electrical Equipment Ltd, London
DAY, R. W. E. — H.Q. D.E.M.E., London
DEVEREUX, A. S. — Joseph Lucas Ltd, London
DOBEDOE, T. J. L. — Ford Motor Co. Ltd, Basildon, Essex
DOWLING, D. B. — Smiths Industries Ltd, London
ELLIOTT, D. R. — The Bendix Corporation, South Bend, Indiana, U.S.A.
ELSEY, C. M. — Army Apprentices College, Reading, Berks.
EMERSON, R. S. — Leslie Hartridge Ltd, Buckingham
EVANS, J. T. — Joseph Lucas Ltd, Birmingham
EVISON, R. A. — Chrysler U.K. Ltd, Coventry
FAWCETT, K. R. — Vauxhall Motors Ltd, Luton, Beds.
FORD, E. H. — Autocar Electrical Equipment Ltd, London
FORD-DUNN, M. D. — Ricardo and Co., Shoreham-by-Sea, Sussex
FRENCH, G. R. — C.A.V. Ltd, London
GEZA, M. — Automotive Research Institute, Budapest, Hungary
GILISSEN, H. P. J. — A.M.P. Holland N.V., den Bosch, Holland
GOODINGE, M. W. — Plessey Co. Ltd, Romford, Essex
GOUGH, T. B. K. — Smiths Industries Ltd, London
GOULD, R. J. — I.T.T. Components Group, Harlow, Essex
GRIFFIN, F. S. — Texas Instruments Ltd, Bedford
HARTOP, C. H. — Vauxhall Motors Ltd, Luton, Beds.
HEATH, J. D. — Rist's Wires and Cables Ltd, Newcastle under Lyme, Staffs.
HEMPSON, J. G. G. — Ricardo and Co., Shoreham-by-Sea, Sussex
HOOD, B. J. — Girling Ltd, Birmingham
HORTON, J. — Joseph Lucas Ltd, Birmingham

HOWE, J. A. — Carr Fastener Co. Ltd, Nottingham
HOYER, J. — Motorola Semiconductors Ltd, Geneva, Switzerland
HUNTER, G. — Ward and Goldstone Ltd, Salford, Lancs.
HURTLEY, D. — University of Warwick, Coventry
IVES, A. P. — Lucas Group Research Centre, Solihull
JAYNE, D. L. — Chloride Automotive Batteries Ltd, Manchester
JOYNSON, E. — R.E.M.E., Chertsey, Surrey
JUDSON, A. M. — British Leyland Motor Corp., Leyland
JUKES, N. A. — Joseph Lucas Ltd, Birmingham
KILMURRY, E. — Chrysler U.K. Ltd, Coventry
LANG, J. — Ward and Goldstone Ltd, Salford, Lancs.
LEDGER, P. — Berks. and Reading Fire Brigade, Reading
LEECH, K. J. — Joseph Lucas Ltd, Birmingham
LENTZ, L. R. — Champion Spark Plug Co., Ohio, U.S.A.
LEONARD, G. H. — C.A.V. Ltd, London
LOCK, C. G. J. — A.C. Delco Division of General Motors Ltd, Dunstable, Beds.
LOUTH, B. — Carr Fastener Co. Ltd, Nottingham
LUMSDEN, W. — British Leyland, Leyland
MAY, F. — Autocar Electrical Equipment Ltd, London
MEISL, C. G. — Britover (Continental) Ltd, London
MELLOR, R. W. — Ford Motor Co. Ltd, Basildon, Essex
MILES, J. F. — Mullard (Mitcham) Ltd, Surrey
MINOZUMA, F. — Hitachi Ltd, and Tokai University, Tokyo
MINTON, L. G. — Triumph Motor Co. Ltd, Coventry
MIZSER, G. — Automotive Research Institute, Budapest, Hungary
MOORE, J. H. — Joseph Lucas Group Research Centre, Solihull
MORRIS, D. W. — Joseph Lucas Ltd, Birmingham
MOWBRAY, D. F. — C.A.V. Ltd, London
MURARI, V. A. — Joseph Lucas Ltd, Birmingham
McARDELL, E. J. — Ford Motor Co. Ltd, Basildon, Essex
M'EWEN, E. — Joseph Lucas Ltd, Birmingham
MACLACHLAN, A. — A.M.P. of G.B. Ltd, Stanmore, Middx.
NELSON, J. H. — Joseph Lucas Ltd, Birmingham
NEVETT, L. J. — Joseph Lucas Ltd, Burnley, Lancs.
NEVILLE, D. J. — Leslie Hartridge Ltd, Buckingham
NICHOLLS, K. D. — Texas Instruments Ltd, Bedford
NORTON, D. W. — Joseph Lucas Ltd, Birmingham
PAGE, I. B. — A.M.P. of G.B. Ltd, Stanmore, Middx.
PARKER, R. C. — Ferodo Ltd, Chapel-en-le-Frith, Stockport, Cheshire
PEARCEY, B. A. — Ministry of Defence, Aldershot, Hants.
PORTLOCK, J. J. — Motorola Semiconductors Ltd, Wembley
RAYNER, C. S. — Joseph Lucas Ltd, Solihull
REED, J. — Pye Electric Ltd, Lowestoft
RIDLEY, J. E. — B.S.A. Group Research Centre, Birmingham
RILEY, P. R. H. — Plessey Dynamics, Romford
RITTMANNSBERGER, N. — Robert Bosch GmbH, Stuttgart, Germany
ROBSON, J. V. B. — Champion Sparking Plug Co., Feltham, Middx.
SAGAR, N. S. — I.T.T. Components Group, Leigh, Lancs.
SAUNDERS, B. K. — Society of Motor Manufacturers and Traders Ltd, London
SCHOLL, H. — Robert Bosch GmbH, Stuttgart, Germany
SENIOR, K. B. — Joseph Lucas (Electrical) Ltd, Birmingham
SHEPHERD, M. W. — Champion Sparking Plug Co. Ltd, Feltham, Middx.
SKINNER, J. W. — Royal Military College of Science, Swindon, Wilts.
SMITH, E. — British Leyland Truck and Bus Division, Preston, Lancs.
SOAR, T. R. — School of Electrical and Mechanical Engineering, Bordon, Hants.
SPENCER, C. W. — Joseph Lucas Ltd, Cannock, Staffs.

STAFFORD, E. M.	The University of Southampton	UEDA, T.	Japan Trade Centre, London
STARTIN, K. J.	A.M.P. of G.B. Ltd, Stanmore, Middx.	WEEKS, M. W.	Petrol Injection Ltd, Plymouth
STRACHAN, D. R.	Joseph Lucas Ltd, Birmingham	WHARTON, E.	Lucas Aerospace Ltd, Hemel Hempstead
STUDER, P.	Bosch Ltd, Watford	WHERRITT, P.	B.L.M.C. Air Pollution Lab., Jaguar Cars Ltd, Coventry
SURRIDGE, C. E.	Automobile Association, Basingstoke, Hants.	WHITE, R. J.	Dept. of the Environment, London
TAYLOR-MOORE, A.	Rolls-Royce Motors, Crewe, Cheshire	WILLIAMS, W. B.	Chloride Automotive Batteries Ltd, Manchester
TIPTON, D. L.	Joseph Lucas Ltd, Birmingham	WINDISCH, M. S.	C.A.V. Ltd, London
TYE, E. S.	Ripaults Ltd, Enfield, Middx.		

Index to Authors and Participants

Names of authors and numbers of pages on which papers begin are printed in bold type.

Subject Index

Titles of papers are in capital letters.

MADE AND PRINTED IN GREAT BRITAIN BY WILLIAM CLOWES & SONS, LIMITED, LONDON, BECCLES AND COLCHESTER